Letters from Sandy Hook—Newtown to the World

Letters from Sandy Hook-Newtown to the World

Compiled and Edited by Suzanne Davenport

KARUNA PUBLICATIONS

Published in 2013 by Karuna Publications
55 Powderhorn Drive
Wayne, NJ 07470

All photos and illustrations are courtesy of various contributors. See page 488 for complete list.

Printed in the United States

Interior book design by Clare Cerullo

Library of Congress Cataloging-in-Publication Data is available upon request.

ISBN 9781939839022

www.karunapublications.org

This book was created in memory of those we have loved.

* * *

Love to my mother, Connie May, and brother Billy.

Acknowledgments

This project was a labor a love from all of us who participated in it. So many people helped turn my initial thought into a reality. "It takes a village to raise a child," and it takes a community to create a book called *Letters from Sandy Hook-Newtown to the World*.

Most important, a sincere thank you to each of you who contributed a letter for the book. For some of you this was a physical hardship to handwrite the letters. For some of you it was a spiritual hardship. For most of you it was an emotional hardship. You will never know how much I appreciate your being willing to listen to my request and then to respond to me. These letters, your letters, show a piece of the life of the wonderful residents who are the heart and soul of our community. Thank you to all my fellow Hookers and Townies.

Thank you to Monsignor Robert Weiss for your support, love, and inspiring foreword; my dear friends Amy Reyen, Andrea Zimmermann, and Cynde DaSilva for proofing letters and helping me get organized; to Shannon Hicks and Sherri Baggett and *The Newtown Bee* for use of their photographs and the Steven Kellogg illustration; to Steven Kellogg for permission to use your illustration; to Phyllis Cortese, Nicole Friedrich, Jim Gaston, Sarah Hemingway, Terry Laslo, and David Lydem for use of photographs; to Steve Cooper of Ware, Fressola, Maguire & Barber LLP, who donated his legal services; to my son Bobby who created the website for the book (www.lettersfromsandyhook-newtown.com), my son Tyler who created the cover of the book, and to the love of my life, husband Bob (who made me write that), who spent hours proofing with me and encouraging me to keep on track. Thank you for all the love and support you have provided to me during these past several months.

Foreword

On a recent trip, I stopped by an art gallery. As I entered, I noticed that there was a large selection of kaleidoscopes. They were all shapes and sizes made from a variety of materials. By definition, a kaleidoscope is a "tubelike instrument containing loose bits of colored glass reflected by several mirrors so that various symmetrical patterns appear as the instrument is rotated." (Webster's New World Dictionary of the American Language). I thought to myself that this is exactly what the community of Newtown is all about. We are all pieces that make a beautiful and intriguing pattern to all who look at us. We have been brought together to create a diversity of patterns that reflect to others the complexity and the simplicity of our lives. We each represent a different color and a different pattern, and yet when all assembled together we create a powerful image that is ever changing and ever new. Each kaleidoscope that I picked up showed something new and unique as I turned it, with ever-changing patterns and colors. So, too, the community of Newtown. We have been described by many as a small, typical New England town. How narrow is that description! We possess a rich history, an ever-changing culture, an intriguing demographic profile, and a community that transcends a typical and stereotyped definition of who we are. We are like a kaleidoscope. The letters in this book reflect the richness of our community. They are written by everyday people whose lives have been enriched by the community in which they live. They tell of faith and citizenship, of commitment to God and to country. They reflect the good times and the hardships, the times of prosperity and struggles, the days when we danced and the days when we sat in silence, the minutes that seemed like hours and the hours that passed too quickly. They reflect our history, our people, our accomplishments, and our everyday stories of life. They celebrate our achievements and our heroes, our place in history from our founding over 300 years ago to this very day. They represent cherished memories and broken hearts, smiles and tears, laughter and anguish. They represent who we are and all that we are about as a community of people. Like a kaleidoscope, we have been tossed and turned through the events of history, but we have held together as a unique community to strengthen and encourage each other in our brightest moments and darkest hours. Pick this book up, as I did those kaleidoscopes, and discover for yourself the richness of the town that we call home. After I sampled each of the unique kaleidoscopes, I noticed a sign that read, "Please do not touch." Too late, I thought to myself. Then I realized that that is a sign that you will never see in Newtown. Open this book, read these letters, and share our memories, and let your hearts be touched by a special and blessed town in New England that is far from small and typical!

Monsignor Robert E. Weiss

Introduction

My husband and I moved to Sandy Hook, CT, in 1991. Our two sons graduated from Newtown High School. To me, Sandy Hook reminds me of Isle of Palms, SC, where I grew up. On Isle of Palms, everyone knew everyone, and as a child, you couldn't get away with much because someone would see you and tell your parents! Although the square miles are bigger here, the attitude is the same. Although the Newtown community covers many miles, we are still "small-town."

As a writing major in college, I took a fact-based opinion writing course. The subject of many of my assignments was my community. My instructor and classmates encouraged me to submit my assignments to a local newspaper. I did, and two of them were published. The idea of writing about our town crept into my soul.

After weeks of reading letters that poured into our community from around the world (over 10,000 that I read personally) as part of the Newtown Documentation Project and then listening to the media describe our town, after just spending a few hours (maybe a few days), I decided that (1) the love that came in needed to go back out, and (2) I was frustrated by people who did not know us try to tell the world who we are. How could they, when they only saw us in sorrow? Thus *Letters from Sandy Hook-Newtown to the World* was born. I reached out to friends and asked them to tell their friends. My request was simple: "I just want you to write a letter about life in Sandy Hook/Newtown. You can write about before December 14, about that day, or about since then. These letters are from each of you—your thoughts, your feelings, and your heart!" That was my request. No more, no less. And the book was born.

Through this experience, I have learned much. I've learned about interesting people who have lived in our town before me. I've learned that I am among the many who enjoy our $2.00 movies at Edmond Town Hall, the ice cream at our two local shops, the Labor Day Parades, and, most of all, our flagpole in the middle of the road. I have felt the sorrow that still fills people's hearts and souls; I have experienced the pride that young adults who have lived their whole lives in our community feel; I share the memories of families whose children played and learned in Sandy Hook School; I embrace my new friendship with an author whose signature is on so many of my children's books; I feel the frustration and anxiety of those who were not home on December 14 and couldn't wait to get back to their families; I share the anger that still flows through our community; I cherish the serenity of beautiful spaces within our town; I remember how much I loved being an involved parent in SHS; I am reminded of the loss one feels when you no longer have a family member to embrace daily; I smile at the fact that someone had the nerve to steal our beloved flag (not once—but twice); my heart hurts with the students from SHS who will have memories that no person should ever have; my heart mourns for the families that have been broken both that day and since and yet they continue on as best they can; my arms ache to hold each and every one of the people who have shared their stories and bared their souls to help me to reach out to the rest of the world to let everyone know who we are . . . a community of love, hate, compassion, anger, caring, sorrow, kindness, and hope—just like so many other communities in the world.

I have also learned that although my request was about our community, many could not write about our community without touching on December 14, 2012. It has forever changed our lives in so many different ways. Some of these letters express how deeply it has affected us.

I have tried to incorporate photos that I have taken (except for those credited otherwise) with letters when possible. Some of the locations are ones that you have seen on television—now I hope you appreciate them as we know these locations—a park where children spend summers at camp, youngsters crawl over playgrounds, water is splashed all over, teams play sports and parents cheer; places of worship in good times and not just bad; our wonderful flagpole that all of the locals know how to navigate around; and our quaint center of Sandy Hook that only takes about one minute to get through, with its wonderful stores, restaurants, and views.

Letters is my way of showing who we really are, not just who you saw on television, with our tears pouring out and our hearts breaking, but *these* letters are the people of Sandy Hook-Newtown. Please get to know us and know what a great community we have. The book is about *us*. And I think we've done a good job of showing that. I did this project out of love. I did this to help us heal. I did this in memory of Anne-Marie and all the others no longer with us. I do this to honor all Sandy Hook-Newtown families. And if one person feels better for being a part of this project—then all the hours spent reading and crying as I received another letter was all worth it. Our hearts have been broken. I'm not sure when they will heal. But I'm hopeful that this project is a start.

* * *

It is also important to me that everyone knows that this was not about making money. All of the profits are going to charitable funds to help our community heal.

Sandy Hook School sign

SAC Field

Baseball field at Treadwell Park

A person's upbringing is the most important stage of their life. The early years are when personality and code of ethics are instilled within us. When I think of Sandy Hook, I think about how lucky I am to have had the life I have. I remember all of the times spent with friends and family over the years. Growing up in a small town like ours, you work your way through school with the same group of kids, year after year. Your classmates are people that you have known from kindergarten through high school. You've watched them grow up, while growing up yourself. I also think back to all of the events shared with my friends over the years, from Sock Hops and Jolly Green Giant Pairs to Prom and Homecoming. I can remember lining up on picture day and playing out on the playground during Field Day. Sandy Hook School and the experiences that I had there, created some of the most important friendships that I have to this day and shaped me into the person that I am today. I can remember every baseball game, whether it be at SHS, SAC Field, on the fields behind (what is now) Reed Intermediate or the fields across the street in Fairfield Hills. When I think of home, I replay the happy memories that came with such an incredible childhood. When others hear that I am from Sandy Hook and at one time walked those very halls myself, they now associate my childhood home with the small glimpse of us that they see on television. However, the negative connotation that our town has gained from their perspective is lost on me. I see my friends and my family. I see the love that our community has demonstrated, and the strength of a bond that can bring a whole town together. I am proud to say that I am from Sandy Hook, Connecticut.

— Bobby Davenport

A person's upbringing is the most important stage of their life. The early years are when personality and code of ethics are instilled within us. When I think of Sandy Hook, I think about how lucky I am to have had the life I had. I remember all of the times spent with friends and family over the years. Growing up in a small town like ours, you work your way through school with the same group of kids, year after year. Your classmates are people that you have known from kindergarten through high school. You've watched them grow up, while growing up yourself. I also think back to all of the events shared with my friends over the years, from Sock Hops and Jolly Green Giant Fairs to Prom and Homecoming. I can remember lining up on picture day and playing out on the playground during Field Day. Sandy Hook School and the experiences that I had there, created some of the most important friendships that I have to this day and shaped me into the person that I am today. I can remember every baseball game, whether it be at SHS, SAC field, on the fields behind (what is now) Reed Intermediate or the fields across the street in Fairfield Hills. When I think of home, I replay the happy memories that came with such an incredible childhood. When others hear that I am from Sandy Hook and at one time walked those very halls myself, they now associate my childhood home with the small glimpse of us that they have seen on television. However, the negative connotation that our town has gained from their perspective is lost on me. I see my friends and my family. I see the love that our community has demonstrated, and the strength of a bond that can bring a whole town together. I am proud to say that I am from Sandy Hook, Connecticut.

Bobby Davenport

Baseball fields behind Reed Intermediate

I am a Hooker who is now a Townie and I am very proud to say so.

So many this could be most confusing and possibly even offensive. But in our town it makes total sense. When someone asks me where I live I say Newtown, because for the last 25 years I have lived in the Newtown area of Newtown. But I was born and raised in the Sandy Hook area of Newtown. Therefore, I am a Hooker who is now a Townie and that is a privilege.

This is just one of the many unique claims one can make in this wonderful town. Newtown—one town with five boroughs, each with its own history and personality. And like people who live in the greater New York City area when you ask them where they are from they will often reply, "the city". But that could mean Brooklyn, Queens, Manhattan or any of the other boroughs. It's the same here in Newtown. You are a Newtowner but you might live in the area of Botsford, Hawleyville, Newtown, Dodgingtown or Sandy Hook. And each area is a very special part of the same town. And like the five fingers on your hand, each one has its own uniqueness but it is part of a team. It's the same here in Newtown.

So therefore, I am a Hooker, who is a Townie and I will be buried in Sandy Hook so I will remain a Hooker.

I am a Hooker who is now a Townie and I am very proud to say so.

To many this could be most confusing and possibly even offensive. But in our town it makes total sense. When someone asks me where I live I say Newtown, because for the last 25 years I have lived in the Newtown area of Newtown. But I was born and raised in the Sandy Hook area of Newtown. Therefore, I am a Hooker who is now a Townie and that is a privilege.

This is just one of the many unique claims one can make in this wonderful town.

Newtown—One town with five boroughs, each with its own history and personality. And like people who live in the greater New York City area when you ask them where they are from they will often reply, "the city". But that could mean Brooklyn, Queens, Manhattan or any of the other boroughs. It's the same here in Newtown. You are a Newtowner but you might live in the area of Botsford, Hawleyville, Newtown, Dodgingtown or Sandy Hook. And each area is a very special part of the same town. And like the five fingers on your hand, each one has its own uniqueness but it is part of a team. It's the same here in Newtown.

So therefore, I am a Hooker, who is a Townie and I will be buried in Sandy Hook so I will remain a Hooker.

Susan Osborne White

Appleberry Farm on scenic Zoar Road

Dear Newtown Students,

This Thursday, June 13, 2013, has been declared "Thank You Thursday" by Newtown High School's Principal's Advisory Committee. PAC would like the entire school to take an opportunity to say thank you to someone who has impacted them in a positive way. This is my thank you to you.

This has been a horribly devastating school year. When Hurricane Sandy blew in and disrupted a week of school and Halloween (again!) in the beginning of the year, we had no idea that was just the beginning. We lost Chris, six educators, twenty first graders, and Ben. Our town was thrown into chaos as the media converged over and over. You attended memorial after memorial. You watched your parents, teachers, coaches, scout leaders, spiritual leaders, first responders, and the other adults in your life lose it in ways you dont see adults lose it too often. And you watched them do it over and over.

It would have been very easy for you to give up. To stop doing school work, stop going to school, to walk away from the adults in your life. To give up, to lay down, and to check out. Some of you did, but not for long. You got back up. You bounced back with kindness. You hugged those adults either physically or with your words and actions. You showed a resiliency that I didn't think was capable from so many young people. Even better, you got involved. You made choices to stand up for what you thought was right. You shared your views, you created art, you voiced your thoughts, you showed the adults in this town that you are going to be OK, that we are all going to be OK. You made a difference.

And you were there not just for the adults, but also for each other. It was beautiful to observe. Don't stop doing that, keep that kindness going. Carry it with you through your lives. And carry that resiliency with you, too. You got through this, you can get through anything the future throws at you. Remember what is important — each other. Remember what helped you and help someone else. Remember that it is ok to ask for help and that help is there if you need it. Remember that you have a town that loves you and will always be here for you. Remember to come home after you graduate and tell us

what great things you have done with
your life.

So, on this first Thank You Thursday,
I thank you for reminding me why I
went into teaching. You are all _incredible_!

With much love,

Lisa Sheridan

Dear Newtown Students,

This Thursday, June 13, 2013, has been declared "Thank You Thursday" by Newtown High School's Principal's Advisory Committee. PAC would like the entire school to take an opportunity to say thank you to someone who has impacted them in a positive way. This is my thank you to you.

This has been a horribly devastating school year. When Hurricane Sandy blew in and disrupted a week of school and Halloween (again!) in the beginning of the year, we had no idea that was just the beginning. We lost Chris, six educators, twenty first graders, and Ben. Our town was thrown into chaos as the media converged over and over. You attended memorial after memorial. You watched your parents, teachers, coaches, scout leaders, spiritual leaders, first responders, and the other adults in your life lose it in ways you don't see adults lose it too often. And you watched them do it over and over.

It would have been very easy for you to give up. To stop doing school work, stop going to school, to walk away from the adults in your life. To give up, to lay down, and to check out. Some of you did, but not for long. You got back up. You bounced back with kindness. You hugged those adults either physically or with your words and actions. You showed a resiliency that I didn't think was capable from so many young people. Even better, you got involved. You made choices to stand up for what you thought was right. You shared your views, you created art, you voiced your thoughts, you showed the adults in this town that you are going to be OK, that we are all going to be OK. You made a difference.

And you were there not just for the adults, but also for each other. It was beautiful to observe. Don't stop doing that, keep that kindness going. Carry it with you through your lives. And carry that resiliency with you, too. You got through this, you can get through anything the future throws at you. Remember what is important—each other. Remember what helped you and help someone else. Remember that it is ok to ask for help and that help is there for you if you need it. Remember that you have a town that loves you and will always be here for you. Remember to come home after you graduate and tell us what great things you have done with your life.

So, on this first Thank You Thursday, I thank you for reminding me why I went into teaching. You are all *incredible*!

With much love,
Lisa Sheridan

Dear Reader,

Newtown's C.H. Booth Library is an historical centerpiece for the town and more recently a fixture of my youth.

Many of my earliest memories include fondly recalled trips to the library filled with hours spent in the towering stacks, nights at the always amusing PJ Story Time, and summer vacations receiving prizes from young volunteers for all the books I had read.

As I grew up, PJ Story Time gave way to midnight release parties for the final Harry Potter novels and participation in a newly formed book trivia contest, The Battle of the Books. I started volunteering at the same Summer Reading Program I had taken part in, and not long after that I joined the staff. Working at a place deemed important enough to warrant annual elementary school field trips, where the most avid patrons come in daily, and the most frequently asked question was, "Is the attic really haunted?" was never a job I took for granted.

However, it wasn't until returning to work over winter break in December of 2012 after my first semester away from home that I realized how essential the Booth Library has always been to the Newtown community. The immediate action of the adult staff in a situation no training could prepare one for was commendable; programs to comfat the public, packs of therapy dogs and counselors, fielding nationwide calls from authors and other good Samaritans, and seas of donated books, movies, and toys were all results of the ceaseless efforts of those at the local library and the generosity of others. Watching the sensitivity and warmth my coworkers demonstrated after December 14th was astounding and made me proud to be an employee of the C. H. Booth Library and a resident of Newtown.

Sincerely,
David, 19 years old

Entrance to C.H. Booth Library

Dear Reader,

Newtown's C. H. Booth Library is an historical centerpiece for the town and more recently a fixture of my youth.

Many of my earliest memories include fondly recalled trips to the library filled with hours spent in the towering stacks, nights at the always amusing PJ Story Time, and summer vacations receiving prizes from young volunteers for all the books I had read.

As I grew up, PJ Story Time gave way to midnight release parties for the final Harry Potter novels and participation in a newly formed book trivia contest, The Battle of the Books. I started volunteering at the same Summer Reading Program I had taken part in, and not long after that I joined the staff. Working at a place deemed important enough to warrant annual elementary school field trips, where the most avid patrons come in daily, and the most frequently asked question was, "Is the attic really haunted?" was never a job I took for granted.

However, it wasn't until returning to work over winter break in December of 2012 after my first semester away from home that I realized how essential the Booth Library has always been to the Newtown Community. The immediate action of the adult staff in a situation no training could prepare one for was commendable; programs to comfort the public, packs of therapy dogs and counselors, fielding nationwide calls from authors and other good Samaritans, and seas of donated books, movies, and toys were all results of the ceaseless efforts of those at the local library and the generosity of others. Watching the sensitivity and warmth my coworkers demonstrated after December 14 was astounding and made me proud to be an employee of the C.H. Booth Library and a resident of Newtown.

Sincerely,
David, 19 years old

Children's Department in the C.H. Booth Library

Cathedral

Come all ye faithful—
the kids are still in school,
no one's on the playground.
Now tell us to "Feast in God",
to believe in your fairy dust salvation.

Come with your lights and teddy bears,
covered in dirty snow.
We forgot that faith comes in the darkest hour.
Remind us of the Gift that came this Christmas;
but your little crosses are too small to bear these ones.

Come with your daylight towers
spoiling the night—there is no rest here.
Take our eyes away from what draws you near—
just beyond the hill around the corner.
"Welcome" says the elementary sign, welcome.

A single candle flickers at the driveway's end,
but whipping rain drowns the flame;
wails from church towers echo
down darkened roads sucking air from lung,
smothering light.

The stained glass windows of this cathedral run red.
Picasso shards that cut too deep into the eyes.
They lie within, yet no salvation comes;
not for those who gave their lives on the altar
where bullets reign supreme.

Go away now—leave them alone!
Your bullet seed from blazing barrels
has ripped their little temples and torn
the fabric of belief in all that's good.
Leave us now—there is mending to be done.

Cathedral   **Gary Winn**

Come all ye faithful—
the kids are still in school,
no one's on the playground.
Now tell us to "Trust in God",
to believe in your fairy dust salvation.

Come with your lights and teddy bears,
covered in dirty snow.
We forgot that faith comes in the darkest hour.
Remind us of The Gift that came this Christmas;
but your little crosses are too small to bear these ones.

Come with your daylight towers
spoiling the night—there is no rest here.
Take our eyes away from what draws you near—
just beyond the hill around the corner.
"Welcome" says the elementary sign, welcome.

A single candle flickers at the driveway's end,
but whipping rain drowns the flame;
wails from church towers echo
down darkened roads sucking air from lungs,
smothering light.

The stained glass windows of this cathedral run red.
Picasso shards that cut too deep into the eyes.
They lie within, yet no salvation comes;
not for these, who gave their lives on the altar
where bullets reign supreme.

Go away now—leave them alone!
Your bulletseed from blazing barrels
has raped their little temples and torn
the fabric of belief in all that's good.
Leave us now—there is mending to be done.

To the world,

On December 14 so many of you came to know our lovely town of Sandy Hook, Connecticut through images you saw on television. There were two images that touched me the most, even as I sat here in Sandy Hook with my eyes glued to the TV.

One image that touched me came from above — showing the bright, beautiful — and now empty — playground at Sandy Hook School and I want to share that playground's story...

Ouch! I had just sat down on the worn, wooden playground at Sandy Hook School. I had been a first grader there for just a few weeks and now had managed to get a splinter just by playing at recess. It took several days for my parents to hold me still long enough to get the splinter out but that was just the beginning of how the splinter changed things at Sandy Hook School.

My Dad became one of very few "PTA Dads." He mentioned at the next meeting that Sandy Hook School should look into building a new playground — and when the cost estimates seemed well above what they should be, he offered to help. He ended up taking the lead on the project — organizing fundraisers, recruiting volunteers and working with the company to get a good deal. It took time — tag sales, Jolly Green Giant fairs, other fundraisers — but eventually the big day had come!

Sandy Hook School was getting a new playground! In an effort to continue saving money, parents and teachers worked after school and on weekends to complete the effort — mixing and pouring cement, placing posts, and tightening bolts. After years of work, Sandy Hook School had new playgrounds — smaller places for younger students and larger equipment for the older ones. There were swings, slides, bridges, stairs, games — and best of all, no wood to give splinters!

Sandy Hook was home to a beautiful new playground — one I have always been incredibly proud of because of all that my Dad did to help make it happen. But when I saw its bright red towers, blue posts and yellow slides sitting empty as helicopters shot scenes from above on December 14 and the days that followed, I couldn't help but cry. No longer will children run and play on a playground that brought so much happiness to thousands of Sandy Hook students.

The other touching image was of the makeshift memorial that appeared at the tree in the center of Sandy Hook — a place that, like the playground, had been home to so many happy memories. Less than two weeks before, thousands of Sandy Hook residents had gathered at the base of that tree to start the holiday season.

The Sandy Hook Tree Lighting is a special evening. The community gathers in Sandy Hook Village enjoying food, cocktails, coffee and hot chocolate from local businesses. There are 3D glasses to make the tree appear even more interesting, face paint, karaoke, caroling and visits from Santa. It was a festive evening – this year, topped off by an incredible honor for me... I got to flip the switch to light the tree. The crowd counted down, and then – flip! – the beautiful lights shone from the tree. There was applause and laughter and real holiday joy.

This same tree was the sight of the memorial less than 2 weeks later. When I saw it, the lights no longer seemed to shine as brightly and the happiness from that night had been sucked away.

But in the months that have now passed, I have seen our community begin to heal and move forward, and know how incredibly strong we are. I know that this December we will again gather in Sandy Hook center – to celebrate the holiday season with the joy, love and peace it should have. The lights will be lit and will shine brightly again.

They say a picture is worth a thousand words. These two images – of an empty playground and a memorial at the tree – are the two that said it all to me. Images that should have been such happiness and joy, forever changed.

With love and pride,
Sarah Hemingway

To the world,

On December 14 so many of you came to know our lovely town of Sandy Hook, Connecticut through images you saw on television. There were two images that touched me the most, even as I sat here in Sandy Hook with my eyes glued to the TV.

One image that touched me came from above—showing the bright, beautiful—and now empty—playground at Sandy Hook School and I want to share that playground's story . . .

Ouch! I had just sat down on the worn, wooden playground at Sandy Hook School. I had been a first grader there for just a few weeks and now had managed to get a splinter just by playing at recess. It took several days for my parents to hold me still long enough to get the splinter out but that was just the beginning of how the splinter changed things at Sandy Hook School.

My Dad became one of very few "PTA Dads." He mentioned at the next meeting that Sandy Hook School should look into building a new playground—and when the cost estimates seemed well above what they should be, he offered to help. He ended up taking the lead on the project—organizing fundraisers, recruiting volunteers and working with the company to get a good deal. It took time—tag sales, Jolly Green Giant Fairs, other fundraisers—but eventually the big day had come!

Sandy Hook School was getting a new playground! In an effort to continue saving money, parents and teachers worked after school and on weekends to complete the effort—mixing and pouring cement, placing posts, and tightening bolts. After years of work, Sandy Hook School had new playgrounds—smaller places for younger students and larger equipment for the older ones. There were swings, slides, bridges, stairs, games—and best of all, no wood to give splinters!

Sandy Hook was home to a beautiful new playground—one I have always been incredibly proud of because of all that my Dad did to help make it happen. But when I saw its bright red towers, blue posts and yellow slides sitting empty as helicopters shot scenes from above on December 14 and the days that followed, I couldn't help but cry. No longer will children run and play on a playground that brought so much happiness to thousands of Sandy Hook students.

The other touching image was of the makeshift memorial that appeared at the tree in the center of Sandy Hook—a place that, like the playground, had been home to so many happy memories. Less than two weeks before, thousands of Sandy Hook residents had gathered at the base of that tree to start the holiday season.

The Sandy Hook Tree Lighting is a special evening. The community gathers in Sandy Hook Village enjoying food, cocktails, coffee and hot chocolate from local businesses. There are 3D glasses to make the tree appear even more interesting, face paint, karaoke, caroling and visits from Santa. It was a festive evening—this year, topped off by an incredible honor for me . . . I got to flip the switch to light the tree. The crowd counted down, and then—flip!—the beautiful lights shone from the tree. There was applause and laughter and real holiday joy.

This same tree was the sight of the memorial less than 2 weeks later. When I saw it, the lights no longer seemed to shine as brightly and the happiness from that night had been sucked away.

But in the months that have now passed, I have seen our community begin to heal and move forward, and know how incredibly strong we are. I know that this December we will again gather in Sandy

Hook center—to celebrate the holiday season with the joy, love and peace it should have. The lights will be lit and will shine brightly again.

They say a picture is worth a thousand words. These two images—of an empty playground and a memorial at the tree—are the two that said it all to me. Images that should have been such happiness and joy, forever changed.

With love and pride,
Sarah Hemingway

Sandy Hook tree lighting, 2012

FOR MY ENTIRE LIFE, 21 YEARS, I HAVE LIVED IN NEWTOWN.
I'VE BEEN LUCKY ENOUGH TO CALL IT MY HOME.
IT'S BEEN THE PLACE WHERE I FIRST LEARNED TO CRAWL,
    WALK AND TALK;
THE PLACE WHERE I LEARNED TO RIDE MY BIKE WITH MY
    BROTHER BY MY SIDE.
MY HOME BECAME MY FIRST MEMORIES AND WHERE I MADE
    MY FIRST TRUE FRIENDS.
IT'S WHERE I LEARNED TO READ AND WRITE, AND CREATED
    BONDS WITH TEACHERS AND PEERS.
NEWTOWN IS MY CHILDHOOD; AND IT'S WHAT MADE ME WHO I
    AM TODAY.

THIS TOWN IS THE ONE WITH A FLAGPOLE IN THE MIDDLE OF
    THE ROAD.
IT IS THE TOWN THAT MY SOFTBALL TEAM BECAME 2010 SWC
    CHAMPIONS IN.
IT IS MAIN STREET; WITH TWO DOLLAR MOVIES AT EDMOND, AND
    SANDWICHES AT THE GENERAL STORE.
IT IS THE PLACE I GO WHEN I'M HOMESICK AT COLLEGE.
IT IS THE PLACE I RETREAT TO WHEN I NEED SUPPORT OR COMFORT.
AND NEWTOWN IS THE ONLY PLACE THAT MAKES ME LIGHT UP
    INSIDE AND FEEL COMPLETELY WHOLE.

NEWTOWN MAKES ME WANT TO BE A BETTER PERSON
IT HELPS ME CREATE AND ACHIEVE MY GOALS.
IT PUSHES ME TO ALWAYS CHOOSE LOVE.
AND HELPS ME STAND UP FOR WHAT I BELIEVE IN.
NEWTOWN HAS ALWAYS BEEN MY HOME.
NEWTOWN HAS ALWAYS BEEN MY STRENGTH.
AND NEWTOWN IS ALWAYS IN MY HEART; AND ALWAYS HAS BEEN

For my entire life, 21 years, I have lived in Newtown.
I've been lucky enough to call it my home.
It's been the place where I first learned to crawl,
    walk and talk;
The place where I learned to ride my bike with my
    brother by my side.
My home became my first memories and where I made
    my first true friends.
It's where I learned to read and write, and created
    bonds with teachers and peers.
Newtown is my childhood; and it's what made me who I
    am today.

This town is the one with a flagpole in the middle of
    the road.
It is the town that my softball team became 2010 SWC
    Champions in.
It is Main Street; with two dollar movies at Edmond, and
    sandwiches at the General Store.
It is the place I go when I'm homesick at college.
It is the place I retreat to when I need support or comfort.
And Newtown is the only place that makes me light up
    inside and feel completely whole.

Newtown makes me want to be a better person.
It helps me create and achieve my goals.
It pushes me to always choose love.
And helps me stand up for what I believe in.
Newtown has always been my home.
Newtown has always been my strength.
And Newtown is always in my heart; and always has been.

NE

Edmond Town Hall lobby of movie theater

Edmond Town Hall seating of movie theater

CHRISTMAS IN NEWTOWN, CONNECTICUT

The ancient Mayans are right: The world ends this week. That doesn't mean I'm not making plans for any event beyond December 21st. In fact, my family just decided that we will be spending Christmas in Newtown this year. But the world as we knew it must end. And I'd like to thank 26 heroes for showing us why.

In 1985, my family moved to Newtown, Connecticut. I attended fifth grade at Sandy Hook Elementary School. I recall the giant green footprints that were painted on the street from Riverside Road up to the school's entrance; I remember Mrs. Paige, my fifth grade teacher; and I recall my friends - carefree, learning, trying to be cool - exactly the way elementary school kids are supposed to be.

I am forever a part of that school and town, and it is forever a part of me. I share a kinship with every person who was a student there, who taught there, who walked those halls, and who had a connection with the building. If you were to draw a line between all of those people and all who knew them, it would include a community of millions of human beings. I'm not only saddened by the atrocity that took place at my old grammar school, I'm broken ... and ready to be rebuilt.

It's been surreal watching 24 x 7 television news plastering images of my childhood everywhere. The police press conferences are being held at Treadwell Park, a place where I've played in hundreds of soccer games. St. Rose of Lima Church is the church where I was confirmed. Sandy Hook center is an intersection I've driven through thousands of times. That firehouse and school - less than one mile from the house I grew up in, and the house where my parents still live — are landmarks that we passed almost every time we went anywhere. I can't help but feel naked and vulnerable as the world peers into my hometown.

But since the world is watching, that amazing community has an opportunity to make a stand and say something both comforting and profound here at the end of the world.

It took 26 angels — most of them young children — to accomplish what no single person could have done alone. They made the world stop turning. They made all of humanity pause. They forced us to ask ourselves, "What's really happening to us?" The ancient Mayans may have predicted the end of the world this week, but these 26 heroes fulfilled it.

These angels all have names: Charlotte Bacon, age 6, Daniel Barden, age 7, Rachel D'Avino, age 29, Olivia Engel, age 6, Josephine Gay, age 7, Ana M. Marquez-Greene, age 6, Dylan Hockley, age 6, Dawn Hochsprung, age 47, Madeleine F. Hsu, age 6, Catherine V. Hubbard, age 6, Chase Kowalski, age 7, Jesse Lewis, age 6, James Mattioli, age 6, Grace McDonnell, age 7, Anne Marie Murphy, age 52, Emilie Parker, age 6, Jack Pinto, age 6, Noah Pozner, age 6, Caroline Previdi, age 6, Jessica Rekos, age 6, Arielle Richman, age 6, Lauren Rousseau, age 30, Mary Sherlach, age 56, Victoria Soto, age 27, Benjamin Wheeler, age 6, and Allison N. Wyatt, age 6.

These fine human beings caused billions of extra hugs in recent days. They started dialogues that need to happen. They woke up a town, a state, a nation and a world to what really matters. They did not die in vain. It's our duty as humans to carry on their legacy.

The person who won't be named is the shooter. Names belong to people. He doesn't deserve his. The 26 angels are all that matter.

But the shooter had his role to play. It took only one monster to remind me that people are good, kind and selfless. Fred Rogers once said, "When I was a boy and I would see scary things in the news, my mother would say to me, 'Look for the helpers. You will always find people who are helping.'"

There was only one monster Friday morning, but hundreds of helpers who ran in — and those are just the first responders. As word spread, you had thousands then millions more who pledged prayers, support and money to help in any way they could.

Even in the darkest corners of this tragedy, we find light. The word "hero" is thrown around too much today, but already we have heard stories of true heroism from Sandy Hook. Victoria Soto, a first grade teacher, thought quickly when she heard shots fired in her school. She hid all of her students in closets and cabinets. When the gunman entered her classroom, she told him her kids were in the gym. The coward then shot the defenseless teacher. She was quick-thinking, brave and selflessly traded her life for those of her students. That is a hero. We should name towns and streets after her. No amount of honor will ever be enough. Each of her students will be greater people because of her. They will guide us into this brave new world.

On Sunday, President Obama visited my quiet hometown to help console the victims' families and a grieving nation. While it was right for him to do so, it saddens me that any United States president would have ever even heard of my little town.

As one of my high school friends pointed out in his Facebook post, "The last time shots were fired like this in Newtown was during the Revolutionary War when Rochambeau's army took practice shots at weather vanes." This stuff doesn't happen in Newtown. It shouldn't happen anywhere.

Of all of the human emotions, "helpless" is the worst. If there was something I could build, I'd build it; something I could fix, I'd fix it; something I could break to undo this, I'd break it. For now, all I can do is prey for those who need our support the most.

When the prayers have been said, and the condolences offered, next I will focus this energy on myself, on my family and those around me. I can be more active in my community. I will try to right the tiny wrongs I encounter in my everyday life. I can hug and appreciate my five-year-old daughter a little more each day. That is a gift 26 angels gave me on Friday.

I moved away from Newtown after college. But I've never lost touch. My parents live there, as do my sister, my uncle and so many friends. Today as I write this from my office in Massachusetts, I've never felt so close to, yet so far away from my hometown. I'll be there for Christmas because there's no place on Earth where hope could shine any brighter. There's no town or village that understands the word "community" better than Newtown. This is a place that comes together to help each other in times of need. They're strong in their faith, conviction and spirit. And that's what this holiday is supposed to be about.

I can't help that the name Newtown will become synonymous with this tragedy. But as the world watches, may they see the light that shines out of every person who shares the unimaginable pain of our neighbors who lost a child, a parent, a spouse, or a friend. Long after the cameras are off and the news vans pull out of town, that light will continue to glow thanks to 26 angels and so many heroes who reminded the world of our humanity.

Yes, the world as we know it has ended, which makes this a time for new beginnings. I'll work each day to make this new world a better place than the old... and Mom and Dad, I'll be in Newtown for Christmas. Newtown is home.

Jeff Belanger
12/16/12

Christmas in Newtown, Connecticut

The ancient Mayans are right: The world ends this week. That doesn't mean I'm not making plans for any event beyond December 21st. In fact, my family just decided that we will be spending Christmas in Newtown this year. But the world as we knew it must end. And I'd like to thank 26 heroes for showing us why.

In 1985, my family moved to Newtown, Connecticut. I attended fifth grade at Sandy Hook Elementary School. I recall the giant green footprints that were painted on the street from Riverside Road up to the school's entrance; I remember Mrs. Paige, my fifth grade teacher; and I recall my friends—carefree, learning, trying to be cool—exactly the way elementary school kids are supposed to be.

I am forever a part of that school and town, and it is forever a part of me. I share a kinship with every person who was a student there, who taught there, who walked those halls, and who had a connection with the building. If you were to draw a line between all of those people and all who knew them, it would include a community of millions of human beings. I'm not only saddened by the atrocity that took place at my old grammar school, I'm broken . . . and ready to be rebuilt.

It's been surreal watching 24×7 television news plastering images of my childhood everywhere. The police press conferences are being held at Treadwell Park, a place where I've played in hundreds of soccer games. St. Rose of Lima Church is the church where I was confirmed. Sandy Hook center is an intersection I've driven through thousands of times. That firehouse and school—less than one mile from the house I grew up in, and the house where my parents still live—are landmarks that we passed almost every time we went anywhere. I can't help but feel naked and vulnerable as the world peers into my hometown.

But since the world *is* watching, that amazing community has an opportunity to make a stand and say something both comforting and profound here at the end of the world.

It took 26 angels—most of them young children—to accomplish what no single person could have done alone. They made the world stop turning. They made all of humanity pause. They forced us to ask ourselves, "What's really happening to us?" The ancient Mayans may have predicted the end of the world this week, but these 26 heroes fulfilled it.

These angels all have names: Charlotte Bacon, age 6, Daniel Barden, age 7, Rachel D'Avino, age 29, Olivia Engel, age 6, Josephine Gay, age 7, Ana M. Marquez-Greene, age 6, Dylan Hockley, age 6, Dawn Hochsprung, age 47, Madeleine F. Hsu, age 6, Catherine V. Hubbard, age 6, Chase Kowalski, age 7, Jesse Lewis, age 6, James Mattioli, age 6, Grace McDonnell, age 7, Anne Marie Murphy, age 52, Emilie Parker, age 6, Jack Pinto, age 6, Noah Pozner, age 6, Caroline Previdi, age 6, Jessica Rekos, age 6, Avielle Richman, age 6, Lauren Rousseau, age 30, Mary Sherlach, age 56, Victoria Soto, age 27, Benjamin Wheeler, age 6, and Allison N. Wyatt, age 6.

These fine human beings caused billions of extra hugs in recent days. They started dialogues that need to happen. They woke up a town, a state, a nation and a world to what really matters. They did not die in vain. It's our duty as humans to carry on their legacy.

The person who won't be named is the shooter. Names belong to people. He doesn't deserve his. The 26 angels are all that matter.

But the shooter had his role to play. It took only one monster to remind me that people are good, kind and selfless. Fred Rogers once said, "When I was a boy and I would see scary things in the news, my mother would say to me, 'Look for the helpers. You will always find people who are helping.'"

There was only one monster Friday morning, but hundreds of helpers who ran in—and those are just the first responders. As word spread, you had thousands then millions more who pledged prayers, support and money to help in any way they could.

Even in the darkest corners of this tragedy, we find light. The word "hero" is thrown around too much today, but already we have heard stories of true heroism from Sandy Hook. Victoria Soto, a first grade teacher, thought quickly when she heard shots fired in her school. She hid all of her students in closets and cabinets. When the gunman entered her classroom, she told him her kids were in the gym. The coward then shot the defenseless teacher. She was quick-thinking, brave and selflessly traded her life for those of her students. *That* is a hero. We should name towns and streets after her. No amount of honor will ever be enough. Each of her students will be greater people because of her. They will guide us into this brave new world.

On Sunday, President Obama visited my quiet hometown to help console the victims' families and a grieving nation. While it was right for him to do so, it saddens me that any United States president would have ever even heard of my little town.

As one of my high school friends pointed out in his Facebook post, "The last time shots were fired like this in Newtown was during the Revolutionary War when Rochambeau's army took practice shots at weather vanes." This stuff doesn't happen in Newtown. It shouldn't happen *anywhere*.

Of all of the human emotions, "helpless" is the worst. If there was something I could build, I'd build it; something I could fix, I'd fix it; something I could break to undo this, I'd break it. For now, all I can do is pray for those who need our support the most.

When the prayers have been said, and the condolences offered, next I will focus this energy on myself, on my family and those around me. I can be more active in my community. I will try to right the tiny wrongs I encounter in my everyday life. I can hug and appreciate my five-year-old daughter a little more each day. That is a gift 26 angels gave me on Friday.

I moved away from Newtown after college. But I've never lost touch. My parents live there, as do my sister, my uncle and so many friends. Today as I write this from my office in Massachusetts, I've never felt so close to, yet so far away from my hometown. I'll be there for Christmas because there's no place on Earth where hope could shine any brighter. There's no town or village that understands the word "community" better than Newtown. This is a place that comes together to help each other in times of need. They're strong in their faith, conviction and spirit. And that's what this holiday is supposed to be about.

I can't help that the name Newtown will become synonymous with this tragedy. But as the world watches, may they see the light that shines out of every person who shares the unimaginable pain of our neighbors who lost a child, a parent, a spouse, or a friend. Long after the cameras are off and the news vans pull out of town, that light will continue to glow thanks to 26 angels and so many heroes who reminded the world of our humanity.

Yes, the world as we know it has ended, which makes this a time for new beginnings. I'll work each day to make this new world a better place than the old . . . and Mom and Dad, I'll be in Newtown for Christmas. Newtown is home.

Jeff Belanger
12/16/12

When we were looking to buy a house in Sandy Hook, everyone told us "the school system was the best." We laughed because we never stayed in one place very long. Matt was only one year old. He's now 24, and we are still here. When I think of Sandy Hook School a few events come to mind...

At Halloween when Danielle was in Kindergarten, all the students and teachers would dress up and "parade" around the courtyard for us parents.

When Matt was in the 5th grade they studied "The Push Cart Wars." The kids choose a partner or two and had to build a cart of some sort, with help from Dad of course. They had to decide on what goods they would sell, whether to buy or make the goods, with help from Mom, and how much they should charge. The night before the "Big Day," they would go to the school and set up their cants (and admire the works of their fellow students). The following day, the kids would sell their goods to the younger students at the school. This was always the Friday before Mother's Day. Danielle would go to school with $3.00 and would be so proud of the items she would come home with. Maybe that's where she found her love of shopping.

Both my kids learned to ride their bikes in the grass and then advanced to the black top at Sandy Hook School.

We have so many great memories of our years in Sandy Hook that we cannot think of a better place to live

When we were looking to buy a house in Sandy Hook, everyone told us "the school system was the best." We laughed because we never stayed in one place very long. Matt was only one year old. He's now 24, and we are still here. When I think of Sandy Hook School a few events come to mind . . .

At Halloween when Danielle was in Kindergarten, all the students and teachers would dress up and "parade" around the courtyard for us parents.

When Matt was in the 5th grade they studied "The Push Cart Wars." The kids choose a partner or two and had to build a cart of some sort, with help from Dad of course. They had to decide on what goods they would sell, whether to buy or make the goods, with help from Mom, and how much they should charge. The night before the "Big Day," they would go to the school and set up their carts (and admire the work of their fellow students). The following day, the kids would sell their goods to the younger students at the school. This was always the Friday before Mother's Day. Danielle would go to school with $3.00 and would be so proud of the items she would come home with. Maybe that's where she found her love of shopping.

Both my kids learned to ride their bikes in the grass and then advanced to the black top at Sandy Hook School.

We have so many great memories of our years in Sandy Hook that we cannot think of a better place to live.

Sandy Hook Green Ribbon Ride May 5, 2013 in Sandy Hook

Heart aches...

... it keeps growing ... spreading
until it bursts ... open ... wide.
Pain spilling ... tumbling ...
over and over and over ...
No place to go to stop it ...

The mouth opens to scream...
there is no sound ...
It's stuck ... deep inside.
Trying to come to the surface
but it can't get past...

... the tears.
The tears flowing over the cheeks
falling into the lap...
down to the floor ...
the trickle turns into a puddle ...
turns into a stream ...
turns into a river...
turns into an ocean ...

which flows, surges and beats
with all the aching hearts...

A tearful Sandy Hooker

Heart aches . . .

. . . it keeps growing . . . spreading
until it bursts . . . open . . . wide.
Pain spilling . . . tumbling . . .
over and over and over . . .
No place to go to stop it . . .

The mouth opens to scream . . .
there is no sound . . .
it's stuck . . . deep inside.
Trying to come to the surface
but it can't get past . . .

. . . the tears.
The tears flowing over the cheeks
falling into the lap . . .
down to the floor . . .
the trickle turns into a puddle . . .
turns into a stream . . .
turns into a river . . .
turns into an ocean . . .

which flows, surges and beats
with all the aching hearts . . .

A tearful Sandy Hooker

I remember my very first day at Sandy Hook School. It was 1997 and I had just turned 7 years old. My family had recently moved from a nearby town to Sandy Hook — a quiet, homey, beautiful section of Newtown. Awkward and shy, with hair so thick and curly you would have thought I'd just had a perm gone wrong, I was nervous to start my first day at a new school full of unfamiliar faces. Sitting Indian style on the floor of Mrs. Roberson's 2nd grade class, I glanced around the room to the fresh faces sitting beside me and missed my old school, my old friends. Distracting me from my gloom, Mrs. Roberson announced to the class that I was new and for everyone to give me a warm welcome. It was then that a small, rosy-cheeked Korean girl wearing round glasses similar to Harry Potter's, turned to me and said "Hi, my name's Irene." In that moment, my nerves disappeared and a smile slowly crossed my face as I realized I had just made my first friend in this comforting and embracing town.

My years at Sandy Hook School came and went in the blink of an eye. The memories I hold from this school are some of the most sacred and dear memories that I have. It was on this schools playground, that I raced my friends to the swings during recess and sat under an old tree gossiping with my girls about our new crushes. It was in this schools court yard that my fellow classmates and I followed clues and miniature footprints to hunt for leprechauns on St. Patrick's Day. It was in this schools' cafeteria that I lost a loose tooth in a taco during lunch. It was in the auditorium that we were taught that "a lot" was two words and not one, and where Traci and I made soap to sell at our 5th grade push-cart day (sadly our hand-made soap wasn't nearly as big of a seller as the candy at the neighboring cart). It was on our class trip to Treadwell Park that I came out of my shy shell and asked out my first boyfriend. In a new town, Sandy Hook School welcomed me with open arms and provided me with memories that I will cherish forever.

On the morning of December 14th, 2012, I was getting ready for another day of waitressing at the town country club when I received a text from a friend saying there had been reports of a shooting at one of the schools. In a town where the biggest crimes committed consist of underage drinking and high school parties, I assumed the shooting was just a scare, or even a mistake. By the time I arrived at work 30 minutes later, every news channel was talking about Sandy Hook. In just a few hours, Newtown went from being a town that nobody had ever heard of, to being the town that was the talk of the world. In between serving tables, I happened to glance at the television and what I saw felt like a punch in the gut. There was my sweet innocent school, my Sandy Hook, on national television from a bird's eye view. Everything about the school looked exactly how I remembered it; the playground, the small baseball field, the court yard in the middle of the square building. It was the same exact school, yet completely different. Police cars lined the streets surrounding the entrance of the school. Every channel we flipped through consisted of different reporters filling the streets that I drive through every day. Mothers, fathers, siblings and friends waited anxiously in the parking lot of the volunteer fire department where I once had a fire safety demonstration, awaiting the news of their loved ones. In just minutes, inside the building where I had once felt the most safe and secure, 26 innocent lives were stolen in the cruelest way possible.

    As someone who rarely cries, especially

in front of other people, I found myself crying every day for months. I was, and still am constantly reminded of what occured on the fateful day. Just driving 5 minutes from my house, you pass by two victim's houses and even the school itself. Most stores in town have decorated their windows with signs showing love and support for our community. Cars are plastered with decals ranging from green ribbons, to stickers with the slogans "We Are Sandy Hook, We Choose Love" and "Proud to be from Newtown". These small symbols are both troubling and reassuring; never letting us forget the pain we've endured yet reminding us of our incredible strength and support for each other. For a while I found myself sometimes lying about where I was from. There were two reasons for this: 1. So I didn't make the other person feel uncomfortable in a casual conversation, and 2. So I wouldn't have to hear the dreaded "Oh...I'm sorry".

And sometimes what was worse than the "I'm sorry" response was the question upon question response: "How is your town holding up?", "Did you know anyone?" or "what was it like going to school there?" Sometimes, it was just easier to lie.

I would do anything to rewind time, to turn Newtown back into the quiet, unknown dot on a map. I would do anything to see my adorable, innocent neighbor run off the school bus or playing basketball with his brother on a warm sunny day, small things he was robbed of the day his young life was taken from him. I would do anything to take the place of any of those beautiful children so they could continue living the life they were supposed to, so they could get their license, go to prom, go to college, have their first legal drink, get their first adult job, start a family of their own; things that many of us take for granted on a daily basis. And I would do anything to just talk to the heroes who selflessly threw themselves in harm's way, the heroes who took bullets and ultimately died trying to save another life. Unfortunately we can't turn back time. All we can do is look forward and try to make the world a better place to honor those who were forced to leave it. And if anything can come out of this tragedy, it's that many of us are working hard to make sure something like this never happens again; that no one ever has to feel the pain Newtown, Columbine, Virginia Tech, Aurora and many others have had to feel. Whether that's gun control, mental health research, or a combination of them both, we are trying, trying, trying. And if anything can come out of this tragedy it's that Newtown is a million times stronger, kinder and more loving than ever before, and I've never felt more proud to say where I come from. - Rachael M.

Stores with the "We are Sandy Hook—We Choose Love" sign throughout Sandy Hook and Newtown

I remember my very first day at Sandy Hook School. It was 1997 and I had just turned 7 years old. My family had recently moved from a nearby town to Sandy Hook—a quiet, homey, beautiful section of Newtown. Awkward and shy, with hair so thick and curly you would have thought I'd just had a perm gone wrong, I was nervous to start my first day at a new school full of unfamiliar faces. Sitting Indian style on the floor of Mrs. Roberson's second grade class, I glanced around the room to the fresh faces sitting beside me and missed my old school, my old friends. Distracting me from my gloom, Mrs. Roberson announced to the class that I was new and for everyone to give me a warm welcome. It was then that a small, rosy-cheeked Korean girl wearing round glasses similar to Harry Potter's, turned to me and said "Hi, my name's Irene." In that moment, my nerves disappeared and a smile slowly crossed my face as I realized I had just made my first friend in this comforting and embracing town.

My years at Sandy Hook School came and went in the blink of an eye. The memories I hold from this school are some of the most sacred and dear memories that I have. It was on this schools playground, that I raced my friends to the swings during recess and sat under an old tree gossiping with my girls about our new crushes. It was in this schools court yard that my fellow classmates and I followed clues and miniature footprints to hunt for leprechauns on St. Patrick's Day. It was in this schools' cafeteria that I lost a loose tooth in a taco during lunch. It was in the auditorium that we were taught that "a lot" was two words and not one, and where Traci and I made soap to sell at our 5th grade push-cart day (sadly our hand-made soap wasn't nearly as big of a seller as the candy at the neighboring cart). It was on our class trip to Treadwell Park that I came out of my shy shell and asked out my first boyfriend. In a new town, Sandy Hook School welcomed me with open arms and provided me with memories that I will cherish forever.

On the morning of December 14th, 2012, I was getting ready for another day of waitressing at the town country club when I received a text from a friend saying there had been reports of a shooting at one of the schools. In a town where the biggest crimes committed consist of underage drinking and high school parties, I assumed the shooting was just a scare, or even a mistake. By the time I arrived at work 30 minutes later, every news channel was talking about Sandy Hook. In just a few hours, Newtown went from being a town that nobody had ever heard of, to being the town that was the talk of the world. In between serving tables, I happened to glance at the television and what I saw felt like a punch in the gut. There was my sweet innocent school, my Sandy Hook, on national television from a bird's eye view. Everything about the school looked exactly how I remembered it; the playground, the small baseball field, the court yard in the middle of the square building. It was the same exact school, yet completely different. Police cars lined the streets surrounding the entrance of the school. Every channel we flipped through consisted of different reporters filling the streets that I drive through every day. Mothers, fathers, siblings and friends waited anxiously in the parking lot of the volunteer fire department where I once had a fire safety demonstration, awaiting the news of their loved ones. In just minutes, inside the building where I had once felt the most safe and secure, 26 innocent lives were stolen in the cruelest way possible.

As someone who rarely cries, especially in front of other people, I found myself crying every day for months. I was, and still am constantly reminded of what occurred on that fateful day. Just driving 5 minutes from my house, you pass by two victim's houses and even the school itself. Most stores in town have decorated their windows with signs showing love and support for our community. Cars are plastered with decals ranging from green ribbons, to stickers with the slogans "We Are Sandy Hook, We Choose Love" and "Proud to be from Newtown." These small symbols are both troubling and re-assuring; never letting us forget the pain we've endured yet reminding us of our incredible strength and support for each other. For a while I found myself sometimes lying about where I was from. There were two reasons for this: 1. So I didn't make the other person feel uncomfortable in a casual con-versation, and 2. So I wouldn't have to hear the dreaded "Oh . . . I'm sorry." And sometimes what was worse than the "I'm sorry" response was the question upon question response: "How is your town holding up?", "Did you know anyone?" or "What was it like going to school there?" Sometimes, it was just easier to lie.

I would do anything to rewind time, to turn Newtown back into the quiet, unknown dot on a map. I would do anything to see my adorable, innocent neighbor run off the school bus or playing basketball with his brother on a warm sunny day, small things he was robbed of the day his young life was taken from him. I would do anything to take the place of any of those beautiful children so they could contin-ue living the life they were supposed to, so they could get their license, go to prom, go to college, have their first legal drink, get their first adult job, start a family of their own; things that many of us take for granted on a daily basis. And I would do anything to just talk to the heroes who selflessly threw themselves in harm's way, the heroes who took bullets and ultimately died trying to save another life. Unfortunately we can't turn back time. All we can do is look forward and try to make the world a better place to honor those who were forced to leave it. And if anything can come out of this tragedy, it's that many of us are working hard to make sure something like this never happens again, that no one ever has to feel the pain Newtown, Columbine, Virginia Tech, Aurora and many others have had to feel. Whether that's gun control, mental health research, or a combination of them both, we are trying, trying, trying. And if anything can come out of this tragedy, it's that Newtown is a million times stron-ger, kinder and more loving than ever before, and I've never felt more proud to say where I come from.

—Rachael M.

I was sitting on the curb outside Newtown High School, in the parking lot, waiting to be picked up from school on my first day as a new 9th grade student after we had just moved to Sandy Hook, at the end of my freshman year of high school in 1984. I was crying and Dr. Breslin, the principal of Newtown High School at the time came down and sat beside me and asked if I was ok. I said "sure" through my tears. He put his arm around me and said, "Tomorrow will be better." That day, my first day of school in a new school, there was a huge food fight in the cafeteria during my lunch period. It was a bad day and Dr. Breslin had no idea I was new but that is who he was. That was my Newtown. That day marked the beginning of a special relationship between Dr. Breslin and I. I struggled as a teenager. Not academically, and by all means, from the outside, I looked quite successful. But inside it was different. I ended up needing psychiatric care as a teenager. Dr. Breslin, his wife and his newborn daughter always visited me. Again, that was my Newtown. I went to undergraduate school in Fairfield, Connecticut and graduate school in the Bronx, New York and subsequently lived in New York for about 10 years. After I got married (at Newtown's Meeting House) I moved back to Newtown. In fact, while I was working in Westport at an outpatient mental health clinic, I was attending a community outreach meeting.

I happened to be sitting across from a teacher who recognized me from high school. As we caught up he asked where I was currently living. As I replied "Newtown", he laughed and added, "I remember when you were in high school you couldn't wait to get out of Newtown". I replied "I know, I know." The fact of the matter is I never said those words nor had I ever even had that individual as a teacher. While this is the sort of thing someone says while they are a teenager and certainly someone from Newtown could have said, I didn't really feel that negatively about Newtown. What I do remember is that I always felt cared for here. I loved this school. I loved the people here; I loved my teachers, the secretaries, my coaches, and the lunch lady in the cafeteria. There was a community of care, concern and love that began long before 12/14. That is my Newtown. This is the community in which I want to raise my son. This is the community in which I want to retire. This is my Newtown, I love Newtown.

Susan Belanger, Ph.D.

I was sitting on the curb outside Newtown High School, in the parking lot, waiting to be picked up from school on my first day as a new 9th grade student after we had just moved to Sandy Hook, at the end of my freshman year of high school in 1984. I was crying and Dr. Breslin, the principal of Newtown High School at the time came down and sat beside me and asked if I was ok. I said "fine" through my tears. He put his arm around me and said, "Tomorrow will be better." That day, my first day of school in a new school, there was a huge food fight in the cafeteria during my lunch period. It was a bad day and Dr. Breslin had no idea I was new but that is who he was. That was my Newtown. That day marked the beginning of a special relationship between Dr. Breslin and I. I struggled as a teenager. Not academically, and by all means, from the outside, I looked quite successful. But inside it was different. I ended up needing psychiatric care as a teenager. Dr. Breslin, his wife and his newborn daughter always visited me. Again, that was my Newtown. I went to undergraduate school in Fairfield, Connecticut and graduate school in the Bronx, New York and subsequently lived in New York for about 10 years. After I got married (at Newtown's Meeting House) I moved back to Newtown. In fact, while I was working in Westport at an outpatient mental health clinic, I was attending a community outreach meeting. I happened to be sitting across from a teacher who recognized me from high school. As we caught up he asked where I was currently living. As I replied "Newtown", he laughed and added, "I remember when you were in high school you couldn't wait to get out of Newtown". I replied "I know, I know." The fact of the matter is I never said those words nor had I ever even had that individual as a teacher. While this is the sort of thing someone says while they are a teenager and certainly someone from Newtown could have said, I didn't really feel that negatively about Newtown. What I do remember is that I always felt cared for here. I loved this school. I loved the people here; I loved my teachers, the secretaries, my coaches, and the lunch lady in the cafeteria. There was a community of care, concern and love that began long before 12/14. That is my Newtown. This is the community in which I want to raise my son. This is the community in which I want to retire. This is my Newtown, I love Newtown.

Susan Belanger, Ph.D.

Newtown High School sign at entrance

I have lived in Newtown for over 40 years
and one of the things I love the most
is Newtown's Main St. It has not
changed over that time and has
retained its character during the years.
I have many fond memories of walking
or riding my bike into town to work
at the General Store, which was an
operating grocery store 30 years ago.
I also enjoyed then & now going to
see movies at the Town Hall. Even
though the price has increased from
$1 to $2 it is still a great value.
During the year there are some festivals
and house tours that occur on Main
St and help bring people to our town
so they can see how great it is.
The houses on Main St hold a lot of
history and the Historic District has done
a great job working with the homeowners
in retaining the charm and feel of
the history. It has been very enjoyable
to take walks around town and
appreciate that some beautiful things
never change, like Newtown's Main St.

I have lived in Newtown for over 40 years and one of the things I love the most is Newtown's Main Street. It has not changed over that time and has retained its character during the years. I have many fond memories of walking or riding my bike into town to work at the General Store, which was an operating grocery store 30 years ago. I also enjoyed then and now going to see movies at the Town Hall. Even though the price has increased from $1 to $2 it is still a great value. During the year there are some festivals and house tours that occur on Main Street and help bring people to our town so they can see how great it is. The houses on Main Street hold a lot of history and the Historic District has done a great job working with the homeowners in retaining the charm and feel of the history. It has been very enjoyable to take walks around town and appreciate that some beautiful things never change, like Newtown's Main Street.

Main Street in Newtown

Enough - enough - enough - enough already.

It isn't loud. But it is getting louder.
Enough with the balloons and ribbons on street signs and mailboxes. Enough with car decals. Enough with wristbands. Enough with tickets to sporting events. Enough with athletes visiting the town. Enough with letting five horrible minutes defining this town. Enough with dwelling in the past.

Yes, Newtown came together after the tragedy. And yes, we showed our resiliency. But Newtown wasn't a community singing Kumbaya before Dec. 14. Budget votes pitted families with children in school against those who pay a lot and receive so little in return. Longtimers resent the development that turned farm land into subdivided properties. The once rural town, dotted with farms and families with roots to the settlers, has become a down-country commuter town without a train station. Newtown has been fragmented for years. Decades, some might say.

And while we held hands and cried together in December, not everything has been a love fest in the ensuing months. And in some ways, those five minutes in that school didn't just leave holes in the cinderblock of Sandy Hook School. It left holes in the community and fragmented it even more. Cracks that are spreading and getting wider. Cracks with talons and tentacles.

Cracks created because the process of grieving is as different as those who experience it. Cracks created from a judgment that those who did not lose a family member should be further into the process of recovery. Cracks created because some have found a comfort zone is grief.

You hear it in private conversations. You hear it in hushed tones. It isn't talked about openly. It is subtle, but it is there. In some corners of Newtown, grief has become a competition.

"Why did she have to take time off from work? She wasn't in the front of the building. I was."
"It happened in Sandy Hook, not Newtown."

"You didn't have kids in the school."

"I don't know why the cops have PTSD. They are trained for this. We weren't."

"I had to walk past bodies in the hall."

Throw into the mix money and gifts and then the hum becomes louder.

"This should be just for the kids at Sandy Hook, not everyone in town."

"How come he got that? He wasn't even on site that day."

"What else are we getting."

While Newtown and the nation grieves with the families for their loss, not all of their actions and opinions have been embraced.

A ripple of comments surfaced when some of the victims' families balked about the delay in disbursing the millions of dollars collected. Should the families get all the money or should some be held for mental health issues the town will certainly face in the future? Should all the money go to the families of those slaughtered in the building, or do those injured and those who escaped deserve a piece of the pie?

Comments that no amount of money can replace a child was said, and not necessarily whispered. So many were vocal in their opinions about who should get what. Politicians made comments about the committee charged with distributing funds. Committee members politely said the politicians didn't have an understanding of the process or a perception of the future.

The hand holding and tear wiping has stopped. In some ways sniping and arguing has taken its place.

The gifts that came into town were from the heart and the intention of bringing healing to a broken community was wonderful. The magnitude was overwhelming, but greed and entitlement reared their ugly heads and took a deep breath. A community give away of gifts sent to the town was an organized grab fest. People arrived with large, dark garbage bags and stuffed it with expensive dolls, toys and any other item they could find. Some tried to skirt the system and sneak out more than their allotment. Residents brought in people from out of town. Posters filled with messages of hope and caring were hung throughout the gymnasium like quilts made to warm the town's soul, but no one was reading them. They were too busy grabbing stuff.

The police department had to institute a lottery system for all gifts donated to the department. The infighting became too loud and divisive.

"He didn't go into the building. I did."

"He didn't see what I saw."

"He already got a lot."

Fire fighters from one department didn't want to share donations sent to their house with the other fire departments in town.

"The money was sent to us."

"They weren't there that day."

Youngsters who don't live in town were admitted to a community concert because their grandparents got them tickets. Employees of the school system who don't live in town and were nowhere near Sandy Hook that day got invited to a James Taylor concert at a local church. And some brought a long line of relatives.

Someone else's loss was their gain.

A small segment of Newtown has found the power in grief and uses it to their advantage.

While the ticket distribution, the gifts and the concerts are winding down, the discussion about building a new school is just heating up. Families with children in Sandy Hook have said they want a $50 million school constructed. Others have said they don't want a nail hammered until a check for the entire amount has been delivered to town officials. And even then, they want to make sure the check has cleared.

And when victim's family members who don't live in Newtown felt compelled to comment on the future of the school site, there was a buzz that they don't pay taxes here, they will never be financially impacted by any decision and need to shut up.

Spending money for a police presence in each school is another topic sending townsfolks scurrying behind two lines drawn in the sand.

"My kid needs to feel protected no matter the cost."

"We don't need a cop in every school. It won't make a difference."

"This was just a fluke. It won't happen again. Let's not get crazy."

And as we creep toward the one-year mark, the scabs will be picked off and the wound inflicted on the town will once again be exposed. A raw hotbed of emotion.

And from those who are sick and tired of the media descending on our town, the debates about money distribution, gun control, and the politics of a tragedy, the crowds who made Newtown a destination to gawk and picture taking and the teddy bears and flowers left for children who are no longer alive, you will hear:

Enough
Enough
Enough already.

Enough—enough—enough—enough already.

It isn't loud. But it is getting louder.

Enough with the balloons and ribbons on street signs and mailboxes. Enough with car decals. Enough with wristbands. Enough with tickets to sporting events. Enough with athletes visiting the town.

Enough with letting five horrible minutes defining this town. Enough with dwelling in the past.

Yes, Newtown came together after the tragedy. And yes, we showed our resiliency. But Newtown wasn't a community singing Kumbaya before Dec. 14. Budget votes pitted families with children in school against those who pay a lot and receive so little in return. Longtimers resent the development that turned farm land into subdivided properties. The once rural town, dotted with farms and families with roots to the settlers, has become a down-county commuter town without a train station.

Newtown has been fragmented for years. Decades, some might say.

And while we held hands and cried together in December, not everything has been a love fest in the ensuing months. And in some ways, those five minutes in that school didn't just leave holes in the cinderblock of Sandy Hook School. It left holes in the community and fragmented it even more. Cracks that are spreading and getting wider. Cracks with talons and tentacles.

Cracks created because the process of grieving is as different as those who experience it. Cracks created from a judgment that those who did not lose a family member should be further into the process of recovery. Cracks created because some have found a comfort zone is grief.

You hear it in private conversations. You hear it in hushed tones. It isn't talked about openly. It is subtle, but it is there. In some corners of Newtown, grief has become a competition.

"Why did she have to take time off from work? She wasn't in the front of the building. I was."

"It happened in Sandy Hook, not Newtown."

"You didn't have kids in the school."

"I don't know why the cops have PTSD. They are trained for this. We weren't."

"I had to walk past bodies in the hall."

Throw into the mix money and gifts and the hum becomes louder.

"This should be just for the kids at Sandy Hook, not everyone in town."

"How come he got that? He wasn't even on site that day."

"What else are we getting?"

While Newtown and the nation grieves with the families for their loss, not all of their actions and opinions have been embraced.

A ripple of comments surfaced when some of the victims' families balked about the delay in disbursing the millions of dollars collected. Should the families get all the money or should some be held for mental health issues the town will certainly face in the future? Should all the money go to the families of those slaughtered in the building, or do those injured and those who escaped deserve a piece of the pie?

Comments that no amount of money can replace a child was said, and not necessarily whispered. So many were vocal in their opinions about who should get what. Politicians made comments about the committee charged with distributing funds. Committee members politely said the politicians didn't have an understanding of the process or a perception of the future.

The hand holding and tear wiping has stopped. In some ways sniping and arguing has taken its place.

The gifts that came into town were from the heart and the intention of bringing healing to a broken community was wonderful. The magnitude was overwhelming, but greed and entitlement reared their ugly heads and took a deep breath. A community give away of gifts sent to the town was an organized grab fest. People arrived with large, dark garbage bags and stuffed it with expensive dolls, toys and any other item they could find. Some tried to skirt the system and sneak out more than their allotment. Residents brought in people from out of town. Posters filled with messages of hope and caring were hung throughout the gymnasium like quilts made to warm the town's soul, but no one was reading them. They were too busy grabbing stuff.

The police department had to institute a lottery system for all gifts donated to the department. The infighting became too loud and divisive.

"He didn't go into the building. I did."

"He didn't see what I saw."

"He already got a lot."

Firefighters from one department didn't want to share donations sent to their house with the other fire departments in town.

"The money was sent to us."

"They weren't there that day."

Youngsters who don't live in town were admitted to a community concert because their grandparents got them tickets. Employees of the school system who don't live in town and were nowhere near Sandy Hook that day got invited to a James Taylor concert at a local church. And some brought a long line of relatives.

Someone else's loss was their gain.

A small segment of Newtown has found the power in grief and uses it to their advantage.

While the ticket distribution, the gifts and the concerts are winding down, the discussion about building a new school is just heating up. Families with children in Sandy Hook have said they want a $50 million school constructed. Others have said they don't want a nail hammered until a check for the entire amount has been delivered to town officials. And even then, they want to make sure the check has cleared.

And when victims' family members who don't live in Newtown felt compelled to comment on the future of the school site, there was a buzz that they don't pay taxes here, they will never be financially impacted by any decision and need to shut up.

Spending money for a police presence in each school is another topic sending town folks scurrying behind two lines drawn in the sand.

"My kid needs to feel protected no matter the cost."

"We don't need a cop in every school. It won't make a difference."

"This was just a fluke. It won't happen again. Let's not get crazy."

And as we creep toward the one-year mark, the scab will be picked off and the wound inflicted on the town will once again be exposed. A raw hotbed of emotion.

And from those who are sick and tired of the media descending on our town, the debates about money distribution, gun control and the politics of a tragedy, the crowds who made Newtown a destination to gawk and picture taking and the teddy bears and flowers left for children who are no longer alive, you will hear:

Enough

Enough

Enough already.

My name is Bonnie A. Fredericks — Newtown native. I started at Sandy Hook school and finished at Newtown High School and so life begins.

I was taught early on; every story has a beginning, a middle and end. The beginning so long ago, the middle I'm there now and end, I hope, is far off. I am who I am because I drank the water, we the people of Newtown, all drank the water and I guess I believe that has made us different. "It's always in the water" It's not special water technically if u tested it., it's just water. But people differ from town to town in character, moral spontaneity. I'd always say with pride "I'm from Newtown", that meant I was loyal, fun and attached to people and places I'd know for half of my life. I also believe I grew up in the "best neighborhood". I still stand by that. Seven Pole Bridge Road, Sandy Hook, Connecticut. Ahhh, I had the Browns, the Longs, the Gervais's, Pandora's and Lombardo's. We had gardens, fields and forts.

People might say we are who we are due to strict parenting, social status and education. I believe it was whom I chose to spend my days with "my friends". Halloween was unbelievable in my neighborhood. Dan Long was a creative genius with haunting = spooky caskets, witches, chains and chasing. Kids would run terrified down Jerimiah Road. Mrs. Long's homemade ginger cookies shaped in bats, witches, and brooms. Jenny and I would decorate for days and many hours for this Halloween treat. Now who does that? Cookies! Homemade! You could find, at any given time "us" the neighborhood kid playing tag, building forts and swimming in Curtis Pond. Lisa, Jenny, Todd, Brett, Matt and I (as well as my brothers Eddie, Billy, A.t. Carl was too little and chris yet to be born). The Warners from Warners "General Store" were neighbors too but we were a bit of a nuisance to them. We made too much noise and could be found daily raiding their expansive vegetable garden. Who could blame us? The tomatoes were "good!" As we grew older, grew boobs and butts and boys were different from girls, we had our first kisses and cuddling.

The ratio was perfect in my neighborhood of boys to girls. Now time was spent in the Sand Pit, which is now a housing development. Sand Pit was for escaping the parents and for riding dirt bikes, go-carts and quads. I believe the fundamental skills of driving came from this, from quads to cars.

I was surrounded by good people and had some important life skills in my pocket and knew everything. I was 15. My Dad was a Jaycee member, mom was a mom, the longs are divorcing but the carnivals tonight so life is pretty good. The ST. Rose Carnival was the place to go, where you look your best and be accompanied by your new best friends and run into your old best friends.

Quickly we grew up, from the carnival to Alberts Hill where the party begins. I'd like to embellish here and make our simple beer and bonfires seem a little wilder, but that would be a stretch. Our parties were just beer and bonfires.

Things were not always perfect, close though. At this point I've failed basic algebra, my jordache jeans were ruined and I have singlehandedly run over the family pet with my fathers car in my own driveway. "Ugh" - how will I survive this? Life sucks, I've killed our dog, I'm failing school and my boyfriend made-out with my best friend - can it get any worse. It can. With cars came crashes, tragedy and loss, we were losing our friends, annoucements were made over intercoms at school. so who coold blame me for failing. Life was failing. How coold shawn, Rob, Terry or Tom at Seventeen or eighteen be gone? Our friends and classmates. It was wrong and raw, so who needed school, "life is short" "live today like there's no tommorrow for today is only here for a little while and tomorrow - well?". But we, I mean me, did get through the loss, day by day, year to next.

So I grew up and grew out of my nice little town, got married, had a couple of kids and moved right back in. "Hair N The Hook" was born, 102 Church Hill Road, Sandy Hook. I may not live here anymore, but this is where my heart is. I am at Home seventeen years strong. Every day I am grateful to you my family in blood and my family in friends for molding me into who I am and supporting my passion in what I do. Many things have changed but many stay the same because I am NewTown STRONG.

Bonnie A. Fredericks
August 2013

My name is Bonnie A. Fredericks—Newtown native. I started at Sandy Hook School and finished at Newtown High School and so life begins.

I was taught early on; every story has a beginning, a middle and end. The beginning so long ago, the middle I'm there now and end, I hope, is far off. I am who I am because I drank the water, we the people of Newtown, all drank the water and I guess I believe that has made us different. "It's always in the water." It's not special water technically if you tested it, it's just water. But people differ from town to town in character, moral spontaneity. I'd always say with pride "I'm from Newtown", that meant I was loyal, fun and attached to the people and places I'd known for half of my life. I also believe I grew up in the "best neighborhood". I still stand by that. Seven Pole Bridge Road, Sandy Hook, Connecticut. Ahhh, I had the Browns, the Longs, the Gervais's, Pandora's, and Lombardo's. We had gardens, fields and forts.

People might say we are who we are due to strict parenting, social status and education. I believe it was whom I choose to spend my days with "my friends." Halloween was unbelievable in my neighborhood. Dan Long was a creative genius with haunting = spooky caskets, witches, chains and chasing. Kids would run terrified down Jerimiah Road. Mrs. Long's homemade ginger cookies shaped in bats, witches, and brooms. Jenny and I would decorate for days and many hours for this Halloween treat. Now who does that? Cookies! Homemade! You could find, at any given time, "us" the neighborhood kids playing tag, building forts and swimming in Curtis Pond. Lisa, Jenny, Todd, Brett, Matt and I (as well as my brothers Eddie, Billy, Art. Carl was too little and Chris yet to be born). The Warners from Warners "General Store" were neighbors too but we were a bit of a nuisance to them. We made too much noise and could be found daily raiding their expansive vegetable garden. Who could blame us? The tomatoes were "good". As we grew older, grew boobs and butts and boys were different from girls, we had our first kisses and cuddling.

The ratio was perfect in my neighborhood of boys to girls. Now time was spent in the Sand Pit, which is now a housing development. Sand Pit was for escaping the parents and for riding dirt bikes, go-carts and quads. I believe the fundamental skills of driving came from this, from quads to cars.

I was surrounded by good people and had some important life skills in my pocket and knew everything. I was 15. My Dad was a Jaycee member, mom was a mom, the Longs are divorcing but the Carnival's tonight so life is pretty good. The St. Rose Carnival was the place to go, where you look your best and be accompanied by your new best friends and run into your old best friends.

Quickly we grew up from the carnival to Alberts Hill where the party begins. I'd like to embellish here and make our simple beer and bonfires seem a little wilder, but that would be a stretch. Our parties were just beer and bonfires.

Things were not always perfect, close though. At this point I've failed basic algebra, my jordache jeans were ruined and I have singlehandedly run over the family pet with my father's car in my own driveway. "Ugh"—how will I survive this? Life sucks, I've killed our dog, I'm failing school and my boyfriend made-out with my best friend—can it get any worse. It can. With cars came crashes, tragedy and loss, we were losing our friends, announcements were made over intercoms at school. So who could blame me for failing. Life was failing. How could Shawn, Rob, Terry or Tom at seventeen or eighteen be gone? Our friends and classmates. It was wrong and raw, so who needed school, "life is short" "live today like there's no tomorrow for today is only here for a little while and tomorrow—well?" But we, I mean me, did get through the loss, day by day, year to next.

So I grew up and grew out of my nice little town, got married, had a couple of kids and moved right back in. "Hair N The Hook" was born, 102 Church Hill Road, Sandy Hook. I may not live here anymore, but this is where my heart is. I am at Home seventeen years strong. Every day I am grateful to you my family in blood and my family in friends for molding me into who I am and supporting my passion in what I do. Many things have changed but many stay the same because I am NEWTOWN STRONG.

Bonnie A. Fredericks
August 2013

Sandy Hook Hair Co. in the center of Sandy Hook

Dear Outsiders,

Newtown is a place that is near and dear to my heart. It's where I grew up, where I went to school and where my friends and family are. It's my home.

I have lived in Newtown since I was one and a half years old. I can't imagine a more perfect place to have been raised. I have so many amazing memories from living here. From $2 movies at Edmond Town Hall, to getting ice cream at the ice cream shop after winning a softball game, to graduating high school with my best friends; I cherish them all.

Some of my favorite memories stem way back to elementary school. My years at Sandy Hook School were some of the most pivotal years in shaping me to be the person I am today. Sandy Hook is where I met my best friends. We went to each other's birthday parties, attended Girl Scouts together and loved the Jolly Green Giant Fair. I am so lucky to still be friends with them today.

I was lucky enough to have some of the greatest teachers that I have had in my educational career at Sandy Hook School. These teachers made school a place that I wanted to go because it was fun! My teachers never just taught us Math, English, History, or Science. They engaged us in our learning through fun activities like selling items on our pushcarts to learn about math, performing plays for our classmates and parents, researching every last detail of our assigned New England state and teaching our classmates what we discovered and building model rockets and launching them on the soccer field. It is because of the seed that these teachers planted in me that I am now a college graduate.

After the recent events, those not from Newtown may think our town has changed. We are a small but strong community, just as we have always been. You are bound to bump into a friendly face at the grocery store, or see a softball team grabbing ice cream at The Ice Cream shop after a win and yes, Edmond still has $2 movies.

Newtown is a place that I am proud to call home.

Sincerely,
Nicole R.

Dear Outsiders,

Newtown is a place that is near and dear to my heart. It's where I grew up, where I went to school and where my friends and family are. It's my home.

I have lived in Newtown since I was one and a half years old. I can't imagine a more perfect place to have been raised. I have so many amazing memories from living here. From $2 movies at Edmond Town Hall, to getting ice cream at the Ice Cream Shop after winning a softball game, to graduating High School with my best friends; I cherish them all.

Some of my favorite memories stem way back to elementary school. My years at Sandy Hook School were some of the most pivotal years in shaping me to be the person I am today. Sandy Hook is where I met my best friends. We went to each other's birthday parties, attended Girl Scouts together and loved the Jolly Green Giant Fair. I am so lucky to still be friends with them today.

I was lucky enough to have some of the greatest teachers that I have had in my educational career at Sandy Hook School. These teachers made school a place that I wanted to go because it was fun! My teachers never just taught us Math, English, History or Science. They engaged us in our learning through fun activities like selling items on our pushcarts to learn about math, performing plays for our classmates and parents, researching every last detail of our assigned New England state and teaching our classmates what we discovered and building model rockets and launching them on the soccer field. It is because of the seed that these teachers planted in me that I am now a college graduate.

After the recent events, those not from Newtown may think that our town has changed. We are a small but strong community, just as we have always been. You are bound to bump into a friendly face at the grocery store, or see a softball team grabbing ice cream at The Ice Cream Shop after a win and yes, Edmond still has $2 movies.

Newtown is a place that I am proud to call home.

Sincerely,
Nicole R.

The Ice Cream Shop in Newtown

I AM PROUD TO SAY NEWTOWN IS MY HOME. I WAS BORN IN UPPER STATE NEW YORK BUT HAVE LIVED IN NEWTOWN SINCE BEFORE I TURNED THREE. I STAND TALL WHEN SOMEONE MENTIONS OUR TOWN, PERK UP AND BEAM WITH PRIDE BECAUSE OF EVERYTHING NEWTOWN REPRESENTS AND EVERYTHING I LOVE ABOUT MY TOWN.

WHEN SOMEONE ASKS ME WHY NEWTOWN IS SO SPECIAL, I FIND IT VERY DIFFICULT TO CHOOSE ONE THING TO RELATE AS TO WHY I LOVE MY TOWN AFTER SPENDING 50 YEARS OF MY LIFE IN ONE PLACE... AND STILL COUNTING.

I REMEMBER ATTENDING HAWLEY SCHOOL, MIDDLE GATE SCHOOL, NEWTOWN MIDDLE SCHOOL, NEWTOWN HIGH SCHOOL AND THE HOMESICK FEELING OF HAVING TO LEAVE TOWN AND ATTEND COLLEGE IN MARYLAND. COLLEGE OPENED MY EYES TO WHAT THE WORLD IS LIKE OUTSIDE OF NEWTOWN, BUT IT ALSO MADE ME YEARN TO COME BACK AND RAISE A FAMILY IN THE ROOTS OF WHERE I GREW UP.

MOVING BACK TO TOWN, ONE OF THE FIRST THINGS I WANTED TO DO WAS TO SEE THE SUNRISE FROM THE TOP OF CASTLE HILL ROAD. WATCH AS THE BEAMING SUN LIT UP MY TOWN, ITS CHURCH STEEPLES, FLAGPOLE, EDMOND TOWN HALL AND MAIN STREET. GROWING UP, THE TREES WERE NOT AS OLD AND MATURE ON MAIN STREET, IT WAS MORE DEFINED BY THE HOUSES THAN THE TREE GROWTH ONE

NOW LOOKS DOWN UPON. VIEWS OF A FULL MOON RISING ARE PRETTY AWESOME TOO.

THERE IS NO PLACE ELSE I KNOW WHERE I CAN STAND IN THE CENTER OF MAIN STREET, LOOK STRAIGHT UP A POLE TO SEE OLD GLORY FLYING HIGH AND MIGHTY. THANK YOU MAE SCHMIDLE FOR OUR HISTORIC LANDMARK AND ALSO A GREAT SOURCE FOR GIVING DIRECTIONS! AS A KID, OUR NEWTOWN LABOR DAY PARADE HAS ALWAYS BEEN A SIGN THAT SUMMER IS COMING TO A CLOSE AND SCHOOL IS STARTING. NOW AS AN ADULT, I LOOK FORWARD TO GATHERING WITH FAMILY AND FRIENDS TO CHEER ON ALL THE CITIZENS PARTICIPATING IN THE PARADE, EVEN THE POLITICIANS, BECAUSE WE ARE PROUD OF OUR TOWN AND HERITAGE AND ARE ABLE TO SHOW THAT EVERY SINGLE LABOR DAY.

I DO MISS THE MUD BOTTOM SWIMMING POOL AT DICKINSON PARK. A BUNCH OF US USED TO SNEAK OVER AFTER THE POOL CLOSED, CLIMB THE FENCE AND COOL OFF DURING THE HOT SUMMER NIGHTS. TWENTY YEARS LATER, MY CHILDREN SHARED IN MANY SIMILAR ACTIVITIES AND ENJOYED PLAYING IN THE SAME PLACES I DID GROWING UP, EVEN SWIMMING IN THE DICKINSON PARK POOL. WHEN I WOULD HEAR FROM MY KIDS "THERE IS NOTHING TO DO IN NEWTOWN", IT WOULD NOT TAKE LONG TO COMPILE A LIST AND WATCH THEM RIDE

OFF ON THEIR BIKES AND NOT SEE THEM FOR HOURS UNTIL DINNER.

A TRIP TO THE GROCERY STORE WOULD ALWAYS TAKE SO LONG AS A KID BECAUSE YOU WOULD SEE SOMEONE YOU KNEW IN EVERY AISLE. I STILL ENJOY GOING TO THE GROCERY STORE AND STILL SEEING PEOPLE IN THE AISLES, CATCHING UP ON WHAT EVERYONE IS DOING. YES, OUR POPULATION HAS GROWN AND WE DON'T KNOW "EVERYONE" IN THE STORES ANYMORE, BUT THERE IS STILL A SENSE OF COMMUNITY THAT I WOULD NOT TRADE FOR A BIG CITY ANYTIME ANYWHERE.

I AM SO FORTUNATE THAT I HAVE BEEN AROUND MY PARENTS AS AN ADULT AND HAVE LEARNED TO APPRECIATE THEM MORE AND MORE EACH DAY. I ALSO APPRECIATE THAT I HAVE BEEN ABLE TO WATCH MY CHILDREN GROW WITH MY PARENTS, WHICH IS A TREASURE IN ITSELF AND HAPPENED IN NEWTOWN.

I AM VERY PROUD TO BE A FIFTH GENERATION SMITH IN NEWTOWN AND APPRECIATE ALL THAT HAS BEEN DONE BY MY GREAT GRANDFATHER, ARTHUR JUDD SMITH, MY GRANDFATHER PAUL SCUDDER SMITH AS WELL AS HOW MY FATHER, R. SCUDDER SMITH, REPRESENTS NEWTOWN TODAY. IT WAS NOT UNTIL SOME YEARS AGO I APPRECIATED BEING A SOLID PART OF THE NEWTOWN BEE AND TO

REPRESENT THE PAPER AND NEWTOWN AND ALL
THAT IT STANDS FOR. My PRIDE WILL NEVER
CHANGE AS IT WILL NEVER WAIVER WHEN I
SPEAK OF NEWTOWN AND WHAT IT MEANS TO ME
TO BE FROM NEWTOWN CONNECTICUT.

Sherri Smith Baggett

Sunrise Easter Service, Castle Hill Road, Newtown

Dickinson Park Pool in Newtown

I am proud to say Newtown is my home. I was born in upper state New York but have lived in Newtown since before I turned three. I stand tall when someone mentions our town, perk up and beam with pride because of everything Newtown represents and everything I love about my town.

When someone asks me why Newtown is so special, I find it very difficult to choose one thing to relate as to why I love my town after spending 50 years of my life in one place . . . and still counting.

I remember attending Hawley School, Middle Gate School, Newtown Middle School, Newtown High School and the homesick feeling of having to leave town and attend college in Maryland. College opened my eyes to what the world is like outside of Newtown, but it also made me yearn to come back and raise a family in the roots of where I grew up.

Moving back to town, one of the first things I wanted to do was to see the sunrise from the top of Castle Hill Road. Watch as the beaming sun lit up my town, its church steeples, flagpole, Edmond Town Hall and Main Street. Growing up, the trees were not as old and mature on Main Street; it was more defined by the houses than the tree growth one now looks down upon. Views of a full moon rising are pretty awesome too.

There is no place else I know where I can stand in the center of Main Street, look straight up a pole to see Old Glory flying high and mighty. Thank you Mae Schmidle for our historic landmark and also a great source for giving directions! As a kid, our Newtown Labor Day Parade has always been a sign that summer is coming to a close and school is starting. Now as an adult, I look forward to gathering with family and friends to cheer on all the citizens participating in the parade, even the politicians, because we are proud of our town and heritage and are able to show that every single Labor Day.

I do miss the mud bottom swimming pool at Dickinson Park. A bunch of us used to sneak over after the pool closed, climb the fence and cool off during the hot summer nights. Twenty years later, my children shared in many similar activities and enjoyed playing in the same places I did growing up, even swimming in the Dickinson Park pool. When I would hear from my kids "there is nothing to do in Newtown", it would not take long to compile a list and watch them ride off on their bikes and not see them for hours until dinner.

A trip to the grocery store would always take so long as a kid because you would see someone you knew in every aisle. I still enjoy going to the grocery store and still seeing people in the aisles, catching up on what everyone is doing. Yes, our population has grown and we don't know "everyone" in the stores anymore, but there is still a sense of community that I would not trade for a big city anytime anywhere.

I am so fortunate that I have been around my parents as an adult and have learned to appreciate them more and more each day. I also appreciate that I have been able to watch my children grow with my parents, which is a treasure in itself and happened in Newtown.

I am very proud to be a fifth generation Smith in Newtown and appreciate all that has been done by my great grandfather, Arthur Judd Smith, my grandfather Paul Scudder Smith as well as how my father, R. Scudder Smith, represents Newtown today. It was not until some years ago I appreciated being a solid part of The Newtown Bee and to represent the paper and Newtown and all that it stands for. My pride will never change as it will never waiver when I speak of Newtown and what it means to me to be from Newtown, Connecticut.

Sherri Smith Baggett

SHADOWS

Born and bred since the age of ten,
I have seen Newtown grow.
Famous people once lived here,
 others come and go.

 Gunfight, Chipper left a scar,
 I have grown since then.
 But for the little ones,
 those feelings start again.

 For those who share the shadows,
 our hearts certainly fell.
 But time will heal for that I'm sure,
 for age has served me well.

 Anonymous

SHADOWS

Born and bred since the age of ten,
I have seen Newtown grow.
Famous people once lived here,
others come and go.

Gunfight, Chipper left a scar,
I have grown since then.
But for the little ones,
those feelings start again.

For those who share the shadows,
our hearts certainly fell.
But time will heal for that I'm sure,
for age has served me well.

Anonymous

Dear World:

At the time of the December 14, 2012 shooting at Sandy Hook Elementary School in Sandy Hook, Connecticut, I had lived in San Jose, California, for six years.

Newtown is my hometown. I attended Sandy Hook Elementary from kindergarten through fifth grade and graduated from Newtown High School in 1985. Both of my parents were teachers. My mother was extremely involved in local politics and served in numerous elected positions including the Board of Education and Legislative Council. While my mother had passed away less than a year ago, my 87-year old father still lived in the house I grew up in.

I was eating breakfast in front of the television on 12/14 when both "Newtown" and "Sandy Hook Elementary" first flashed on the screen. Hearing the name of my once obscure hometown on the news pierced my consciousness. I had spent a lifetime explaining to people that Newtown was approximately eighty miles north of New York City, east of Danbury, and was NOT spelled or pronounced "Newton," but rather "New-town" as two words sandwiched together. Instinctively, 3,000 miles away in San Jose, I knew that my little town was in trouble.

Although it was relatively early in California, I immediately connected with my father and friends in town via the phone and social media. Together, we tried to piece together the information that we learned from different sources. As is well known now, the official reports changed throughout the day and the facts grew progressively worse until we were all ultimately confronted with the heartbreak of twenty-six fatalities that included twenty children and six educators.

The next few days were a blur. I cried on the couch, watched the news, monitored Facebook posts from my Newtown friends, answered phone calls from friends who knew that I was from Newtown, attended a vigil in Sunnyvale, California, and stayed connected to my father. I called various town offices in Newtown looking for a way for the class of '85 to help. I had plenty of connections to the elected officials and town employees through my mother's activism, and my classmates were standing by on facebook looking for direction. However, the Newtown communications infrastructure had been overwhelmed amidst the crisis. The phones did not ring.

Waves of memories from my time at Sandy Hook Elementary rushed through my mind. I saw myself sitting in each of my six classrooms, listening to teachers, chatting with friends, kicking a soccer ball at recess, and playing violin in the orchestra. Yet, my happy reflections lasted only moments. The horror of what I imagined to have happened on 12/14 intruded on my thoughts like an unwelcome guest, the fear of administrators as they saw an assailant at the school's door, the "pop" of gun fire, the screams of innocent children, and the sights and smells of death. The two different realities merged to form an entirely new landscape, one that would never again bear mention of Sandy Hook Elementary without acknowledgement of the 12/14 massacre. In an instant, my own history had been rewritten, forever.

I arrived in Newtown four days after the shooting for a pre-planned holiday visit. My father had warned me that the town was crowded with people, but I was not prepared for what I encountered. The single-lane roads were jammed with cars, as people had come from all over to pay their respects at the makeshift memorials, and see the town that had suffered the unthinkable tragedy. Dignitaries travelled in and out of Newtown with police escorts, as they communicated their offers of assistance and ~~and~~ condolences to the victims' families and town officials. News trucks lined the roads with satellite dishes that beamed the sounds and images of a grieving community for all of America and the world to see.

Police cruisers were parked in the driveways of every family that had lost a loved one to provide protection from a prying public and a dogged media. Friends and neighbors provided food, transportation, and other assistance to each of the families under a veil of community privacy. Police contained the media, managed crowds and traffic, and provided escorts for every funeral procession.

Shortly after I arrived home, I drove to the center of town in ballgame-like gridlock. Police sirens sounded, and the traffic pulled to the side of the road to make way for a funeral procession. I sobbed over my steering wheel as I watched a long line of cars stream by me on Main Street and make the turn that led to the town cemetary. Furthermore, I was keenly aware that I knew some of the people in the cars that had passed.

Like so many others, I was desperate to do something to help, but it was not obvious how to best contribute. It seemed that everyone was trying to do something and the grass roots efforts included a wide array of activities such as the creation of memorials around town, fundraisers for specific causes, entertainment for the community, professional counseling services, massages, comfort dogs, or in-kind donation collections. It was clear that many Newtowners were searching for a way to make a positive impact on the community.

Unbeknownst to me at the time, the American Red Cross (ARC) had classified the Newtown shooting as a disaster and deployed its resources to assist the town. The ARC quickly came to the aid of Newtown volunteers who had taken the first steps to create a local call center. Every town office, school office, community organization, and religious organization had been overwhelmed with phone calls, emails, and written letters. The volunteers speculated that a call center could help the town and school officials to deal with the outpouring of support that Newtown received from around the world. Sanctioned by the town, the group came to be known as the Newtown Volunteer Task Force (NVTF). I joined immediately.

American Red Cross representatives from Washington D.C. met with the NVTF team to share their disaster relief expertise. As I sat with the core group of volunteers, I learned more about disasters from the Red Cross team than I had ever thought about in a lifetime. The experts explained what to expect in terms of a national response, the accompanying emotions, and recapped what actions had been taken for other disasters. The NVTF conveyed the realization that no one in Newtown had lost a home or place of employment, as had happened in the Northeast corridor during super storm Sandy. The Red Cross representatives praised and encouraged our efforts. We were the first community to attempt a volunteer call center without the oversight of a federal agency. They also correctly anticipated that the people who called us wanted to speak to someone in Newtown, rather than a professional call center representative located somewhere else.

With donated office space, donated tables and chairs, donated office supplies, donated computers, and donated WIFI, the NVTF call center opened in five days. Initially, we responded to the thousands of phone calls that had already been received throughout town to numerous town offices, schools, and other organizations. We quickly expanded to take in-bound calls with a toll-free number, and then moved to answering more than ten thousand emails. We steered people to the official Sandy Hook Support Fund for financial contributions, provided a shipping address for in-kind donations, collected contact information for offers of professional services, and recorded high-value goods and services from corporations in a donor database for further review by town officials.

The NVTF core team managed more than eighty volunteers each day to staff the various call center tasks. For several weeks, I served as the full-time training coordinator and helped to manage the work of the volunteers on the floor of the call center. I conducted training six times a day, for six shifts of volunteers who arrived from Newtown, surrounding towns, and sometimes New York and Massachusetts. During each training session, I tried to prepare the new volunteers for the emotional scope of the range of tasks on-going at the call center and provided hands-on training for the software that we used to track donations.

I shared the first two (return) calls that I had made myself, both to mothers who had lost their own elementary age children. Both women wanted to provide very specific gifts. One mother was a jewelry designer and wanted to design bracelets for every mother in Newtown who had lost her child. The second mother had written a book on grieving that was designed for a child to read to him/herself. I described how one person had paid for twenty-six stars to be named after the twenty-six shooting victims and partnered with a scientific equipment company to donate a telescope to the Newtown School District, so that kids could look up at the sky and "see" their lost classmates.

I also explained that the information we had received at the call center was often incorrect or incomplete. When I personally returned the call to someone name "Nikki Shoes," I was shocked to find myself connected with the marketing department at Nike, Inc. The company wanted to make a gift of sports equipment to the town, and was looking for advice as to how their donation could make the biggest impact. Similarly, Scholastic Publishing sent catalogues for Newtown teachers to freely "shop" for educational materials. The corporate donors were not looking for publicity; they simply wanted to help Newtown. Most importantly, I counseled the volunteers to show respect for the generosity of the public that was calling with offers of assistance. In some regard, the greatest challenge was explaining to people that we needed time to process the thousands of offers that we received.

Across town, the NVTF organized volunteers to staff a massive warehouse to receive the mountains of teddy bears, toys, clothes, school supplies, books, paper snowflakes, memorial items, and everything else that was shipped to Newtown. Another volunteer organization, ACS (Adventist Community Services) supervised the warehouse activity, as more than twenty NVTF volunteers a day staffed shifts to open boxes, sort items, and repack donations into boxes of the appropriate size to stack on pallets. Twenty-six large boxes lined the wall of the warehouse, as items addressed directly to victims' families were separated from the bulk donations. ACS placed all items under inventory control for eventual distribution. Elsewhere in Newtown, more volunteers gathered to sort through the more than 100,000 pieces of mail and wrote thank you notes to the senders.

Daily, more and more items arrived in town. Due to the volume of goods, town officials formally requested that donors redirect gifts to their local communities. At the call center, we urged the same and suggested to callers that they make donations in their local community "...in honor of the Newtown victims." We asked callers to share a picture of their activity, or gift, on the NVTF Facebook page as a way to connect with us directly in Newtown. We hoped to start a movement as acts of kindness spread across the country.

I extended my holiday visit in Newtown to work at the NVTF Call Center for several weeks. Upon my return to California, I joined the Silicon Valley Chapter of the Red Cross and completed the training for its Disaster Action Team. I was amazed at what I had learned through my Newtown experience and was able to apply in my formal training and deployments.

I have moved back to Newtown since 12/14 to be closer to my father, and hope to continue my disaster-oriented volunteer work in the future. Despite the town's association with the events of 12/14, I am proud to once again call Newtown my home.

Kelley T. Johnson
Sandy Hook, CT

Dear World:

At the time of the December 14, 2012 shooting at Sandy Hook Elementary School in Sandy Hook, Connecticut, I had lived in San Jose, California for six years.

Newtown is my hometown. I attended Sandy Hook Elementary from kindergarten through fifth grade and graduated from Newtown High School in 1985. Both of my parents were teachers. My mother was extremely involved in local politics and served in numerous elected positions including the Board of Education and Legislative Council. While my mother had passed away less than a year ago, my 87-year old father still lived in the house that I grew up in.

I was eating breakfast in front of the television on 12/14 when both "Newtown" and "Sandy Hook Elementary" first flashed on the screen. Hearing the name of my once obscure hometown on the news pierced my consciousness. I had spent a lifetime explaining to people that Newtown was approximately eighty miles north of New York City, east of Danbury, and was NOT spelled or pronounced "Newton," but rather "New-town" as two words sandwiched together. Instinctively, 3,000 miles away in San Jose, I knew that my little town was in trouble.

Although it was relatively early in California, I immediately connected with my father and friends in town via the phone and social media. Together, we tried to piece together the information that we learned from different sources. As is well known now, the official reports changed throughout the day and the facts grew progressively worse until we were all ultimately confronted with the heartbreak of twenty-six fatalities that included twenty children and six educators.

The next few days were a blur. I cried on the couch, watched the news, monitored Facebook posts from my Newtown friends, answered phone calls from friends who knew that I was from Newtown, attended a vigil in Sunnyvale, California, and stayed connected to my father. I called various town offices in Newtown looking for a way for the Class of '85 to help. I had plenty of connections to the elected officials and town employees through my mother's activism, and my classmates were standing by on Facebook looking for direction. However, the Newtown communications infrastructure had been overwhelmed amidst the crisis. The phones did not ring.

Waves of memories from my time at Sandy Hook Elementary rushed through my mind. I saw myself sitting in each of my six classrooms, listening to teachers, chatting with friends, kicking a soccer ball at recess, and playing violin in the orchestra. Yet, my happy reflections lasted only moments. The horror of what I imagined to have happened on 12/14 intruded on my thoughts like an unwelcome guest, the fear of administrators as they saw an assailant at the school's door, the "pop" of gun fire, the screams of innocent children, and the sights and smells of death. The two different realities merged to form an entirely new landscape, one that would never again bear mention of Sandy Hook Elementary without acknowledgement of the 12/14 massacre. In an instant, my own history had been rewritten, forever.

I arrived in Newtown four days after the shooting for a pre-planned holiday visit. My father had warned me that the town was crowded with people, but I was not prepared for what I encountered. The single-lane roads were jammed with cars, as people had come from all over to pay their respects at the makeshift memorials, and see the town that had suffered the unthinkable tragedy. Dignitaries travelled in and out of Newtown with police escorts, as they communicated their offers of assistance and condolences to the victims' families and town officials. News trucks lined the roads with satellite dishes that beamed the sounds and images of a grieving community for all of America and the world to see.

Police cruisers were parked in the driveways of every family that had lost a loved one to provide protection from a prying public and a dogged media. Friends and neighbors provided food, transportation, and other assistance to each of the families under a veil of community privacy. Police contained the media, managed crowds and traffic, and provided escorts for every funeral procession.

Shortly after I arrived home, I drove to the center of town in ballgame-like gridlock. Police sirens sounded, and the traffic pulled to the side of the road to make way for a funeral procession. I sobbed over my steering wheel as I watched a long line of cars stream by me on Main Street and make the turn that led to the town cemetery. Furthermore, I was keenly aware that I knew some of the people in the cars that had passed.

Like so many others, I was desperate to do something to help, but it was not obvious how to best contribute. It seemed that everyone was trying to do something and the grass roots efforts included a wide array of activities such as the creation of memorials around town, fundraisers for specific causes, entertainment for the community, professional counseling services, massages, comfort dogs, or in-kind donation collections. It was clear that many Newtowners were searching for a way to make a positive impact on the community.

Unbeknownst to me at the time, the American Red Cross (ARC) had classified the Newtown shooting as a disaster and deployed its resources to assist the town. The ARC quickly came to the aid of Newtown volunteers who had taken the first steps to create a local call center. Every town office, school office, community organization, and religious organization had been overwhelmed with phone calls, emails, and written letters. The volunteers speculated that a call center could help the town and school officials to deal with the outpouring of support that Newtown received from around the world. Sanctioned by the town, the group came to be known as the Newtown Volunteer Task Force (NVTF). I joined immediately.

American Red Cross representatives from Washington D.C. met with the NVTF team to share their disaster relief expertise. As I sat with the core group of volunteers, I learned more about disasters from the Red Cross team than I had ever thought about in a lifetime. The experts explained what to expect in terms of a national response, the accompanying emotions, and recapped what actions had been taken for other disasters. The NVTF conveyed the realization that no one in Newtown had lost his/her home, or place of employment, as had happened in the Northeast corridor during super storm Sandy. The Red Cross representatives praised and encouraged our efforts. We were the first community to attempt a volunteer call center without the oversight of a federal agency. They also correctly anticipated that the people who called us wanted to speak to someone in Newtown, rather than a professional call center representative located somewhere else.

With donated office space, donated tables and chairs, donated office supplies, donated computers, and donated WIFI, the NVTF call center opened in five days. Initially, we responded to the thousands of phone calls that had already been received throughout town to numerous town offices, schools, and other organizations. We quickly expanded to take in-bound calls with a toll-free number, and then moved to answering more than ten thousand emails. We steered people to the official Sandy Hook Support Fund for financial contributions, provided a shipping address for in-kind donations, collected contact information for offers of professional services, and recorded high-value goods and services from corporations in a donor database for further review by town officials.

The NVTF core team managed more than eighty volunteers each day to staff the various call center tasks. For several weeks, I served as the full-time training coordinator and helped to manage the work of the volunteers on the floor of the call center. I conducted training six times a day for six shifts of volunteers who arrived from Newtown, surrounding towns, and sometimes New York and Massachusetts. During each training session, I tried to prepare the new volunteers for the emotional scope of the range of tasks on-going at the call center and provided hands-on training for the software that we used to track donations.

I shared the first two (return) calls that I had made myself, both to mothers who had lost their own elementary age children. Both women wanted to provide very specific gifts. One mother was a jewelry designer and wanted to design bracelets for every mother in Newtown who had lost her child. The second mother had written a book on grieving that was designed for a child to read to him/herself. I described how one person had paid for twenty-six stars to be named after the twenty-six shooting victims and partnered with a scientific equipment company to donate a telescope to the Newtown School District, so that the kids could look up at the sky and "see" their lost classmates.

I also explained that the information we had received at the call center was often incorrect or incomplete. When I personally returned the call to someone named "Nikki Shoes," I was shocked to find myself connected with the marketing department at Nike, Inc. The company wanted to make a gift of sports equipment to the town, and was looking for advice as to how their donation could make the biggest impact. Similarly, Scholastic Publishing sent catalogues for Newtown teachers to freely "shop" for educational materials. The corporate donors were not looking for publicity; they simply wanted to help Newtown. Most importantly, I counseled the volunteers to show respect for the generosity of the public that was calling with offers of assistance. In some regard, the greatest challenge was explaining to people that we needed time to process the thousands of offers that we received.

Across town, the NVTF organized volunteers to staff a massive warehouse to receive the mountains of teddy bears, toys, clothes, school supplies, books, paper snowflakes, memorial items, and everything else that was shipped to Newtown. Another volunteer organization, ACS (Adventist Community Services) supervised the warehouse activity, as more than twenty NVTF volunteers a day staffed shifts to open boxes, sort items, and repack donations into boxes of the appropriate size to stack on pallets. Twenty-six large boxes lined the wall of the warehouse, as items addressed directly to victims' families were separated from the bulk donations. ACS placed all items under inventory control for eventual distribution. Elsewhere in Newtown, more volunteers gathered to sort through the more than 100,000 pieces of mail and wrote thank you notes to the senders.

Daily, more and more items arrived in town. Due to the volume of goods, town officials formally requested that donors redirect gifts to their local communities. At the call center, we urged the same and suggested to callers that they make donations in their local communities ". . . in honor of the

Newtown victims." We asked callers to share a picture of their activity, or gift, on the NVTF Facebook page as a way to connect with us directly in Newtown. We hoped to start a movement as acts of kindness spread across the country.

I extended my holiday visit in Newtown to work at the NVTF Call Center for several weeks. Upon my return to California, I joined the Silicon Valley Chapter of the Red Cross and completed the training for its Disaster Action Team. I was amazed at what I had learned through my Newtown experience and was able to apply in my formal training and deployments.

I have moved back to Newtown since 12/14 to be closer to my father, and hope to continue my disaster-oriented volunteer work in the future. Despite the town's association with the events of 12/14, I am proud to once again call Newtown my home.

Kelley T. Johnson
Sandy Hook, CT

Center of Sandy Hook behind the Foundry Kitchen & Tavern

August 15, 2013

This is an open letter of gratitude to the first responders who took care of our town on the day of the tragedy and the months that followed. And of course to those who continue to care for us all. There was a cocoon of safety provided by not only Newtown's own police officers, firefighters, and EMTs, but from the municipalities all across our state and region that so generously sent their personnel to help. Officers from our state and our federal government were here too. Quietly taking on the most difficult tasks or helping our kids to feel safe going back to school. Helping us to feel it was okay to go out to the grocery store or post office. They created a strong, safe, silent wall of protection that came from their commitment to serve. There is no way to fully express what this means to a community in crisis.

Thank you,

Brenda McKinley

August 15, 2013

This is an open letter of gratitude to the first responders who took care of our town on the day of the tragedy and the months that followed. And of course to those who continue to care for us all. There was a cocoon of safety provided by not only Newtown's own police officers, firefighters, and EMTs, but from the municipalities all across our state and region that so generously sent their personnel to help. Officers from our state and our federal government were here too. Quietly taking on the most difficult tasks or helping our kids to feel safe going back to school. Helping us to feel it was okay to go out to the grocery store or post office. They created a strong, safe, silent wall of protection that came from their commitment to serve. There is no way to fully express what this means to a community in crisis.

Thank you,
Brenda McKinley

Newtown Police Department Honor Guard at the 2013 Labor Day Parade

Dear Newtown,

I want to start off by saying 'I love you.' I love my beautiful hometown. I love the landscape, I love the history, and I love the people. The person who I am today has been largely influenced by you, Newtown, and for that I am eternally grateful.

I have no memories of the time in my life before I lived in Newtown so for all intents and purposes I lived in Newtown for my entire childhood. Though at times I felt, as most teenagers do, that there is 'nothing to do in Newtown,' I adored my hometown the majority of the time.

Though I have a great family, my parents' divorce was challenging for me and my siblings. Having the supportive love of Newtown residents and teachers helped me to get through this difficult life event. At a time when my family was shifting and changing, Newtown was my constant family.

I cannot say enough good things about the Newtown schools. School was always a comfortable and enjoying place for me. While middle school may have not been the best years of my life, as I'm certain it is not for the majority of children, my years in the Newtown school system were spectacular. I will not even try to name specific teachers and staff members who made my experience so lovely, because there are far too many. When I went off to college and would reflect about my primary schooling with classmates, they were often amazed at what a wonderful experience I had. As I made friends who grew up in places other than Newtown, I truly began to realize how lucky I was.

On Friday, December 14, 2012, I woke up and looked at BBC World News on my computer. Because I currently live in the Pacific Time Zone, the front page of BBC displayed the picture we saw on most of the media of children being lead out of Sandy Hook School. I could not believe what I was seeing and reading. I texted my family members to find out information - learning that my sister was in lock down at Newtown High School. My mom who is a nurse at the Danbury Hospital Emergency Department and was at work that day simply told me that 'this is bad.' I didn't know what to think as I started getting ready for work that morning. As more news started trickling in I began to understand how truly bad this is. As the death toll rose, my heart sank. When I came home from my first job and prepared to head to my second job, I turned on the news and cried as President Obama shed a tear for my beautiful town. I decided to go to my other job as a science instructor at an after school program and was haunted by the thought that someone gunned down children as small and innocent as many of my students. It was terrible and wonderful to be around children that day, but overall it gave me extra appreciation for the strong and courageous Sandy Hook School staff.

My flight to return to Newtown for Christmas was scheduled for the following week. As Saturday, 12/15 approached, however, I could not handle waiting that long to return to my broken town. I knew that if I went home I could find some way to help and I knew that I would not be able to make it an entire week being so far away from my home. When I returned to Newtown, it was clear that I made the right decision. I was able to find ways to volunteer and help in some small way, but again it was Newtown that truly helped me. The people of Newtown and many others from across the country and world came together in this tragedy. The support and love that poured out after this tragedy helped me to remember that there is still so much good in the world. Once again, I set out to help my town, but instead my town helped me. Although the Sandy Hook School shooting has permanently impacted us, it does not define who we are. Newtown is defined by the love and caring we show each other. Newtown is a place where you cannot leave your house without seeing at least one person you know. Newtown is the ultimate hometown, the place where grown children cannot wait to return to. Newtown is my town and for that I am eternally grateful.

Love always,
Allie Clement

Dear Newtown,

I want to start off by saying 'I love you.' I love my beautiful hometown. I love the landscape, I love the history, and I love the people. The person who I am today has been largely influenced by you, Newtown, and for that I am eternally grateful.

I have no memories of the time in my life before I lived in Newtown so for all intents and purposes I lived in Newtown for my entire childhood. Though at times I felt, as most teenagers do, that there is 'nothing to do in Newtown,' I adored my hometown the majority of the time.

Though I have a great family, my parents' divorce was challenging for me and my siblings. Having the supportive love of Newtown residents and teachers helped me to get through this difficult life event. At a time when my family was shifting and changing, Newtown was my constant family.

I cannot say enough good things about the Newtown schools. School was always a comfortable and enjoying place for me. While middle school may have not been the best years of my life, as I'm certain it is not for the majority of children, my years in the Newtown school system were spectacular. I will not even try to name specific teachers and staff members who made my experience so lovely, because there are far too many. When I went off to college and would reflect about my primary schooling with classmates, they were often amazed at what a wonderful experience I had. As I made friends who grew up in places other than Newtown, I truly began to realize how lucky I was.

On Friday, December 14, 2012, I woke up and looked at BBC World News on my computer. Because I currently live in the Pacific Time Zone, the front page of BBC displayed the picture we saw on most of the media of children being lead out of Sandy Hook School. I could not believe what I was seeing and reading. I texted my family members to find out information—learning that my sister was in lock down at Newtown High School. My mom who is a nurse at the Danbury Hospital Emergency Department and was at work that day simply told me that 'this is bad.' I didn't know what to think as I started getting ready for work that morning. As more news started trickling in I began to understand how truly bad this is. As the death toll rose, my heart sank. When I came home from my first job and prepared to head to my second job, I turned on the news and cried as President Obama shed a tear for my beautiful town. I decided to go to my other job as a science instructor at an after school program and was haunted by the thought that someone gunned down children as small and innocent as many of my students. It was terrible and wonderful to be around children that day, but overall it gave me extra appreciation for the strong and courageous Sandy Hook School staff.

My flight to return to Newtown for Christmas was scheduled for the following week. As Saturday, 12/15 approached, however, I could not handle waiting that long to return to my broken town. I knew that if I went home I could find some way to help and I knew that I would not be able to make it an entire week being so far away from my home. When I returned to Newtown, it was clear that I made the right decision. I was able to find ways to volunteer and help in some small way, but again it was Newtown that truly helped me. The people of Newtown and many others from across the country and world came together in this tragedy. The support and love that poured out after this tragedy helped me to remember that there is still so much good in the world. Once again, I set out to help my town, but instead my town helped me. Although the Sandy Hook School shooting has permanently impacted us, it does not define who we are. Newtown is defined by the love and caring we show each other. Newtown is a place where you cannot leave your house without seeing at least one person you know. Newtown is the ultimate hometown, the place where grown children cannot wait to return to. Newtown is my town and for that I am eternally grateful.

Love always,
Allie Clement

June 22, 2013

Over the past twenty-eight years
of living in Newtown/Sandy Hook, CT
and raising our two sons, my wife
and I have always wondered if they
liked growing up in this smaller
bedroom community. Their response
was always the same, "Yes dad,
it always felt like home."

My perspective as a child and young
adult, who grew up in the second
largest metropolitan city in the
good old USA, was they felt a deep
rooted emotional connection to the
town. I have good memories of
growing up where I did, but what
I don't have and they do, is a
sense of belonging to a community,
an extension to their birth family.

The emotional connection comes in
so many ways. Having your dad as
the coach of your baseball or soccer
team year after year, allowed
them to get to know and grow

up with some of the same
kids year after year, it was
like having so many brothers
and sisters as an extension to
their families. Sharing the emotions
of winning and losing with some
of these same kids game after
game, brought them together in a
very special way. Working on
community projects like the
annual haunted yard as a fund
raiser, gave them a sense of pride
and connection to the community.
Delivering food baskets to families
in need around the holidays, gave
them a deeper sense of appreciating
what they had and they were doing
something to help others in their
town.

This is why, when the Sandy Hook
tragedy of 12-14-12 occurred, our
sons felt so much personal pain.
Someone had violated their town,
their community and in a way,
their home.

Newtown/Sandy Hook has been
and will continue to be a
wonderful community to raise a
family, because it is like an extension
to your own home.

With deepest regards,

Bob Gaines

Gardens at The Pleasance in Newtown

June 22, 2013

Over the past twenty-eight years of living in Newtown/Sandy Hook, Connecticut and raising our two sons, my wife and I have always wondered if they liked growing up in this smaller bedroom community. Their response was always the same. "Yes dad, it always felt like home."

My perspective from a child and young adult, who grew up in the second largest metropolitan city in the good old USA, was they felt a deep rooted emotional connection to the town. I have good memories of growing up where I did, but what I don't have and they do, is a sense of belonging to a community, an extension to their birth family.

The emotional connection comes in so many ways. Having your dad as the coach of your baseball or soccer team year after year, allowed them to get to know and grow up with some of the same kids year after year, it was like having so many brothers and sisters as an extension to their families. Sharing the emotions of winning and losing with some of these same kids game after game, brought them together in a very special way. Working on community projects like the annual haunted yard as a fund raiser, gave them a sense of pride and connection to the community. Delivering food baskets to families in need around the holidays, gave them a deeper sense of appreciating what they had and they were doing something to help others in their town.

This is why, when the Sandy Hook tragedy of 12-14-12 occurred, our sons felt so much personal pain. Someone had violated their town, their community and in a way, their home.

Newtown/Sandy Hook has been and will continue to be a wonderful community to raise a family, because it is like an extension to your own home.

With deepest regards,
Bob Gaines

Lutheran Home of Southbury

A Program of Lutheran Social Services

Rev. Leo E. McIlrath, Ecumenical Chaplain
Lutheran Home of Southbury
990 Main Street
Southbury, CT 06488

June 14, 2013

My 26 New Friends,

Si Vales, bene est, Valeo! Such is the way that the great Roman Orator, Marcus Tullius Cicero, began many of his letters. I am certain that you have already met him — and all the wonderful people of the earth—who greeted you upon your arrival in the glorious halls of heaven —

I am also certain that I need no translate the above greeting for you because you have already mastered all of the world's languages — and that you understand them just as the people of the Apostolic Times could understand what St. Peter was saying when he, filled with the Holy Spirit, told them about Jesus and his wish to welcome them into the Kingdom of God.

But just in case others reading this letter, do not understand Cicero's Latin, it means; "If you are well, it is well. I am well!"

I pray that your loving family and friends will realize that you are truly well and that when they are well, totally healed from their grieving,

the world of Newtown / Sandy Hook will
be well again — Pray for them and for
all of us — For you have greater vision
and know what / who Love really is —
You have experienced, already, Teachers
and children, "Love", face to face —
You, dear friends, already have
what we, still on earth, long for: the
fullness of Love — Joy — Peace. and
realizing that we are all in communion
with one another, ask the good Lord to
share that peace with the nations of the
earth — and our little town of Newtown.
Your time on earth was very
brief — and we wish that it was longer —
But life is relatively brief for all humans.
Thankfully, in your new and better life,
"a day is like a thousand years" — So, you
can enjoy an eternity of complete happiness —
and just one more thing — Help
us who do not yet have your knowledge
and wisdom, to forgive Adam and all those
who do harm to others — in body, mind and
spirit — to forgive them — for they do not
really know what they have done !
you are well ! It is well !

Love + Prayers

Leo

Newtown Meeting House sign

Newtown Meeting House on Main Street

My 26 New Friends,   June 14, 2013

Si vales, bene est, valeo! Such is the way that the great Roman orator, Marcus Tullius Cicero, began many of his letters. I am certain that you have already met him—and all the wonderful people of the earth—who greeted you upon your arrival in the glorious halls of heaven.

I am also certain that I need not translate the above greeting for you because you have already mastered all of the world's languages—and that you understand them just as the people of the Apostolic times could understand what St. Peter was saying when he, filled with the Holy Spirit, told them about Jesus and his wish to welcome them into the Kingdom of God.

But just in case others reading this letter, do not understand Cicero's Latin, it means: "If you are well, it is well, I am well!" I pray that your loving family and friends will realize that you are truly well and that when they are well, totally healed from their grieving, the world of Newtown/Sandy Hook will be well again—pray for them and for all of us. For you have greater vision and know what/who Love really is. You have experienced, already, teachers and children, 'Love' face to face.

You, dear friends, already have what we, still on earth, long for: the fullness of Love—Joy—Peace. And realizing that we are all in communion with one another, ask the good Lord to share that peace with the nations of the earth—and our little town of Newtown.

Your time on earth was very brief—and we wish that it was longer. But life is relatively brief for all humans. Thankfully, in your new and better life, "a day is like a thousand years." So, you can enjoy an eternity of complete Happiness.

And just one more thing. Help us who do not yet have your knowledge and wisdom, to forgive Adam and all those who do harm to others—in body, mind and spirit—to forgive them—for they do not really know what they have done.

You are well! It is well!

Love and prayers,
Leo

Sometimes life just isn't fair! Sometimes you can't even imagine how difficult it can be. Everything you thought about the world has been crushed. Does anyone realize what you are going through? Does anyone truly care?

You share your feelings, fears, and sadness with so many people. Sadly they leave. Never again do you want to share your story.

In the distance you spot something that gives you peace. Something you can't explain happens inside you. Your heart which has been crushed feels alive. You feel safe and for the first time you don't have to share your story. You cuddle up against the soft fur of this new friend. You are not judged!

The comfort dogs were a place to come to... for shelter... for unconditional caring... for sharing all the support you need. No words are spoken! No words need to be!

This is who you want to turn to. You don't need answers from them — just a look. They understood and reinforced that you could love something without it leaving you. You feel incredibly special!

The comfort dogs are the reason you can walk through the doors of a place that no longer feels the same.

As a parent, these sweet animals were the only reason you could get your child to go to school. The reason you smile! There are no lies they speak to you! They help you to be brave.

The bond you feel between you is unimaginable, unexplainable, and we are so grateful!

The situation is impossible, but somehow you make things possible. The humans who love you love my child too! You hold on tightly when you are scared. The bond is unbreakable. We will always be in love with you! We will always be grateful!

Love,
Jill and Samantha Kuruc

Sometimes life just isn't fair! Sometimes you can't even imagine how difficult it can be. Everything you thought about the world has been crushed. Does anyone realize what you are going through? Does anyone truly care?

You share your feelings, fears, and sadness with so many people. Sadly they leave. Never again do you want to share your story.

In the distance you spot something that gives you peace. Something you can't explain happens inside you. Your heart which has been crushed feels alive. You feel safe and for the first time you don't have to share your story. You cuddle up against the soft fur of this new friend. You are not judged!

The comfort dogs were a place to come to . . . for shelter . . . for unconditional caring . . . for sharing all the support you need. No words are spoken! No words need to be!

This is who you want to turn to. You don't need answers from them—just a look. They understood and reinforced that you could love something without it leaving you. You feel incredibly special!

The comfort dogs are the reason you can walk through the doors of a place that no longer feels the same.

As a parent, these sweet animals were the only reason you could get your child to go to school. The reason you smile! There are no lies they speak to you! They help you to be brave.

The bond you feel between you is unimaginable, unexplainable, and we are so grateful!

The situation is impossible, but somehow you make things possible. The humans who love you love my child too! You hold on tightly when you are scared. The bond is unbreakable. We will always be in love with you! We will always be grateful!

Love,
Jill and Samantha Kuruc

Dear Santa,
Thank you for waching over me.
You make a difference in childrens lives.
I also know that Christmas is not about
presents. When I get a presents it means
I was loyal, nice, helpful and that's all
Jesus was about. I go to the school that
had a shooting. I thought I was not going
to make it out. I was scared, but every
time I thought about you I was not scared
at all. I would like for elfie a girl elf. I
had been thinking. He is lonley.
                              Love,
                              Samantha Kuruc
                              Samantha Kuruc

Dogs

Dogs are a cuddly
companions,
They always have your
back,
They will snuggle you,
They will be your
best friends forever,

Dear Santa,

Thank you for watching over me. You make a difference in childrens lives. I also know that Christmas is not about presents. When I get a present it means I was loyal, nice, helpful and that's all Jesus was about. I go to the school that had a shooting. I thought I was not going to make it out. I was scared, but every time I thought about you I was not scared at all. I would like for elfie a-girl elf. I had been thinking. He is lonely.

Love,
Samantha Kuruc

Dogs
Dogs are a cuddly
companions,
They always have your
back,
They will snuggle you,
They will be your
Best Friends Forever.

Dear Reader:

How things "are" in a place is an expression of the different "spaces" one occupies — culturally, economically, emotionally and politically. At the very outset, I think it's important to emphasize that the Newtown we live in today is a multidimensional space built on a firm New England foundation. We pursue every sort of activity, cultivate every kind of talent and follow every school of thought and faith. As a result, we move between groups and gather acquaintances over generations, decades or (mere) years of residency.

Now that our kids are grown, my primary "space" in town is the annual summer book sale sponsored by the Friends of the C.H. Booth Library to benefit our town library. Physically, the sale occupies almost 24,000 square feet of one wing of our newest school, the Reed Intermediate School. The event is the fruit of cooperation among the hard-working Friends volunteers; the people who donate the books, CDs, DVDs, LPs, etc. offered for sale; town officials — in particular, our First Selectman, Pat Llodra; school staff; and local businesses. The book sale has grown to be one of the largest in the Northeast, and due to its financial success the Friends have been able to underwrite approximately 90% of our library's acquisitions budget in recent years, as well as funding most programs and many projects.

Yes, I want you to grasp that a book sale in a small Connecticut town can earn a major amount of money. That is a reflection of a particular New England ethos: Control governmental expenditures and/or make up for tight governmental budgets by mounting a community-based fundraiser.

That's not what's unique about Newtown, however. What is unique is the "space" the book sale volunteers occupy in terms of social and emotional bonds that compel them to come through each year to mount the book sale. We are of all ages, faiths and philosophies, economic stations, political affiliations, genders and orientations, and yet we pull together to work all year round and particularly hard during two weeks in July, abetted by even more volunteers, to put on the book sale. The list of adult volunteers comprises almost 100 names; add the local students who performed community service at the sale, the town and school personnel who were involved, and the local business-people who provided support, and the number would surely top 160, out of a population of perhaps 28,000. Over almost four decades, hundreds of Newtown residents have actualized their common faith in the power of the written word—and in each other—by holding the book sale.

On Dec. 14, 2012 the president of the Friends had just called our monthly board meeting to order when we were bombarded by a cacophony of sirens outside the library and cell phones inside the boardroom. How appropriate for us to have been there together at that time. Whatever our other affiliations – and, remember, we each occupy various "spaces" in this town – in the aftermath all of the volunteers knew that the booksale sorting rooms and office were areas to retreat to for conversation and consolation. Some of us became part of the team at the warehouse processing donated books, some of us pitched in to help the library staff shield patrons from the media onslaught and address private needs, some of us met for intimate coffee klatches, some of us stayed in touch by phone or e-mail. Our emotional space–carved out by an annual, boisterous celebration of books and media – embraced us and held us firmly upright.

Newtown remains strong.

Denise A. Kaiser
Chairwoman, 2013 Annual Summer Book Sale
On behalf of the Friends of the C.H. Booth Library

Dear Reader:

How things "are" in a place is an expression of the different "spaces" one occupies—culturally, economically, emotionally and politically. At the very outset, I think it's important to emphasize that the Newtown we live in today is a multidimensional space built on a firm New England foundation. We pursue every sort of activity, cultivate every kind of talent and follow every school of thought and faith. As a result, we move between groups and gather acquaintances over generations, decades or (mere) years of residency.

Now that our kids are grown, my primary "space" in town is the annual summer book sale sponsored by the Friends of the C.H. Booth Library to benefit our town library. Physically, the sale occupies almost 24,000 square feet of one wing of our newest school, the Reed Intermediate School. The event is the fruit of cooperation among the hard-working Friends volunteers; the people who donate the books, CDs, DVDs, LPs, etc. offered for sale; town officials—in particular, our First Selectman, Pat Llodra; school staff; and local businesses. The book sale has grown to be one of the largest in the Northeast, and due to its financial success the Friends have been able to underwrite approximately 90% of our library's acquisitions budget in recent years, as well as funding most programs and many projects.

Yes, I want you to grasp that a book sale in a small Connecticut town can earn a major amount of money. That is a reflection of a particular New England ethos: Control governmental expenditures and/or make up for tight governmental budgets by mounting a community-based fundraiser.

That's not what's unique about Newtown, however. What is unique is the "space" the book sale volunteers occupy in terms of social and emotional bonds that compel them to come through each year to mount the book sale. We are of all ages, faiths and philosophies, economic stations, political affiliations, genders and orientations, and yet we pull together to work all year round and particularly hard during two weeks in July, abetted by even more volunteers, to put on the book sale. The list of adult volunteers comprises almost 100 names; add the local students who performed community service at the sale, the town and school personnel who were involved, and the local businesspeople who provided support, and the number would surely top 160, out of a population of perhaps 28,000. Over almost four decades, hundreds of Newtown residents have actualized their common faith in the power of the written word—and in each other—by holding the book sale.

On Dec. 14, 2012 the president of the Friends had just called our monthly board meeting to order when we were bombarded by a cacophony of sirens outside the library and cell phones inside the boardroom. How appropriate for us to have been there together at that time. Whatever our other affiliations—and, remember, we each occupy various "spaces" in this town—in the aftermath all of the volunteers knew that the book sale sorting rooms and office were areas to retreat to for conversation and consolation. Some of us became part of the team at the warehouse processing donated books, some of us pitched in to help the library staff shield patrons from the media onslaught and address private needs, some of us met for intimate coffee klatches, some of us stayed in touch by phone or e-mail. Our emotional space—carved out by an annual, boisterous celebration of books and media—embraced us and held us firmly upright.

Newtown remains strong.

Denise A. Kaiser
Chairwoman, 2013 Annual Summer Book Sale
On behalf of the Friends of the C.H. Booth Library

We are Sandy Hook,
We choose Love

Love is finding the perfect home to raise your family in.

Love is seeing the flagpole and knowing that you are home.

Love is knowing that a movie will cost no more that $2 at Edmond Town Hall

Love is cutting oranges and purchasing snacks for baseball, softball or soccer teams

Love is watching the Labor Day Parade, even in the rain from the back of the family car.

Love is birthday parties, pumpkin picking and corn mazes at Paproski's Farm.

Love is not knowing what you want to eat and going to the Blue Colony Diner (Exit 10) and having hundreds of choices.

Love is the welcoming green "Giant" footprints on the road to Sandy Hook School.

Love is helping run Picture Day and the Ice Cream Social at Sandy Hook School. We call it SHS not SHES.

Love is summer camp at Dickinson Park and Treadwell Park.

Love is lobster dinner at the Sandy Hook Fire House annual Lobster Fest.

Love is walking in the woods at Fairfield Hills with your dogs.

Love is the summer reading program at the Booth Library.

Love is getting bags of reduced or free books at the annual Book Sale.

Love is watching Mr. Porco dump hundreds of rubber ducks into the Pootatuck River at the annual Duck Race.

Love is being the cookie mom for Girl Scout Troop 23.

Love is watching dad make a perfect pinewood derby car.

Love is the Holy Cow Ice Cream Shop and the Ferris Creamery.

Love is the Christmas Tree Lighting at Ram Pasture and Sandy Hook Center.

Love is Trick-or-Treating and the House Tours on Main Street.

Love is making life-long friends in Sandy Hook

Love is watching Sandy Hook's transformation in the worst of times

We are Sandy Hook,
         we choose Love

WE ARE SANDY HOOK, WE CHOOSE LOVE

Love is finding the perfect home to raise your family in.

Love is seeing the flagpole and knowing that you are home.

Love is knowing that a movie will cost no more than $2 at Edmond Town Hall.

Love is cutting oranges and purchasing snacks for baseball, softball or soccer teams.

Love is watching the Labor Day Parade, even in the rain from the back of the family car.

Love is birthday parties, pumpkin picking and corn mazes at Paproski's Farm.

Love is not knowing what you want to eat and going to the Blue Colony Diner (Exit 10) and having hundreds of choices.

Love is the welcoming green "Giant" footprints on the road to Sandy Hook School.

Love is helping run Picture Day and the Ice Cream Social at Sandy Hook School. We call it SHS not SHES.

Love is summer camp and swimming at Dickinson Park and Treadwell Park.

Love is lobster dinner at the Sandy Hook Fire House annual Lobster Fest.

Love is walking in the woods at Fairfield Hills with your dogs.

Love is the summer reading program at the Booth Library.

Love is getting bags of reduced or free books at the annual Book Sale.

Love is watching Mr. Porco dump hundreds of rubber ducks into the Pootatuck River at the annual Duck Race.

Love is being the cookie mom for Girl Scout Troop 23.

Love is watching dad make a perfect pinewood derby car.

Love is the Holy Cow Ice Cream shop and the Ferris Creamery.

Love is the Christmas Tree Lighting at Ram Pasture and Sandy Hook Center.

Love is Trick-or-Treating and the House Tours on Main Street.

Love is making life-long friends in Sandy Hook.

Love is watching Sandy Hook's transformation in the worst of times.

WE ARE SANDY HOOK, WE CHOOSE LOVE

Baseball field at Treadwell Park

Castle Hill Farm corn maze

Blue Colony Diner at night with lights

Cullens Memorial sign for the Boy Scout camp

Sandy Hook fire engine at the Labor Day Parade

Edmond Town Hall

View of seats at Edmond Town Hall

Treadwell Pool

Labor Day Parade 2013

Fairfield Hills

Lobsterfest crowd eating

Ducks being released

Liberty baseball field

Woods at Fairfield Hills

It is a blessing when you witness the power of love even in the midst of the most incredible and difficult circumstances. And yet that is exactly what happened on December 14, 2012 in our community. As I stood in the midst of school children assembled in the bays of the firehouse not sure whether they wanted to stay with their friends or go home with their parents, among teachers who were absolutely the most valiant in their efforts to bring calm and strength to their students, side by side with first responders trying to make sense out of chaos and finally with families who could not find their child and had to wait for the news that their lives had changed forever. I saw love at its best. I also saw love as husbands embraced wives, as parents embraced parents, as friends embraced friends. I saw love in the midst of tears from hearts broken, in the gasps of parents trying to catch their lost breath, in the strength of one person holding another who was collapsing from grief. I saw love in the volunteers who brought water and tissues hoping to bring some comfort, in the screams of a family member wanting to know where her loved one was and in the medical personnel who were just waiting to do what they could. I found love in the embrace of the clergy who were there to console, in the folded hands of people just praying that this really was not happening and in the common prayer of all in one room who had to learn to walk a new path through life. I saw it as thousands gathered wherever they could just to be together. As local officials tried to bring a sense of calm and as more and more help kept arriving to lift up a community whose town had been violated in the worst possible manner. I listened as I heard small groups singing Christmas carols. As candlelight filled the town with lightness among so much darkness and as people of all ages simply stood side by side looking for hope. I saw love through the eyes of the seniors who never thought they would live to see so much violence in our world, in the eyes of young parents hoping their children would be safe from anything that might harm them and in the eyes of children who were afraid and confused. I saw it as one after another spoke that evil had visited our land but goodness had overcome it, that darkness is overcome by light and that hate will be conquered by the love that brought us together. Being asked over and over again by the media if I thought this was God's hand or why God allowed this to happen. I knew that this was not the hand of God but rather the power of evil that had overtaken us for a brief moment. We saw evil face to face. but we also saw love. light and hope. It is not a matter of choosing love; we know love. We know its power to heal, its grace to conquer and its hope in the midst of despair. We are Newtown. We did not simply choose love, we choose to live it.

God bless,
Monsignor Robert Weiss
Pastor
Saint Rose of Lima Parish
Newtown, CT

Saint Rose of Lima Church

It is a blessing when you witness the power of love even in the midst of the most incredible and difficult circumstances, and yet that is exactly what happened on December 14, 2012 in our community. As I stood in the midst of school children assembled in the bays of the fire house not sure whether they wanted to stay with their friends or go home with their parents, among teachers who were absolutely the most valiant in their efforts to bring calm and strength to their students, side by side with first responders trying to make sense out of chaos and finally with families who could not find their child and had to wait for the news that their lives had changed forever, I saw love at its best. I also saw love as husbands embraced wives, as parents embraced parents, as friends embraced friends. I saw love in the midst of tears from hearts broken, in the gasps of parents trying to catch their lost breath, in the strength of one person holding another who was collapsing from grief. I saw love in the volunteers who brought water and tissues hoping to bring some comfort, in the screams of a family member wanting to know where her loved one was and in the medical personnel who were just waiting to do what they could. I found love in the embrace of the clergy who were there to console, in the folded hands of people just praying that this really was not happening and in the common prayer of all in one room who had to learn to walk a new path through life. I saw it as thousands gathered wherever they could just to be together, as local officials tried to bring a sense of calm and as more and more help kept arriving to lift up a community whose town had been violated in the worst possible manner. I listened as I heard small groups singing Christmas carols, as candlelight filled the town with brightness among so much darkness and as people of all ages simply stood side by side looking for hope. I saw love through the eyes of the seniors who never thought they would live to see so much violence in our world, in the eyes of young parents hoping their children would be safe from anything that might harm them and in the eyes of children who were afraid and confused. I saw it as one after another spoke that evil had visited our land but goodness had overcome it, that darkness is overcome by light and that hate will be conquered by the love that brought us together. Being asked over and over again by the media if I thought this was God's hand or why God allowed this to happen, I knew that this was not the hand of God but rather the power of evil that had overtaken us for a brief moment. We saw evil face to face, but we also saw love, light and hope. It is not a matter of choosing love; we know love. We know its power to heal, its grace to conquer and its hope in the midst of despair. We are Newtown. We did not simply choose love, we choose to live it.

God Bless,
Monsignor Robert Weiss
Pastor
Saint Rose of Lima Parish
Newtown, CT

What does Newtown mean to me? That should really be a very easy question for someone who came to town as a newborn in 1935 from Bridgeport Hospital and took up residence on Main Street, at that time two doors down from the Hawley Manor. It was a good place to grow up; we never locked up the house, Mr. Boyson delivered fresh milk to our doorsteps, during heavy winter storms a horse and plow would often go up the sidewalk on our side of the street and go back down across the way, and there were no strangers in the lobby of the Post Office at the Edmond Town Hall. We knew just about everyone.

I would like to think that the Town was special because, as a fourth generation of the Smith family in town, many had gone before me and helped make Newtown a good place to be. Three generations ago a Smith was one of the guiding lights in the Congregational Church, helping people with their religious life and assisting in the times of need. Two generations ago my grandfather and great uncle bought and ran The Bee, keeping readers up with all that was happening in town, including such things as cows being born and people making day trips to Bridgeport for some extravagant shopping. My father left a job in New York City and moved back to town to take up the reins of The Bee, where he worked for over 50 years, championing such things as town and school budgets and zoning regulations that passed a town meeting by two votes. Things which were done by those three generations, many that I never knew about, I like to think made Newtown a better place for all of us to live. But when I think about what Newtown really means to me I always reflect back to the fun times we had living on Main Street, where we could walk to the library for books, to the town hall for movies and bowling, and to the General Store or the A&P for a Coke and box of Cracker-Jacks for about a dime. From the time I could walk, my best friend, the late Danny Desmond also lived on Main Street, but across the road and opposite the Booth Library. Some of our experiences remain fresh in my memory, such as the time we made a snowball with a cherry bomb inside and, after lighting it, tossed it well up into the air for it to explode. At the time we were standing at the driveway entrance to the Town Hall, and it went off with a bang. We loved it, but the excitement faded quickly when we found a police car with the town resident state trooper, Sgt. Jim Costello, drawn up beside us.

He said something like "if you go right home, probably your parents will never know about this". We high-tailed it down the street. Then there was a Halloween night when we trick or treated Honan's Funeral parlor, only to find a wake taking place, casket and all. That led to another fast trip down the street. And then there were the Thanksgiving morning walks up the hill to the deserted castle; evening ball games in the vacant lot between our house and my grandparents house next door; and horseback rides on an unpaved Wendover Road with Mr. Bounty, who lived two doors down from Trinity Church and Kept two horses in his barn. And one last Danny story... The Rev. Paul Cullens, long-time minister at the Congregational Church, picked Danny and myself to take part in a special church service one Sunday to introduce two new flags, an American flag and a church flag to the congregation. Dressed in our best, we were given the flags just inside the entrance and had to walk up the stairs and down the aisle to the front of the church. We acted as if we were leading a parade down Park Avenue, clowning a bit and paying little attention, when the end of my pole with a cross on top, hit the door jam going into the church and the cross snapped in half. It was not fixable, but the ceremony went on and one person mentioned that "half a cross is better than no cross."

So from prior to Miss Fanel's kindergarten school on South Main Street, through grade eight at Hawley school, I had a great time growing up and can thank Newtown for its part in it. After prep school, the Marine Corps and college, there was no question of where to live and raise a family. That was over 50 years ago, and still liking it.

R Scudder Smith

What does Newtown mean to me? That should really be a very easy question for someone who came to town as a newborn in 1935 from Bridgeport Hospital and took up residence on Main Street, at that time two doors down from the Hawley Manor. It was a good place to grow up; we never locked up the house, Mr. Boyson delivered fresh milk to our doorsteps, during heavy winter storms a horse and plow would often go up the sidewalk on our side of the street and go back down across the way, and there were no strangers in the lobby of the post office at the Edmund Town Hall. We knew just about everyone.

I would like to think that the town was special because, as a fourth generation of the Smith family in town, many had gone before me and helped make Newtown a good place to be. Three generations ago a Smith was one of the guiding lights in the Congregational Church, helping people with their religious life and assisting in the times of need. Two generations ago my grandfather and great uncle bought and ran The Bee, keeping readers up with all that was happening in town, including such things as cows being born and people making day trips to Bridgeport for some extravagant shopping. My father left a job in New York City and moved back to town to take up the reins of The Bee, where he worked for over 50 years, championing such things as town and school budgets and zoning regulation that passed a town meeting by two votes. Things which were done by those three generations, many that I never knew about, I like to think made Newtown a better place for all of us to live. But when I think about what Newtown really means to me I always reflect back to the fun times we had living on Main Street, where we could walk to the library for books, to the town hall for movies and bowling, and to the General Store or the A&P for a Coke and box of Cracker-Jacks for about a dime. From the time I could walk, my best friend, the late Danny Desmond also lived on Main Street, but across the road and opposite the Booth Library. Some of our experiences remain fresh in my memory, such as the time we made a snowball with a cherry bomb inside and, after lighting it, tossed it well up into the air for it to explode. At the time we were standing at the driveway entrance to the town hall, and it went off with a bang. We loved it, but the excitement faded quickly when we found a police car with the town resident state trooper, Sgt. Jim Costello, drawn up beside us. He said something like "if you go right home, probably your parents will never know about this." We high-tailed it down the street. Then there was a Halloween night when we trick or treated Honan's Funeral parlor, only to find a wake taking place, casket and all. That led to another fast trip down the street. And then there were the Thanksgiving morning walks up the hill to the deserted castle; evening ball games in the vacant lot between our house and my grandparent's house next door; and horseback rides on an unpaved Wendover Road with Mr. Bounty, who lived two doors down from Trinity Church and kept two horses in his barn. And one last Danny story . . . The Rev. Paul Cullens, long-time minister at the Congregational Church, picked Danny and myself to take part in a special church service one Sunday to introduce two new flags, an American flag and a church flag to the congregation. Dressed in our best, we were given the flags just inside the entrance and had to walk up the stairs and down the aisle to the front of the church. We acted as if we were leading a parade down Park Avenue, clowning a bit and paying little attention, when the end of my pole with a cross on top, hit the door jam going into the church and the cross snapped in half. It was not fixable, but the ceremony went on and one person mentioned that "half a cross is better than no cross."

So from prior to Miss Farrel's kindergarten school on South Main Street, through grade eight at Hawley School, I had a great time growing up and can thank Newtown for its part in it. After prep school, the Marine Corps and college, there was no question of where to live and raise a family. That was over 50 years ago, and still liking it.

R. Scudder Smith

8.22.13

I read this quote by Henry David Thoreau once, he stated: *Things do not change. We change.* It is often said to embrace change and value what it brings to your life. But me? I choose to cherish what stays the same. Too often, change is out of your hands, and takes place too fast, too soon, or too late. I have realized that in this ever-changing world, it is the things that do not change that become refreshing.

Newtown is my sameness, my constant. I now attend college seven hours away, and haven't spent more than a few weeks in my old room during the past few years. Yes, my parents have grown older, and friends have moved away, nevertheless some things here remain untouched by time: like the rasberry bush in my backyard that blooms every summer and how the best picnics are those at the top of Holcomb's Hill. The breakfast sandwiches from the General Store that will always be $1.25 ($1.33 with tax to be exact), and the two dollar movies at Edmond Town Hall. The view from the top of Castle Hill that is beautiful every day of the year. How Head O Meadow Elementary School will always be my "H.O.M.E" and my tile that will forever hang in the Reed Intermediate School lobby. And how there's hardly a place you could go to where you wouldn't run into a friend, or a friend of a friend. I whole-heartedly agree with the band O.A.R., that tells us in their song *I Feel Home*: "there are few things pure in this world anymore, and home is one of the few." Time and time again, it's these little snapshots of life in Newtown that keep me connected when I'm so far away.

This past July I decided to drive home to surprise my family one weekend. After pulling into the driveway I grabbed my bags out of the car and placed them on the front porch. The sky was a perfect blue, the tiger lilies in my mom's garden were in full bloom, the grass freshly cut by my dad, and the sun shining through the pine trees. There before me sat the same house I had come home to for 21 years. How lucky was I?

-JMR

I read this quote by Henry David Thoreau once, he stated: *Things do not change. We change.* It is often said to embrace change and value what it brings to your life. But me? I choose to cherish what stays the same. Too often, change is out of your hands, and takes place too fast, too soon, or too late. I have realized that in this ever-changing world, it is the things that do not change that become refreshing.

Newtown is my sameness, my constant. I now attend college seven hours away, and haven't spent more than a few weeks in my old room during the past few years. Yes, my parents have grown older, and friends have moved away, nevertheless some things here remain untouched by time: Like the raspberry bush in my back yard that blooms every summer and how the best picnics are those at the top of Holcomb's Hill. The breakfast sandwiches from the General Store that will always be $1.25 ($1.33 with tax to be exact), and the two dollar movies at Edmond Town Hall. The view from the top of Castle Hill that is beautiful every day of the year. How Head O Meadow Elementary School will always be my "H.O.M.E" and my tile that will forever hang in the Reed Intermediate School lobby. And how there's hardly a place you could go to where you wouldn't run into a friend, or a friend of a friend. I whole-heartedly agree with the band O.A.R., that tells us in their song *I Feel Home:* "there are few things pure in this world anymore, and home is of the few." Time and time again, it's these little snap-shots of life in Newtown that keep me connected when I'm so far away.

This past July I decided to drive home to surprise my family one weekend. After pulling into the driveway, I grabbed my bags out of the car and placed them on the front porch. The sky was a perfect blue, the tiger lilies in my mom's garden were in full bloom, the grass freshly cut by my dad, and the sun shining through the pine trees. There before me sat the same house I had come home to for 21 years. How lucky was I?

JMR

General Store, Main Street, Newtown

She twirled in her driveway, completely and utterly carefree. Her long hair lifted by the freedom in the movement. She was innocent, joyous and full of life. Waiting for the morning bus was a simple, daily routine. Watching her dance and twirl, she created joy in an ordinary moment.

I only got to watch her for as long as it took the stoplight to flicker from red to green, but her dance of innocence kept a lift in my spirit for quite a stretch down the road. How wonderful and rewarding to have witnessed this zest for life created by a young child.

For most of Sandy Hook there is only one main road. You know what side of the morning schedule you are on based on whether you are in front or in back of the bus. You see the same children, usually with the same parent, waiting at the end of the driveway every school-day morning. Seeing this little girl wait in the drive for the morning bus had become part of a routine. I looked forward to seeing her. You don't have to know someone for them to become a part of your life.

I don't remember the day, or even the day of the week she danced in the driveway. All I know is that day was different. What she felt, what she shared, in that moment was palpable. It was as if she generated an energy of joy and forced it into the Road — into the line of traffic congested with those focused on little more than beating the light and making their way to the highway. It was as if she was telling everyone that life is to be lived, and felt, and loved and not just muddled through.

There was something so beautiful and so captivating in those few fleeting moments.

I didn't see her dance and twirl again. I didn't have to. Her spinning feet left prints in my memory. From that day on, all I would have to do is catch a glimpse of her, or pass her house, and I would smile. Alone in the car, the radio buzzing, I would smile at the memory of her dance. I didn't know her name. I knew nothing but the joy she brought to me that morning. And in that joy, I felt a gratitude and a connection.

Joy turned to sorrow on Dec. 15. Parked like a tombstone in the driveway that was once the site of boundless energy, was a gray Connecticut State Police car. I didn't need to wait for a list of the victims. I knew, I just knew. Anyone who drove by the house that day knew. Passing the house brought a gasp from deep within. A shortness of breath likely repeated by each driver who passed the house that day.

No more dancing and twirling. No need to look to see if she was in the driveway. The bus wouldn't be stopping there again.

Once the list of names was released and faces were put to the names, I saw her. I saw a girl with an impish smile. I saw a girl full of energy and life. In so many of the pictures released by the family, she was dancing or running. Life and energy captured in ordinary moments.

Waiting at the red light I remember her twirling and outstretching arms to catch every moment of life. The bus may no longer need to stop there, but we need to stop. We need to stop and remember. We need to remember the exuberance of a dancing child. We need to feel free and enjoy it. We need to celebrate the ordinary moments. We need to remember what the children have taught us. And, even if for a fleeting moment, we need to twirl in the driveway.

Eileen Byrnes

She twirled in her driveway, completely and utterly carefree. Her long hair lifted by the freedom in the movement. She was innocent, joyous and full of life. Waiting for the morning bus was a simple, daily routine. Watching her dance and twirl, she created joy in an ordinary moment.

I only got to watch her for as long as it took the stoplight to flicker from red to green, but her dance of innocence kept a lift in my spirit for quite a stretch down the road. How wonderful and rewarding to have witnessed this zest for life created by a young child.

For most of Sandy Hook there is only one main road. You know what side of your morning schedule you are on based on whether you are in front or in back of the bus. You see the same children, usually with the same parent, waiting at the end of the driveway every school-day morning. Seeing this little girl wait in the drive for the morning bus had become part of a routine. I looked forward to seeing her. You don't have to know someone for them to become a part of your life.

I don't remember the day, or even the day of the week, she danced in the driveway. All I know is that day was different. What she felt, what she shared, in that moment was palpable. It was as if she generated an energy of joy and forced it out into the road—into the line of traffic congested with those focused on little more than beating the light and making their way to the highway. It was as if she was telling everyone that life is to be lived, and felt, and loved and not just muddled through.

There was something so beautiful and so captivating in those few fleeting moments.

I didn't see her dance and twirl again. I didn't have to. Her spinning feet left prints in my memory. From that day on, all I would have to do is catch a glimpse of her, or pass her house, and I would smile. Alone in the car, the radio buzzing, I would smile at the memory of her dance. I didn't know her name. I knew nothing but the joy she brought to me that morning. And in that joy, I felt a gratitude and a connection.

Joy turned to sorrow on Dec. 15. Parked like a tombstone in the driveway that once was the site of boundless energy, was a gray Connecticut State Police car. I didn't need to wait for a list of the victims. I knew, I just knew. Anyone who drove by the house that day knew. Passing the house brought a gasp from deep within. A shortness of breath likely repeated by each driver who passed the house that day.

No more dancing and twirling. No need to look to see if she was in the driveway. The bus wouldn't be stopping there again.

Once the list of names was released and faces were put to the names, I saw her. I saw a girl with an impish smile. I saw a girl full of energy and life. In so many of the pictures released by the family, she was dancing or running. Life and energy captured in ordinary moments.

Waiting at the red light, I remember her twirling and outstretching arms to catch every moment of life. The bus may no longer need to stop there, but we need to stop. We need to stop and remember. We need to remember the exuberance of a dancing child. We need to feel free and enjoy it. We need to celebrate the ordinary moments. We need to remember what the children have taught us. And, even if for a fleeting moment, we need to twirl in the driveway.

Eileen Byrnes

Newtown is rich in youth athletic programs starting at age five (or in some cases younger) through high school. These programs include football, baseball, basketball, soccer, lacrosse, swimming, tennis, track and more. Many of my favorite memories of my 23 years in Newtown come from my association with youth sports. I was involved with Parks and Rec with basketball and baseball for several years but my largest involvement and greatest memories comes from the Newtown Soccer Club.

I was associated with the club as a coach/manager/grounds keeper for 12 years. I started with my son at age five and retired (for the third time) when my daughter was 15 and a sophomore in high school. Both my kids started at five and went from the Rec league to the Travel Teams to Premier Teams and finally terminating their soccer careers on the high school varsity teams. Though I experienced great joy watching my kids grow and progress in their soccer skills I also enjoyed watching the same growth for hundreds of kids that I probably would not have met if not for the Newtown Soccer

CLUB. IN ADDITION, I MADE MANY FRIENDS WITH THE PARENTS OF THESE KIDS AND TODAY MY BEST FRIENDS IN NEWTOWN ALL ORIGINATED WITH YOUTH SOCCER.

THE CLUB EMPHASIZED LEARNING SOCCER SKILLS, TEAM WORK AND MOST IMPORTANTLY... HAVING FUN. I HAVE MANY GREAT STORIES ABOUT THE GROWTH OF THE KIDS BOTH AS SOCCER PLAYERS BUT MORE IMPORTANTLY AS YOUNG ADULTS. I STILL GET GREAT PLEASURE OUT OF RUNNING INTO ONE OF THEM IN NEWTOWN AND LEARNING ABOUT WHAT THEY HAVE ACCOMPLISHED SINCE I LAST SAW THEM. ALL OF THEM ARE THROUGH COLLEGE AND HAVE STARTED ON CAREERS OR ARE DOING GRADUATE WORK. SOME WENT ON AFTER HIGH SCHOOL AND PLAYED SOCCER IN COLLEGE BUT MOST DID NOT. MANY NEVER PLAYED MORE THAN REC BUT LEARNED THE VALUE OF TEAM WORK AND ENJOYING COMPETITION FROM THAT EXPERIENCE.

I KEEP THREATENING MY WIFE THAT I WILL COME OUT OF RETIREMENT AND START COACHING A REC TEAM AGAIN. SHE JUST GIVES ME THAT "YOU'RE CRAZY" LOOK. WELL,

MAYBE I AM A LITTLE CRAZY BUT I THINK I MAY WANT TO MAKE SOME NEW FRIENDS IN NEWTOWN.

Soccer field at Treadwell Park

Newtown is rich in youth athletic programs starting at age five (or in some cases younger) through high school. These programs include football, baseball, basketball, soccer, lacrosse, swimming, tennis, track and more. Many of my favorite memories of my 23 years in Newtown come from my association with youth sports. I was involved with Parks and Rec with basketball and baseball for several years but my largest involvement and greatest memories comes from the Newtown Soccer Club.

I was associated with the club as a coach/manager/grounds keeper for 12 years. I started with my son at age five and retired (for the third time) when my daughter was 15 and a sophomore in high school. Both my kids started at five and went from the Rec league to the Travel Teams to Premier Teams and finally terminating their soccer careers on the high school varsity teams. Though I experienced great joy watching my kids grow and progress in their soccer skills I also enjoyed watching the same growth for hundreds of kids that I probably would not have met if not for the Newtown Soccer Club. In addition, I made many friends with the parents of these kids and today my best friends in Newtown all originated with youth soccer.

The club emphasized learning soccer skills, team work and most importantly . . . having fun. I have many great stories about the growth of the kids both as soccer players but more importantly as young adults. I still get great pleasure out of running into one of them in Newtown and learning about what they have accomplished since I last saw them. All of them are through college and have started on careers or are doing graduate work. Some went on after high school and played soccer in college but most did not. Many never played more than Rec but learned the value of team work and enjoying competition from that experience.

I keep threatening my wife that I will come out of retirement and start coaching a Rec team again. She just gives me that "you're crazy" look. Well, maybe I am a little crazy but I think I may want to make some new friends in Newtown.

Christmas In January

It was a bleak day back in the beginning of January as I sat parked in my patrol car, still just as dumbfounded by recent events. It was early in the day and I was taking a deep breath before I had to face the day ahead. Suddenly I heard a knock at my car window and I looked down to see a little boy with big eyes staring up at me.

The little boy's mom stood sheepishly behind her son. I stepped out of my car and asked the little boy (who barely was as tall as my waist) how I could help him. His mom explained that her son had a Christmas gift for me. With those words, the little boy confidently held up a small paper bag for me to take from him. I looked in the bag and saw several pieces of candy and a homemade card that read: "Thank you for your hard work. We ♡ you. Griffin + Reid!" I could feel the lump in my throat form as my eyes started to water. I thanked the little boy and asked if I could hug him. He responded with a big smile on his face and said that I could.

When I composed myself I asked the little boy if he knew how much I needed a Christmas present THAT day. And the little boy simply responded; "I know you did..... THAT'S WHY I PICKED YOU!"

Officer Maryhelen McCarthy
Newtown Police Department

Christmas in January

It was a bleak day back in the beginning of January as I sat parked in my patrol car, still just as dumbfounded by recent events. It was early in the day and I was taking a deep breath before I had to face the day ahead. Suddenly I heard a knock at my car window and looked down to see a little boy with big eyes staring up at me.

The little boy's mom stood sheepishly behind her son. I stepped out of my car and asked the little boy (who barely was as tall as my waist) how I could help him. His mom explained that her son had a Christmas gift for me. With those words, the little boy confidently held up a small paper bag for me to take from him. I looked in the bag and saw several pieces of candy and a homemade card that read: "Thank you for your hard work. We (heart) you. Griffin & Reid." I could feel the lump in my throat form as my eyes started to water. I thanked the little boy and asked if I could hug him. He responded with a big smile on his face and said that I could.

When I composed myself I asked the little boy if he knew how much I needed a Christmas present *THAT* day. And the little boy simply responded; "I know you did. . . THAT'S WHY I PICKED YOU!"

Officer Maryhelen McCarthy
Newtown Police Department

Newtown Police Department

The thing I have come to realize is that we, the people of Newtown, are a compassionate, incredibly strong, peace loving group of people. I guess I never had to think about that out loud before but it is so evident after all that has occurred to us in the last eight months.

Maybe we are naive, or maybe we have just carved out this beautiful little family oriented happy place town just so we can live out our American Dreams together. I never knew how lucky I was to be a part of all this. Now, all of a sudden in a blink of an eye, this town Newtown, means so much more to me than ever before.

Never in our wildest dreams would any of us have ever imagined what happened on 12/14. It still continues to haunt me. How could we have suffered like this at the hands of one insane man? How will we heal? How will our children heal? How will we move forward with a new normal?

What I have come to realize is that we have all grown up a bit; the fantasy is somehow tarnished. It will be hard to feel completely safe.

Many of us feel and crumbled for awhile. We walked around in a post traumatic stress haze, unable to do the most routine of chores. Our eyes were wide and dazed with a perpetual lump in our throats that would move up and flow out into tears in a millisecond.

The moms ... oh the moms suffered. Not to say the dads did not but I'm writing this from my mom perspective and its all I know. Moms are supposed to be able to protect and nuture their babies. We as moms also love and nuture our friends, relatives and neighbors babies as well. When those children were massacred we felt as though we lost a part of ourselves. We knew it could have been any of our school aged children. We put ourselves into that place of loss, the most intense loss a mom could ever suffer.

What I have also come to realize as these months continue to pass is that in order to for us as a community to start moving forward, we need to be heard.

For the first few months and even now eight months later I have listened to clients and friends tell their stories. The need to be heard is great. There is healing that occurs as people tell their story; where they were, who they knew, how it affected them and their children. The need to talk is great. We want to tell people how we cried, how we explained the unfairness to our children, how our children were affected and how they are working through their feelings, how we prayed or did not pray or how we decided to turn to God or away from God. We need to talk about how we got so busy with volunteering and other things in town so as not to have to think about what happened or so you could try to squash the never ending thoughts of sadness and just take a break from thinking about it all.

I joined the Newtown Documentation Project so I would have a place to go and sit and be with others who wanted to help. We all found an outlet of warmth and support.

We sat for hours sifting through hundreds of thousands of letters and words of love that were sent to our town. We organized and sorted the letters and at the same time we talked and listened. Somehow our pain was being organized and sorted.

I have spent the past eight months listening to friends and clients and I now understand that talking is a way to put the pieces back into some order. Human nature is an interesting thing; we are one in our basic needs. We need to be heard and validated. We need to feel safe and nurtured and loved. Grieving takes time. We need to keep helping one another in our town and in other towns.

Newtown made history in an awful way on 12/14 but my hope is that as we move forward, we will make history again in the best of ways. Time will tell. We have a lot of determined people in our town. Until then we are changed, we move forward with some blackness in our hearts but we keep pushing forward for our kids and ourselves. Our hearts will always ache for the families who lost their children and loved ones.

We love our town and all its been through. We are thankful for our great leaders and the first responders and everyone who has helped or made a difference in anyway at all. Love Wins!

Nicole Friedrich LMT

The thing I have come to realize is that we, the people of Newtown, are a compassionate, incredibly strong, peace loving group of people. I guess I never had to think about that out loud before but it is so evident after all that has occurred to us in the last eight months.

Maybe we are naïve, or maybe we have just carved out this beautiful little family oriented happy place town just so we can live out our American Dreams together. I never knew how lucky I was to be a part of all this. Now, all of a sudden in a blink of an eye, this town Newtown, means so much more to me than ever before.

Never in our wildest dreams would any of us have ever imagined what happened on 12/14. It still continues to haunt me. How could we have suffered like this at the hands of one insane man? How will we heal? How will our children heal? How will we move forward with a new normal?

What I have come to realize is that we have all grown up a bit; the fantasy is somehow tarnished. It will be hard to feel completely safe.

Many of us fell and crumbled for a while. We walked around in a post traumatic stress haze, unable to do the most routine of chores. Our eyes were wide and dazed with a perpetual lump in our throats that would move up and flow out into tears in a millisecond.

The moms . . . oh the moms suffered. Not to say the dads did not but I'm writing this from my mom perspective and it's all I know. Moms are supposed to be able to protect and nurture their babies. We as moms also care and nurture our friends, relatives and neighbors babies as well. When those children were massacred we felt as though we lost a part of ourselves. We knew it could have been any of our school aged children. We put ourselves into that place of loss, the most intense loss a mom could ever suffer.

What I have also come to realize as these months continue to pass is that in order for us as a community to start moving forward, we need to be heard.

For the first few months and even now eight months later I have listened to clients and friends tell their stories. The need to be heard is great. There is healing that occurs as people tell their story; where they were, who they knew, how it affected them and their children. The need to talk is great. We want to tell people how we cried, how we explained the awfulness to our children, how our children were affected and how they are working through their feelings, how we prayed or did not pray or how we decided to turn to God or away from God. We need to talk about how we got so busy with volunteering and other things in town so as not to have to think about what happened or so you could try to squash the never ending thoughts of sadness and just take a break from thinking about it all.

I joined the Newtown Documentation Project so I would have a place to go and sit and be with others who wanted to help. We all found an outlet of warmth and support. We sat for hours sifting through hundreds of thousands of letters and words of love that were sent to our town. We organized and sorted the letters and at the same time we talked and listened. Somehow our pain was being organized and sorted.

I have spent the past eight months listening to friends and clients and I now understand that talking is a way to put the pieces back into some order. Human nature is an interesting thing; we are one in our basic needs. We need to be heard and validated. We need to feel safe and nurtured and loved. Grieving takes time. We need to keep helping one another in our town and in other towns.

Newtown made history in an awful way on 12/14 but my hope is that as we move forward, we will make history again in the best of ways. Time will tell. We have a lot of determined people in our town. Until then we are changed, we move forward with some blackness in our hearts but we keep pushing forward for our kids and ourselves. Our hearts will always ache for the families who lost their children and loved ones.

We love our town and all its been through. We are thankful for our great leaders and the first responders and everyone who has helped or made a difference in any way at all. Love wins!

Nicole Friedrich L.M.T.

According to his wife, the only phone number her husband, my son, has memorized is my number at work. When he was deployed to Iran and Afghanistan he would call the C.H. Booth Library and ask to speak to me as if he were still a kid in high school in need of research materials. All of my children used their mother as their personal librarian, (they didn't know what an overdue fine was until they moved out of the house) but I'm okay with that. That's what I love, matching people and books. For 16 years I've been the children's librarian at the public library in Newtown. I love children, children's literature and children's authors—you could say I love my job.

One of the most rewarding and exciting things about being a librarian in this part of the country has been the opportunity to meet so many wonderful authors and illustrators. Newtown is the home of many famous authors. We have a special section of the library dedicated to their books. Stop by some time, you'll be amazed at all of the talented people who live here. If you visit the Children's department, you can't miss the three handmade colorful quilts hanging on the wall featuring the signatures of several well-loved children's authors and illustrators. The idea to create a quilt built around the signatures of famous people came from a quilter and friend, Peg Jacques. We were about to celebrate the library's 75th birthday and I wanted to do something special in the Children's department for the Gala Auction, Peg's idea to make Friendship Author Quilts sounded like a great idea. So we sent out signature requests and when they came back, we had the makings for three beautiful quilts. Peg and her friends from "the Sew Together Gals," taught workshops on quilting. Teams of children and adults created blocks to build the quilts. When it came time for the auction it was clear those who labored so hard to make the quilts were struggling with giving them up for auction. They had become attached. The quilts were too precious to sell to the highest bidder.

After much discussion, we decided the quilts belonged in the library. You can't put a price on some things. The support of family, friends and the power of story, these are the things that help us through the darkest times in our life's journey. This is what I will remember about working in Newtown. Oh, did I say I really love children's books and the talented people who wrote them?

Alana Bennison
C.H. Booth Library Children's Librarian

Quilts in Children's Department of C.H. Booth Library

According to his wife, the only phone number her husband, my son, has memorized is my number at work. When he was deployed to Iran and Afghanistan he would call the C.H. Booth Library and ask to speak to me as if he were still a kid in high school in need of some research materials. All of my children used their mother as their personal librarian, (they didn't know what an overdue fine was until they moved out of the house) but I'm okay with that. That's what I love, matching people and books. For 16 years I've been the children's librarian at the public library in Newtown. I love children, children's literature and children's authors—you could say I love my job.

One of the most rewarding and exciting things about being a librarian in this part of the country has been the opportunity to meet so many wonderful authors and illustrators. Newtown is the home of many famous authors. We have a special section of the library dedicated to their books. Stop by some time, you'll be amazed at all of the talented people who live here. If you visit the children's department, you can't miss the three handmade colorful quilts hanging on the wall featuring the signatures of several well-loved children's authors and illustrators. The idea to create a quilt built from the signatures of famous people came from a quilter and friend, Peg Jacques. We were about to celebrate the library's 75th birthday and I wanted to do something special in the children's department for the Gala Auction, Peg's idea to make Friendship Author Quilts sounded like a great idea. So we sent out signature requests and when they came back, we had the makings for three beautiful quilts. Peg and her friends from "The Sew Together Gals," taught workshops on quilting. Teams of children and adults created blocks to build the quilts. When it came time for the auction it was clear those who labored so hard to make the quilts were struggling with giving them up for auction. They had become attached. The quilts were too precious to sell to the highest bidder. After much discussion, we decided the quilts belonged in the library. You can't put a price on some things. The support of family, friends, and the power of story, these are the things that help us through the darkest times in our life's journey. This is what I will remember about working in Newtown. Oh, did I say I really love children's books and the talented people who write them?

Alana Bennison
C.H. Booth Library Children's Librarian

My husband and I moved to Newtown four years ago, lured by the open spaces and the enormous welcoming American flag as it waved us to our new home and the start of our life together. It is the perfect combination of small town country with its horse farms and homemade ice cream stand and only a little over an hour away from New York City.

When we moved into our Newtown neighborhood we were instantly embraced by our surrounding neighbors. Cookies were left on our doorstep, drinks and seats around the fire-pit were offered, lawn care machines were lent out and spare keys to each other's houses were exchanged. Now, a few years later, neighbors have moved away and new ones have given us the chance to continue this outreach of welcoming. We have become a family bonded by our everyday occurrence in each other's lives.

But my love of Newtown didn't start when my husband and I became proud residents of the town. It reaches further back. Since high school, my father and I have had movie dates at the Edmund Town Hall. We had a routine established - he would go to the ticket window and I would get the usual from the concession stand; a large popcorn with butter (which we would finish before we could settle in for the movie), a large root beer and of course a free candy and then we would meet to add salt and grab napkins. This was a treat, not only because we didn't have to splurge to have snacks with our movie, but I had a night alone with my dad, and being one of four children, that was rare. Now, being married and holding a job in which I work late into the evening, our movie date night is even rarer. Yet, every time I drive by the Edmund Town Hall I always check out the sign to see what movie is playing and feel a smile start to erupt at the cherished memory.

Not long ago, one of our dogs became ill and had to be brought to an emergency care vet at eight o'clock on a Saturday night. We were unsure about bringing him to someone other than our normal vet and wary that we may be walking into a place where unnecessary tests would be run and false hope given while our money was continuously pulled out of our pockets. We carried one of the most precious members of our family into Newtown Veterinary Specialists. There we were treated with the most caring and kind hearted people we have ever met. While crucial decisions had to be made quickly, procedures explained and financial matters handled, we were never rushed. We were given options with complete honesty. In our time of hurt we needed guidance and that is exactly what we were given. During one of the hardest nights of our lives we were comforted by compassion, sympathy and understanding. The Newtown community is abundant with these traits. Days later while we were still trying to deal with our grief we not only received a heartfelt letter from one of our neighbors, a standard one from the NVS, but also a personal handwritten letter of condolence from the veterinarian himself. These cards helped us know that we were not alone and that there were people who genuinely cared that we were hurting.

It wasn't until recently that I was even conscious of how much this town has a special place in my heart. I was in conversation with someone I had just met. He was telling me that he was in the market for a new house in the area - yet he didn't like Newtown. It was as if he had socked me in the gut. Not like Newtown? Was he crazy? I was at a loss for more than one word... why? It was at that moment, that feeling of personal insult and the want to protect and defend, that I realized how much I love this town.

Eriy & Kevin Albohn

My husband and I moved to Newtown four years ago, lured by the open spaces and the enormous welcoming American flag as it waved us to our new home and the start of our life together. It is the perfect combination of small town country with its horse farms and homemade ice cream stand and only a little over an hour away from New York City.

When we moved into our Newtown neighborhood we were instantly embraced by our surrounding neighbors. Cookies were left on our doorstep, drinks and seats around the fire-pit were offered, lawn care machines were lent out and spare keys to each other's houses were exchanged. Now, a few years later, neighbors have moved away and new ones have given us the chance to continue this outreach of welcoming. We have become a family bonded by our everyday occurrence in each other's lives.

But my love of Newtown didn't start when my husband and I become proud residents of the town. It reaches further back. Since high school, my father and I have had movie dates at the Edmund Town Hall. We had a routine established—he would go to the ticket window and I would get the usual from the concession stand; large popcorn with butter (which we would finish before we could settle in for the movie), a large root beer and of course a free candy and then we would meet to add salt and grab napkins. This was a treat, not only because we didn't have to splurge to have snacks with our movie, but I had a night alone with my dad, and being one of four children, that was rare. Now, being married and holding a job in which I work late into the evening, our movie date night is even rarer. Yet, every time I drive by the Edmund Town Hall I always check out the sign to see what movie is playing and feel a smile start to erupt at the cherished memory.

Not long ago, one of our dogs became ill and had to be brought to an emergency care vet at eight o'clock on a Saturday night. We were unsure about bringing him to someone other than our normal vet and wary that we may be walking into a place where unnecessary tests would be run and false hope given while our money was continuously pulled out of our pockets. We carried one of the most precious members of our family into Newtown Veterinary Specialists. There we were treated with the most caring and kind hearted people we have ever met. While crucial decisions had to be made quickly, procedures explained and financial matters handled, we were never rushed. We were given options with complete honesty. In our time of hurt we needed guidance and that is exactly what we were given. During one of the hardest nights of our lives we were comforted by compassion, sympathy and understanding. The Newtown community is abundant with these traits. Days later while we were still trying to deal with our grief we not only received a heartfelt letter from one of our neighbors, a standard one from the NVS, but also a personal handwritten letter of condolence from the veterinarian himself. These cards helped us know that we were not alone and that there were people who genuinely cared that we were hurting.

It wasn't until recently that I was even conscious of how much this town has a special place in my heart. I was in conversation with someone I had just met. He was telling me that he was in the market for a new house in the area—yet he didn't like Newtown. It was as if he had socked me in the gut. Not like Newtown? Was he crazy? I was at a loss for more than one word . . . why? It was at that moment, that feeling of personal insult and the want to protect and defend, that I realized how much I love this town.

Erin & Kevin Albohn

June 6, 2013

"I am LOVE. I am NEWTOWN."

These are the words I painted on a sign the morning of December 15, 2012. I was compelled to make a message to the world about my town. I sat at the exit 10 ramp with the Blue Colony Diner behind me. I wanted to be the first thing the throngs of people flooding in saw as they entered or left town. My message was simple, yet profound. It was all I had to say — nothing more.

It is still my message.

Little did I know that at that moment messages from all over the world were flooding in to our town. Hundreds of thousands of them — in letter, card, art, banner, gifts and many other forms. The town workers were thrust into managing an outpouring of an unprecedented magnitude.

I walked into the municipal center in late January to see the display of all this mail and I was utterly blown away. It was stunning to see the sheer volume of it all. The entire length of the building was covered in banners, quilts, posters and tray after tray of mail. For some it was emotionally unmanageable to witness, but for me it felt like a giant hug. It was beautiful. Such an immense outpouring of love and support from all over the world.

I wondered what would happen to all of it since the town could not possibly keep it all. I heard it would eventually be burned and reduced to "sacred ash" for cement in a future memorial. At that moment I knew I had to figure out a way to document all of it. I asked if I could start taking photos of everything. I felt a tremendous responsibility to make sure that others could see these messages too.

That is how the Newtown Documentation Project began. On January 26th I began photographing every single letter I could. Soon I gathered many volunteers and we have been working ever since. Our goal is to record as much as possible and share these messages of love and support through a website. We feel compelled to let everyone know that we received their letters and hold them sacred. That we feel the love and care. I never considered any of this simply "mail" or "historical documents." Each and every letter is a person wishing they could give a hug and say: "I love you, I care."

There have been so many layers to what this project means. Yes, it is an archive. Yes, it is witness. But most importantly it is the representation of the true nature of human beings -- kindness. Ironically in this day and age where technology rules how we communicate, nothing could ever

Compare to the handwritten letter or handmade card when someone is grieving. It is also the tangible manifestation of connection in a way that the internet could never replicate. These letters have connected me to neighbors and others I may never have met otherwise. I have become connected to my community and the world through this horrific massacre in ways I could not have predicted.

All of us have been doing our part to help care for and hold sacred the bond that pain creates. I have a deep insight into the people of this beautiful town through the outreach of millions of others across the globe. THAT's community. That's my Newtown. We are all love. We are ALL Newtown.

All my love,

June 6, 2013

"I am LOVE. I am NEWTOWN."

These are the words I painted on a sign the morning of December 15th 2012. I was compelled to make a message to the world about my town. I sat at the exit 10 ramp with the Blue Colony Diner behind me. I wanted to be the first thing the throngs of people flooding in saw as they entered or left town. My message was simple, yet profound. It was all I had to say—nothing more.

It is still my message.

Little did I know that at that moment messages from all over the world were flooding in to our town. Hundreds of thousands of them—in letter, card, art, banner, gifts and many other forms. The town workers were thrust into managing an outpouring of an unprecedented magnitude.

I walked into the municipal center in late January to see the display of all this mail and I was utterly blown away. It was stunning to see the sheer volume of it all. The entire length of the building was covered in banners, quilts, posters and tray after tray of mail. For some it was emotionally unmanageable to witness, but for me it felt like a giant hug. It was beautiful. Such an immense outpouring of love and support from all over the world.

I wondered what would happen to all of it since the town could not possibly keep it all. I heard it would eventually be burned and reduced to "sacred ash" for cement in a future memorial. At that moment I knew I had to figure out a way to document all of it. I asked if I could start taking photos of everything. I felt a tremendous responsibility to make sure that others could see these messages too.

That is how the Newtown Documentation Project began. On January 26th I began photographing every single letter I could. Soon I gathered many volunteers and we have been working ever since. Our goal is to record as much as possible and share these messages of love and support through a website. We feel compelled to let everyone know that we received their letters and hold them sacred. That we feel the love and care. I never considered any of this simply "mail" or "historical documents." Each and every letter is a person wishing they could give a hug and say: "I love you, I care."

There have been so many layers to what this project means. Yes, it is an archive. Yes, it is witness. But most importantly it is the representation of the true nature of human beings—kindness. Ironically in this day and age where technology rules how we communicate, *nothing* could ever compare to the handwritten letter or handmade card when someone is grieving. It is also the tangible manifestation of connection in a way that the internet could never replicate. These letters have connected me to neighbors and others I may never have met otherwise. I have become connected to my community and the world through this horrific massacre in ways I could not have predicted.

All of us have been doing our part to help care for and hold scared the *bond* that pain creates. I have a deep insight into the people of this beautiful town through the outreach of millions of others across the globe. THAT'S community. That's my Newtown. We are all love. We are ALL Newtown.

All my love,
Yolie

Thousands upon thousands of letters and banners sent to the Newtown Municipal Center

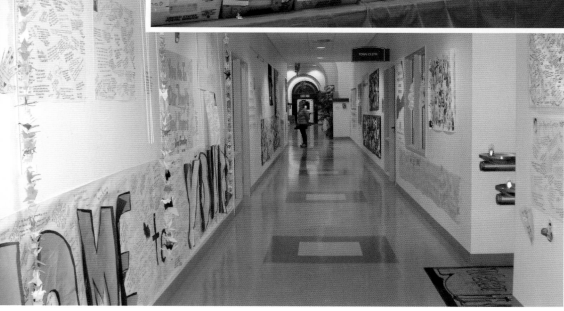

The Newtown Bee

When children visit the offices of Bee Publishing Co. for tours, usually for tours with a Boy or Girl Scout group, one of the things they are asked is "Why do you think your hometown newspaper is called The Newtown Bee?," with an emphasis on that final word.

After a few tentative — and sometimes very creative — guesses, we explain that the bee is an old-fashioned symbol for the newspaper industry. Honey bees live in their hives, we tell them, and they go out from there to collect pollen. They then return to the hive, "do their magic" (we don't get too graphic with these young, impressionable guests), and eventually produce honey from that pollen. The honey benefits the bees, as well as humans, they are told.

Then we draw the parallels, with newspaper reporters taking on the roles of bees, our office becoming the beehive. The Bee's reporters head out into the world to collect information that is then turned into stories. Our honey is those stories, which are printed on the pages of The Newtown Bee each week. The dual benefits are that the stories are shared with our readers, and they also continue the ongoing, permanent record of Newtown's history.

The Newtown Bee has been Newtown's hometown newspaper for 136 years. The paper's first issue was dated June 28, 1877. Four years later the paper was purchased by Reuben Hazen Smith, and it has remained in the Smith family since then.

Aside from the occasional week when Founding Publisher John T. Pearce did not feel the urge to print the paper, The Bee has been published every week, even after a particularly difficult winter storm named

Alfred knocked power out to thousands of homes and businesses for a number of days, including The Bee's landmark building at 5 Church Hill Road and its printing facility on Commerce Road, a few years ago. That week, the staff pulled up its collective bootstraps, burned a lot of late night oil, and worked very creatively to make sure there was a print edition for Friday, November 4, 2011. There was no question that it would be done. The paper would be printed. It's tradition.

Current owner and Publisher R. Scudder Smith has been leading the company since 1973, when he took over as Editor from his retiring father, Paul.

It has always been the mission of <u>The Newtown Bee</u> to share the news of this town (and in years past, the western Connecticut region) with its residents, those who visit it, and even those who have moved away. The newspaper has an independence few others have, thanks to the single-family ownership — not an outside corporation nor even a board of directors — that has led the company for more than a century. The Smith family not only owns the newspaper, its members are personally invested. Today there are three generations of the family who work full-time in various departments.

The staff is committed to telling Newtown's stories; not just news of its events, but also the stories of her residents.

Those stories continue to be printed on broadsheet-size newsprint. It's a wider paper than most, but it works for <u>The Bee</u>. Reporters leave the building carrying not only their notebooks, but also cameras, challenged with the dual roles of writer and photographer. Yes its different than most other papers, where an employee is one or the other but again, it works for The Bee.

Employees of the newspaper have known about the comforting

presence of dogs in the workplace for years. For well over two decades, dogs have been part of working here. The animals have been owned by Smith family members, but they are loved and spoiled by many of those who call this place our second home.

Visitors to the office are regularly greeted by the dogs (it usually adds a few minutes to those Scouts tours we have, when dogs and kids all meet up in the front lobby and everyone wants to meet each other). Today the canine crew includes two golden retrievers, Rosie and Piper; and Tigue, a chocolate lab. Their presence only adds to the first impression many have when they walk through the front door. From the folk art that covers walls and counters, hangs in windows and even—like the three carousel figures I can see from my desk—takes up plenty of floor space, to the layout of a building constructed during the very early 20th Century, customers and other guests know they have not found a typical office space when they enter 5 Church Hill Road.

Some of The Bee's employees have been with the company for a few months. Others have been here for the majority of their lives. I count myself firmly among the latter.

I was called early to a career in journalism. I put my toe through the entrance of The Newtown Bee for the first time, in 1986. That year, I took a part-time job in the newspaper's mailroom.

I haven't looked back—or elsewhere—since, taking additional duties first as a typesetter, then becoming a sports writer, and then The Bee's arts editor. I have been an associate editor for The Newtown Bee since January 2006.

It can be a difficult job, this one I have chosen, but it is what I love to do, and where I love to be. There are very good days on this job, occasional extremely difficult ones, and many that fall somewhere in between. It is a job that constantly challenges, and educates.

I am proud to be part of the newspaper produced in Newtown every week. (Not to mention The Bee's website, NewtownBee.com. Launched in March 1995, ours was the first newspaper in the State to present constantly updated news and information to its readers online. And that juggling of additional duties I mentioned earlier? Add website maintenance/updating to the work handled in-house by The Bee staff. Most editors and reporters post their own stories and photos, too.) We are all dedicated to presenting all of Newtown's news — good and bad, serious and light-hearted, breaking and continuing.

Finally, it is important to remember that the members of The Bee's Editorial department may be those whose names appear attached to stories and/or photographs each week, there are many others who work behind the scenes who keep this operation working. There are sales representatives, accountants, graphic designers, pressmen and typesetters, a copy editor, a proof reader, front office employees, and the entire staff of our sister publication, <u>Antiques and The Arts Weekly</u>. This entire team works very hard to put out a newspaper that offers coverage of everything that happens within the 60-plus square miles that many of us call home.

Shannon Hicks
September 2013

The Newtown Bee

When children visit the offices of Bee Publishing Co. for tours, usually for tours with a Boy or Girl Scout group, one of the things they are asked is "Why do you think your hometown newspaper is called *The Newtown Bee*?" with an emphasis on that final word.

After a few tentative—and sometimes very creative—guesses, we explain that the bee is an old-fashioned symbol for the newspaper industry. Honey bees live in their hives, we tell them, and they go out from there to collect pollen. They then return to the hive, "do their magic" (we don't get too graphic with these young, impressionable guests), and eventually produce honey from that pollen. The honey benefits the bees, as well as humans, they are told.

Then we draw the parallels, with newspaper reporters taking on the roles of bees, our office becoming the beehive. The Bee's reporters head out into the world to collect information that is then turned into stories. Our honey is those stories, which are printed on the pages of *The Newtown Bee* each week. The dual benefits are that the stories are shared with our readers, and they also continue the ongoing, permanent record of Newtown's history.

The Newtown Bee has been Newtown's hometown newspaper for 136 years. The paper's first issue was dated June 28, 1877. Four years later the paper was purchased by Reuben Hazen Smith, and it has remained in the Smith family since then.

Aside from the occasional week when Founding Publisher John T. Pearce did not feel the urge to print the paper, *The Bee* has been published every week, even after a particularly difficult winter storm named Alfred knocked power out to thousands of homes and businesses for a number of days, including The Bee's landmark building at 5 Church Hill Road and its printing facility on Commerce Road, a few years ago. That week, the staff pulled up its collective bootstraps, burned a lot of late night oil, and worked very creatively to make sure there was a print edition for Friday, November 4, 2011. There was no question that it would be done. The paper would be printed. It's tradition.

Current owner and Publisher R. Scudder Smith has been leading the company since 1973, when he took over as Editor from his retiring father, Paul.

It has always been the mission of *The Newtown Bee* to share the news of this town (and in years past, the western Connecticut region) with its residents, those who visit it, and even those who have moved away. The newspaper has an independence few others have, thanks to the single-family ownership—not an outside corporation nor even a board of directors—that has led the company for more than a century. The Smith family not only owns the newspaper, its members are personally invested. Today there are three generations of the family who work full-time in various departments.

The staff is committed to telling Newtown's stories: not just news of its events, but also the stories of her residents.

Those stories continue to be printed on broadsheet-size newsprint. It's a wider paper than most, but it works for *The Bee.* Reporters leave the building carrying not only their notebooks, but also cameras, challenged with the dual roles of writer and photographer. Yes it's different than most other papers, where an employee is one or the other but again, it works for The Bee.

Employees of the newspaper have known about the comforting presence of dogs in the workplace for years. For well over two decades, dogs have been part of working here. The animals have been owned by Smith family members, but they are loved and spoiled by many of those who call this place our second home.

Visitors to the office are regularly greeted by the dogs (it usually adds a few minutes to those Scout tours we have, when dogs and kids all meet up in the front lobby and everyone wants to meet each other). Today the canine crew includes two golden retrievers, Rosie and Piper; and Tique, a chocolate lab. Their presence only adds to the first impression many have when they walk through the front door. From the folk art that covers walls and counters, hangs in windows and even—like the three carousel figures I can see from my desk—takes up plenty of floor space, to the layout of a building constructed during the very early 20th Century, customers and other guests know they have not found a typical office space when they enter 5 Church Hill Road.

Some of The Bee's employees have been with the company for a few months. Others have been here for the majority of their lives. I count myself firmly among the latter.

I was called early to a career in journalism. I put my toe through the entrance of The Newtown Bee for the first time in 1986. That year, I took a part-time job in the newspaper's mailroom.

I haven't looked back—or elsewhere—since, taking additional duties first as a typesetter, then becoming a sports writer, and then *The Bee*'s arts editor. I have been an associate editor for *The Newtown Bee* since January 2006.

It can be a difficult job, this one I have chosen, but it is what I love to do, and where I love to be. There are very good days on this job, occasional extremely difficult ones, and many that fall somewhere in between. It is a job that constantly challenges, and educates.

I am proud to be part of the newspaper produced in Newtown every week. (Not to mention The Bee's website, NewtownBee.com. Launched in March 1995, ours was the first newspaper in the state to present constantly updated news and information to its readers online. And that juggling of additional duties I mentioned earlier? Add website maintenance/updating to the work handled in-house by The Bee staff. Most editors and reporters post their own stories and photos, too.) We are all dedicated to presenting all of Newtown's news—good and bad, serious and light-hearted, breaking and continuing.

Finally, it is important to remember that the members of The Bee's Editorial department may be those whose names appear attached to stories and/or photographs each week, there are many others who work behind the scenes who keep this operation working. There are sales representatives, accountants, graphic designers, pressmen and typesetters, a copy editor, a proof reader, front office employees, and the entire staff of our sister publication, *Antiques and The Arts Weekly*. This entire team works very hard to put out a newspaper that offers coverage of everything that happens within the 60-plus square miles that many of us call home.

—Shannon Hicks
September 2013

Inside the Newtown Bee with Piper and Rosie Baggett

Andrew Mangold

'Message from Newtown'

This letter was written in December a few days after, and was released online. The original format was text, but I have edited-down and hand-written three of the seven pages as neatly as I can to match this publication. The whole piece is available online at www.newfarmpark.tk under 'Response'.

———

I have lived in Newtown all of my life. I graduated from Newtown High School, my phone number starts with 203, I have Nighthawk clothes, and so on... I did not know anyone in the school, specifically, but that does not matter. It is a pretty close town. Everyone is affected, and I could have just as well known these kids when they grew up.

There are news reporters all over our town. They ask a lot of questions. Some of them that I see are doing a very respectful job, with constructive messages. Other times it feels like they are fishing for useless, gossipy details.

These are the stories that I feel are especially important to share. They are about my experience in Newtown, immediatly after and long before this event.

I am 21. One thing that the reporters ask people my age is whether or not we knew the person who committed the act in Sandy Hook School. I have not heard anyone answer 'yes'. This was really not a known person.

Yesterday I remembered however, that I do know who this person was. There was an individual in high school who I always saw, and wondered about. This was Lanza.

S So far, whenever someone asked me whether I knew him, I would say 'who cares', because I felt like I was being asked just to satisfy a gross curiosity.

But now I realize something.
People are calling him a monster.

The person that I remember was not a monster.

He was an extremely shy and awkward kid who, as far as I know, had no one to call a friend.

He wore tan dress pants that were too big, and always had on a buttoned, collared shirt. He rarely looked people in the eye, and walked quickly through the halls, very close to the wall. If he happened to speak, it was in a hushed voice. Usually his lips were pinched shut.

He carried a briefcase instead of a backpack.

I am not aware of anyone who bullied him. I felt sympathy for him and tried to be nice when I could, but I never took any big steps to be a friend. I am not aware of anyone who really went out of their way to connect with him. He had some favorite rooms, and otherwise hurried through the school. That was it.

The person I remember was a shy, nervous and awkward kid, much different than what people are calling him now.

Maybe the conversation could be different.

If, when we were in high school, more people had thought about Adam, and realized that this was a person who needed connection or someone who might have a problem, then maybe things could have been different. Maybe we could have helped him or understood him and maybe if we had, we would all be okay.

If I or anyone else had taken a moment out of typical busy-ness and offered our support to this individual who seemed like they needed it, maybe it would have made the difference.

Now I remember who it was, and I have wondered if it is better just to let things be, or take the opportunity to open up another conversation. I feel as if people want to hear about how twisted this person was, but I can discern a different story... about mental health, who this person was, why things happened the way they did and how much we can learn.

This is a terrible, terribly sad and tragic event.....

What I am seeing though, are people come together. Last night I left the interfaith vigil that the President spoke at and walked with the people of our town, and our supporters. What I did not expect to feel, were any positive emotions, but on my way home, I was overcome by how 'cool' it is that people are together. Everyone that I saw was caring, listening, patient, compassionate, and thoughtful. It was reassuring. It felt good.

Passing a corner with gifts, lights and prayers for the children, I ran into some friends, Oskar, Matt & Gina, who I hadn't seen for months. How beautiful it felt to connect. We chatted with a woman I had never met, about what it means to recognize the important things in life. Afterward, my friend Matt looked around and said "you see all of these people? I could go up to any one of these people and have a great conversation..."

He remarked that he could stay here all night, without a problem, talking to everyone that was there. Meanwhile, the memorials grew into beautiful, glowing sculptures around us.

Back in my car, I waited at as stoplight and looked to my left. I saw someone who I used to perform with in the high school drumline. 'James', I said after rolling down the window. He crossed the street and had just enough time to clasp my hand and say 'Good to see you, Man', before the light turned green. 'Take care' I told him.

I thought of how special it is that everyone is so open, and how great it would be if we can hold such a way-of-being long into the future. Maybe that is what the black [and green] ribbons could represent. Something to remind us of our priorities, of how beautiful life can be, and to sustain this heart-opening state where there are no strangers.

If this tragedy can bring communities together, then that is a beautiful thing. It is so rare that people genuinly connect nowadays, and if this can bring our town and the rest of the world together, then that is a miraculous thing.

Some people in town are upset about all of the cameras that are here, but behind every camera are millions of people who would be here if they could be to support. In some ways, they are here.

If in every city there are people who are touched and moved, tuning in with us and sending their love and their thoughts.... Then that is something beautiful. Thank you all, it means so much!!!

This is a terrible tragedy, but if the whole world is watching and if the whole world is connected, then together, let us make something miraculous.

I think that this is a wakeup call....

Maybe it is the final wakeup call that 'all is not well in this world'... It is time for us all to say that 'we don't want things to be this way anymore'.

We can come out of this tragedy stronger, and make deep changes to our world so that things get better. It is not about left politics, it is not about right politics, and it is not about whether there should be sides at all. It is about recognizing that this whole circus, this whole charade has been misguided, and much of our way of life doesn't work anymore.

I thought that the president's speech was very nice. I was at the high school with my little sister to listen. It was too difficult to get in, but we waited outside with the police, the American Red Cross, a set of large sound amplifiers and the rest of the town who wanted to be there. The president's message is a good one. I was at the edge of my seat when he ASKED whether our society is 'doing enough'. Thank goodness that he answered 'no'.

How can we make things better?
What in our world causes people to be more likely to commit a violent crime?
How can we keep people well?

That is the place that I am driven to focus my efforts.

Let the victims lives be remembered for something wonderful. I disagree that we should get back to 'business as usual' or 'normalize'. The old way is unacceptable. Don't go back. Now, we do better.

The solution is different for everyone. What can you do to increase the physical and mental health of yourself and the people around you? For me, this looks like public plantings of fruit trees, nuts, herbs and native plants. My greatest vision is for an interactive 'Farm Park' that is accessible by paths to local schools, which demonstrates effective ways to increase sustainability while offering a recreational space for community

It is not one park or one town though. Broadly, prioritize the healing of people, and the healing of places. Connect. From now on, breathe. Be alive, look people in the eye, listen, focus, feel, and live the best life possible while encouraging the best world possible. Enjoy making this planet a better place to live. It is long past time. Better late though, than never.

Andrew Mangold

Andrew Mangold
"Message from Newtown"

This letter was written in December a few days after, and released online. The original format was text, but I have edited-down and hand-written three of the seven pages as neatly as I can to match this publication. The whole piece is available online at www.newfarmpark.tk under 'response'.

I have lived in Newtown all of my life. I graduated from Newtown High School, my phone number starts with 203, I have Nighthawk clothes, and so on . . . I did not know anyone in the school, specifically, but that does not matter. It is a pretty close town. Everyone is affected, and I could have just as well known these kids when they grew up.

There are news reporters all over our town. They ask a lot of questions. Some of them that I see are doing a very respectful job, with constructive messages. Other times it feels like they are fishing for useless, gossipy details.

These are the stories that I feel are especially important to share. They are about my experience in Newtown, immediately after and long before this event.

I am 21. One thing that the reporters ask people my age is whether or not we knew the person who committed the act in Sandy Hook School. I have not heard anyone answer 'yes'. This was really not a known person.

Yesterday I remembered however, that I do know who this person was. There was an individual in high school who I always saw, and wondered about. This was Lanza.

So far, whenever someone asked me whether I knew him, I would say 'who cares', because I felt like I was being asked just to satisfy a gross curiosity.

But now I realize something.

People are calling him a monster.

The person that I remember was not a monster.

He was an extremely shy and awkward kid who, as far as I know, had no one to call a friend.

He wore tan dress pants that were too big, and always had on a buttoned, collared shirt. He rarely looked people in the eye, and walked quickly through the halls, very close to the wall. If he happened to speak, it was in a hushed voice. Usually his lips were pinched shut.

He carried a briefcase instead of a backpack.

I am not aware of anyone who bullied him. I felt sympathy for him and tried to be nice when I could, but I never took any big steps to be a friend. I am not aware of anyone who really went out of their way to connect with him. He had some favorite rooms, and otherwise hurried through the school. That was it.

The person I remember was a shy, nervous and awkward kid, much different than what people are calling him now.

Maybe the conversation could be different.

If, when we were in high school, more people had thought about Adam, and realized that this was a person who needed connection or someone who might have a problem, then maybe things could have been different. Maybe we could have helped him or understood him and maybe if we had, we would all be okay.

If I or anyone else had taken a moment out of typical busy-ness and offered our support to this individual who seemed like they needed it, maybe it would have made the difference.

Now I remember who it was, and I have wondered if it is better just to let things be, or take the opportunity to open up another conversation. I feel as if people want to hear about how twisted this person was, but I can discern a different story . . . about mental health, who this person was, why things happened the way they did and how much we can learn.

This is a terrible, terribly sad and tragic event. . . .

What I am seeing though, are people come together. Last night I left the interfaith vigil that the President spoke at and walked with the people of our town, and our supporters. What I did not expect to feel, were any positive emotions, but on my way home, I was overcome by how 'cool' it is that people are together. Everyone that I saw was caring, listening, patient, compassionate, and thoughtful. It was reassuring. It felt good.

Passing a corner with gifts, lights and prayers for the children, I ran into some friends, Oskar, Matt & Gina, who I hadn't seen for months. How beautiful it felt to connect. We chatted with a woman I had never met, about what it means to recognize the important things in life. Afterward, my friend Matt looked around and said, "You see all of these people? I could go up to any one of these people and have a great conversation . . ."

He remarked that he could stay here all night, without a problem, talking to everyone that was there. Meanwhile, the memorials grew into beautiful, glowing sculptures around us.

Back in my car, I waited at a stoplight and looked to my left. I saw someone who I used to perform with in the high school drumline. 'James', I said after rolling down the window. He crossed the street and had just enough time to clasp my hand and say 'good to see you man', before the light turned green. 'Take care' I told him.

I thought of how special it is that everyone is so open, and how great it would be if we can hold such a way-of-being long into the future. Maybe that is what the black [and green] ribbons could represent. Something to remind us of our priorities, of how beautiful life can be, and to sustain this heart-opening state where there are no strangers.

If this tragedy can bring communities together, then that is a beautiful thing. It is so rare that people genuinely connect nowadays, and if this can bring our town and the rest of the world together, then that is a miraculous thing.

Some people in town are upset about all of the cameras that are here, but behind every camera are millions of people who WOULD be here if they could be, to support. In some ways, they are here.

If in every city there are people who are touched and moved, tuning in with us and sending their love and their thoughts. . . . then that is something beautiful. Thank you all, it means so much!!!

This is a terrible tragedy, but if the whole world is watching and if the whole world is connected, then together, let us make something miraculous.

I think that this is a wakeup call. . . .

Maybe it is the final wake-up call that 'all is not well in this world' . . . It is time for us all to say that 'we don't want things to be this way anymore'.

We can come out of this tragedy stronger, and make deep changes to our world so that things get better. It is not about left politics, it is not about right politics, and it is not about whether there should be sides at all. It is about recognizing that this whole circus, this whole charade has been misguided, and much of our way of life doesn't work anymore.

I thought that the president's speech was very nice. I was at the high school with my little sister to listen. It was too difficult to get in, but we waited outside with the police, the American Red Cross, a set of large sound amplifiers and the rest of the town who wanted to be there. The president's message is a good one. I was at the edge of my seat when he asked whether our society is 'doing enough'. Thank goodness that he answered 'no'.

How can we make things better?

What in our world causes people to be more likely to commit a violent crime?

How can we keep people well?

That is the place that I am driven to focus my efforts.

Let the victim's lives be remembered for something wonderful. I disagree that we should get back to 'business as usual' or 'normalize'. The old way is unacceptable. Don't go back. Now, we do better.

The solution is different for everyone. What can you do to increase the physical and mental health of yourself and the people around you? For me, this looks like public plantings of fruit trees, nuts, herbs and native plants. My greatest vision is for an interactive 'farm park' that is accessible by paths to local schools, which demonstrates effective ways to increase sustainability while offering a recreational space for community.

It is not one park or one town though. Broadly, prioritize the healing of people, and the healing of places. Connect. From now on, breathe. Be alive, look people in the eye, listen, focus, feel, and live the best life possible while encouraging the best world possible. Enjoy making this planet a better place to live. It is long past time. Better late though, than never.

Andrew Mangold

I remember the first time.
My hair was pulled back.
The goose bumps rose on my legs.
while my arms remained safe
under my dad's extra large navy sweater.
I sat on the bottom stoop
of the front steps to tie the last lace
of my black All Star Converse sneaker.
The keys were grasp tight in my hand,
making them sweat.

I looked over at the car,
a small tan one,
who cares if I knew the style,
I couldn't wait to get behind the wheel.
The car roared as I turned the key,
my eyes lit like a dog at the sight of a treat.
I felt the freedom,
the control,
the potential adventure.

The car and I made our way
away from my welcoming country home
to accept an invitation from the road.
With the windows rolled halfway down,
I could smell the cool crisp air,
with a distant hint of wood burning
in the neighbor's fireplace.
The scent was inspiring.

Trees on all sides of me
as I drove on,
I couldn't help but see myself
inside a painter's dream.
The vibrant Autumn leaves-
crimson reds, golden yellows,
ginger oranges and olive greens
scattered along yard after yard.

The temptation arose to drive
through the town.
The Sandy Hook center
flocked with people strolling by stores
and admiring the calming river
from the view of the bridge.

Townees leisurely walking past
the library, the General Store,
the Town Hall, and the charming country homes
that sit on Main Street,
enjoying the view of the flagpole,
our town's landmark, raised high.

A young couple sat deep in love and laughter,
by the pond at Rams Pasture,
the place my mother and I would feed the geese
when we came across stale bread.

A short ride later and I found myself
at my favorite place to view the whole town,
Castle Hill.
I sat at the bench remembering the first time.

I was remembering the first time
I got an A in school,
the first sleepover,
and my first zit.

I remembered my first soccer game
and trip to the ice cream store.

Now, I will remember my first drive,
when I sat at the bench, on top of the town,
in awe of the breath taking view
remembering memories
that help me call what I saw, home.

Michelle Rahtelli

Ram Pasture with flowers

I remember the first time.
My hair was pulled back.
The goose bumps rose on my legs
while my arms remained safe
under my dad's extra large navy sweater.
I sat on the bottom stoop
of the front steps to tie the last lace
of my black All Star Converse sneaker.
The keys were grasp tight in my hand,
making them sweat.

I looked over at the car,
a small tan one,
who cares if I knew the style,
I couldn't wait to get behind the wheel.
The car roared as I turned the key,
my eyes lit like a dog at the sight of a treat.
I felt the freedom,
the control,
the potential adventure.

The car and I made our way
away from my welcoming country home
to accept an invitation from the road.
With the windows rolled halfway down,
I could smell the cool crisp air,
with a distant hint of wood burning
in the neighbor's fireplace.
The scent was inspiring.

Trees on all sides of me
as I drove on,
I couldn't help but see myself
inside a painter's dream.
The vibrant autumn leaves—
crimson reds, golden yellows,
ginger oranges and olive greens,
scattered along yard after yard.

The temptation arose to drive
through the town.
The Sandy Hook center
flocked with people strolling by stores
and admiring the calming river
from the view of the bridge.

Townees leisurely walking past
the library, the General Store,
the Town Hall, and the charming country homes
that sit on Main Street,
enjoying the view of the flagpole,
our town's landmark, raised high.

A young couple sat deep in love and laughter,
by the pond at Rams Pasture,
the place my mother and I would feed the geese
when we came across stale bread.

A short ride later and I found myself
at my favorite place to view the whole town,
Castle Hill.
I sat at the bench remembering the first time.

I was remembering the first time
I got an A in school,
the first sleepover,
and my first zit.

I remembered my first soccer game
and trip to the ice cream store.

Now, I will remember my first drive,
when I sat at the bench, on top of the town,
in awe of the breath taking view
remembering memories
that help me call what I saw, *home*.

Michelle Rahtelli

My name is Joan Glover Ceick living at 7 Glover Avenue, Newtown, Ct. I am the 10th generation of the Glover family living in Newtown. I am directly related to John Glover, one of the first founders of Newtown.

I want to tell you about my school years here at Newtown. I attended Hawley School, Church Hill Rd. Newtown — grades 1 through 12 — The elementary kids were on the first floor and the High School kids were on the second floor. We all knew each other. What a grand time! Since I lived too close to the school, I could not ride a school bus, which was always my desire. I walked to school.

With the arrival of Coaches Ann Anderson and Harold DeGroat, we had the "best" athletic program around. I just loved that as I was a 3-sport athlete and lived for each one. Due to the small size of the school's gym, we walked up Church Hill Rd. to the Edmond Town Hall gym for our basketball practice and that's where all our home games were played.

I have so many wonderful memories of that school — friends, walking to school and home, playing softball and soccer on Taylor Field, seeing the little kids (on the first floor) looking at us as if were their idols. They, anxiously awaiting the day when they could go up the stairs.

I, one of 29, graduated in 1950 and hated to leave my home of Twelve years. My memories are so dear to me and I am still in touch with some of my classmates.

Memories of Main St.

I lived on Main St. until I was 9 years old and then moved to The Glover House on Glover Avenue which was built by my Granfather, William B. Glover, in 1915.

Main St. was our playground. We kids skated on the sidewalks, sold apples on the street, lived at the Library with Sarah Beers Mitchell, played softball in the open lot and then there was "Halloween".

It was so special to us as we knew most of the residents, which we had to "trick" in order to get candy. Of course, we all ended up with some eventually. That was our "Trick or Treat". Today is so different.

Joan Glover Crick

Hawley School, Church Hill Road, Newtown

My name is Joan Glover Crick living at 7 Glover Avenue, Newtown, Connecticut. I am the 10th generation of the Glover family living in Newtown. I am directly related to John Glover, one of the first founders of Newtown.

I want to tell you about my school years here at Newtown. I attended Hawley School, on Church Hill Rd., Newtown—grades I through 12—The elementary kids were on the first floor and the High School kids were on the second floor. We all knew each other. What a grand time! Since I lived too close to the school, I could not ride a school bus, which was always my desire. I walked to school.

With the arrival of Coaches Ann Anderson and Harold DeGroat, we had the "best" athletic program around. I just loved that as I was a 3-sport athlete and lived for each one. Due to the small size of the school's gym, we walked up the Church Hill Road hill to the Edmond Town Hall gym for our basketball practice and that's where all our home games were played.

I have so many wonderful memories of that school—friends, walking to school and home, playing softball and soccer on Taylor Field, seeing the little kids (on the first floor) looking at us as if we were their idols. They, anxiously awaiting the day when they could go up the stairs.

I, one of 29, graduated in 1950 and hated to leave my home of twelve years. My memories are so dear to me and I am still in touch with some of my classmates.

Memories of Main St.

I lived on Main Street until I was nine years old and then moved to the Glover House on Glover Avenue which was built by my Grandfather, William B. Glover, in 1915.

Main St. was our playground. We kids skated on the sidewalks, sold apples on the street, lived at the library with Sarah Beers Mitchell, played softball in the open lot and then there was "Halloween".

It was so special to us as we knew most of the residents, which we had to "trick" in order to get candy. Of course, we all ended up with some eventually. That was our "Trick or Treat." Today is so different.

Joan Glover Crick

December 17, 2012

My Heart is Still in Sandy Hook

We moved to Phoenix, Arizona from Sandy Hook, Connecticut.

Sandy Hook School was my son's school. I use the possessive because that is how he felt about the school: it is a place to which he belonged and at the same time a place that he felt somehow belonged to him.

We took a trip back home at the end of October and went for a drive to see some of the places of our memories: the house we lived in, the town ice cream stand, the famous flagpole in the middle of the road and my son's old school. It was late on a Friday afternoon, and there were lots of young kids running around in costumes, obviously celebrating a fall festival. We remarked on how small they seemed, and how although so much time has passed it seems like just yesterday we lived there.

My son and I walked through the halls that he said seemed much smaller than he remembered. I imagine that his perspective from a height of six feet is a bit different from his perspective as an elementary school student. We read each teacher's name outside of each classroom, to see if any of my son's teachers were still there. One teacher saw us wandering the halls and very politely inquired if she could help us. She looked familiar and I explained that my son had gone to school here years ago, that we were visiting from Phoenix, and that we were on a little trip down memory lane. When I told her our names, she remembered my son even though he had not been her student. I later remembered that her husband and my husband had been Cub Scout leaders there together. My son inquired about the whereabouts of his former teachers and she was able to tell him who had retired and who had gone where.

Last Friday morning, my son called to tell me that there had been a shooting at Sandy Hook school. As the morning wore on, the news got worse and worse. For five years I was a mother with a young child at that school. Listening to the news I was transported back to the time when he was a student there and I could totally imagine being one of the mothers rushing to the school to find out about my child.

I called my son and asked if I could meet him for lunch. That would be nice, he said. I need a hug I told him. So do I he said.

When he was a student at Sandy Hook School, my son had written a poem entitled "The Empty Chair". A student at the school had just lost her father to cancer, and my son had been thinking about how there would always be an empty chair at the dinner table where her father used to sit. His teacher showed the poem to the principal who thought the poem was so good he called The Newtown Bee and asked if they could do a story about him. The Newtown Bee came to the school and interviewed my son, took his picture and printed his poem in the paper. Last Friday, after our lunch, I sent my son a text: 26 EMPTY CHAIRS IN SANDY HOOK. My son said that was when he cried.

My younger son once made the front page of The Newtown Bee because his ice cream cone was melting. The temperature had reached a record-breaking 103 degrees, and his expression at the loss of his ice cream was the illustration for an article on the heat wave.

I always thought of The Newtown Bee as a small town newspaper printing the kind of articles that only local folk can appreciate: the kind of articles that do not make it to the wire services but do make it to the refrigerators of families all over town.

Today, the articles are quite different. We are saddened to think of how drastically the world has changed for the children we had seen running and laughing at the school.

Many people have asked if we knew any of the victims. We did not. People sigh with relief when we say this, but that bothers me very much: just because we didn't know them does not mean that we don't mourn them. We feel profound sadness for all the children, the families, the school and the town.

Someone asked me how I see the town now after the horrible events. I realized that my family is lucky — our memories are good ones. We remember Sandy Hook as a lovely place where my children were happy. Eighteen years later, my heart is still in Sandy Hook; it just feels as though part of it has stopped beating.

Shari Keith

December 17, 2012

My Heart is Still in Sandy Hook

We moved to Phoenix, Arizona from Sandy Hook, Connecticut.

Sandy Hook School was my son's school. I use the possessive because that is how he felt about the school: it is a place to which he belonged and at the same time a place that he felt somehow belonged to him.

We took a trip back home at the end of October and went for a drive to see some of the places of our memories: the house we lived in, the town ice cream stand, the famous flagpole in the middle of the road and my son's old school. It was late on a Friday afternoon, and there were lots of young kids running around in costumes, obviously celebrating a fall festival. We remarked on how small they seemed, and how although so much time has passed it seems like just yesterday we lived there.

My son and I walked through the halls that he said seemed much smaller than he remembered. I imagine that his perspective from a height of six feet is a bit different from his perspective as an elementary school student. We read each teacher's name outside of each classroom, to see if any of my son's teachers were still there. One teacher saw us wandering the halls and very politely inquired if she could help us. She looked familiar and I explained that my son had gone to school here years ago, that we were visiting from Phoenix, and that we were on a little trip down memory lane. When I told her our names, she remembered my son even though he had not been her student. I later remembered that her husband and my husband had been Cub Scout leaders there together. My son inquired about the whereabouts of his former teachers and she was able to tell him who had retired and who had gone where.

Last Friday morning, my son called to tell me that there had been a shooting at Sandy Hook School. As the morning wore on, the news got worse and worse. For five years I was a mother with a young child at that school. Listening to the news I was transported back to the time when he was a student there and I could totally imagine being one of the mothers rushing to the school to find out about my child.

I called my son and asked if I could meet him for lunch. That would be nice, he said. I need a hug I told him. So do I he said.

When he was a student at Sandy Hook School, my son had written a poem entitled "The Empty Chair". A student at the school had just lost her father to cancer, and my son had been thinking about how there would always be an empty chair at the dinner table where her father used to sit. His teacher showed the poem to the principal who thought the poem was so good he called The Newtown Bee and asked if they could do a story about him. The Newtown Bee came to the school and interviewed my son, took his picture and printed his poem in the paper. Last Friday, after our lunch, I sent my son a text: 26 EMPTY CHAIRS IN SANDY HOOK. My son said that was when he cried.

My younger son once made the front page of The Newtown Bee because his ice cream cone was melting. The temperature had reached a record-breaking 103 degrees, and his expression at the loss of his ice cream was the illustration for an article on the heat wave.

I always thought of The Newtown Bee as a small town newspaper printing the kind of articles that only local folk can appreciate: the kind of articles that do not make it to the wire services but do make it to the refrigerators of families all over town.

Today, the articles are quite different. We are saddened to think of how drastically the world has changed for the children we had seen running and laughing at the school.

Many people have asked if we knew any of the victims. We did not. People sigh with relief when we say this, but that bothers me very much: just because we didn't know them does not mean that we don't mourn them. We feel profound sadness for all the children, the families, the school and the town.

Someone asked me how I see the town now after the horrible events. I realized that my family is lucky—our memories are good ones. We remember Sandy Hook as a lovely place where my children were happy. Eighteen years later, my heart is still in Sandy Hook; it just feels as though part of it has stopped beating.

Shari Keith

Dear Reader,

I'd like to tell the story of a teacher. She is a teacher I happened to witness for a little while as she taught her class soon after returning to school after the events of December 14.

Once the students arrived in her classroom, she wasted no time, as there was no time to waste and much to do. She began by placing the students in their new seats: 'Jack, you sit here, and Amber, you... I think you should sit here.' Part of the challenge was figuring out not only student placement, but also the new foreign classroom they all found themselves in. How would it work? What's the best way to use the space? Should those materials be placed along that wall, or in the back of the room? So much to consider, but as so many things had been during the last few weeks, she'd have to figure it out as she went. One thing she was sure of, though, was what she wanted to accomplish. That soon became clear. Once everyone was in the right seat, the lesson began.

I was in awe. I had never seen a class conducted like this. She was a force whose energy was incredible. She taught with focused abandon, leading the students through the lesson and they were captivated. They followed every direction with an enthusiasm only a masterful teacher could elicit. They were working hard but enjoying it too. She knew which students needed what "tweaks" and immediately addressed them and had them try again successfully. She moved deftly through the activity at a pace that kept every student engaged, while giving them time to take a breather when needed. They worked together, persevered together, solved problems together and laughed together. And what they created together in that room that morning was truly beautiful. Her passion for teaching was evident, even under the most challenging circumstances and it was extraordinary. After everything she had faced just weeks before, she was able to work magic with her class. I'd guess that this day's lesson was planned down to the minute, but I could also tell that every day was like this in her classroom, full of hard work and positive energy. It was also clear that this day, and every day after, was not just another day for her and her students. Every day was a step forward. Every lesson was progress of many kinds. And the students that left her class were leaving with a hugely positive experience.

Her energy seemingly spent after this class, she dismissed the students to their next class, and as they filed out, a parent filed in to say hello. They looked at each other and immediately hugged, strongly, tightly, and tears began to flow. There was clearly a common bond and a common understanding about what they were both going through, and I had the impression that this wasn't the first time they had checked in with each other.

I didn't see every teacher in the building that day, but I'd be willing to bet that this one anonymous teacher exemplifies the strength, professionalism, and passion of the rest of the staff of Sandy Hook School. Finally, as soon as the last student from the previous class stepped out into the hallway, the next class came in. It was time again. Time to get back up for this next group of students, to give them her all once again, with passion, energy, joy and love.

- Anonymous

Dear Reader,

I'd like to tell the story of a teacher. She is a teacher I happened to witness for a little while as she taught her class soon after returning to school after the events of December 14.

Once the students arrived in her classroom, she wasted no time, as there was no time to waste and much to do. She began by placing the students in their new seats: 'Jack, you sit here, and Amber, you . . . I think you should sit here.' Part of the challenge was figuring out not only student placement, but also the new foreign classroom they all found themselves in. How would it work? What's the best way to use the space? Should those materials be placed along that wall, or in the back of the room? So much to consider, but as so many things had been during the last few weeks, she'd have to figure it out as she went. One thing she was sure of, though, was what she wanted to accomplish. That soon became clear. Once everyone was in the right seat, the lesson began.

I was in awe. I had never seen a class conducted like this. She was a force whose energy was incredible. She taught with focused abandon, leading the students through the lesson and they were captivated. They followed every direction with an enthusiasm only a masterful teacher could elicit. They were working hard but enjoying it too. She knew which students needed what "tweaks" and immediately addressed them, and had them try again successfully. She moved deftly through the activity at a pace that kept every student engaged, while giving them time to take a breather when needed. They worked together, persevered together, solved problems together and laughed together. And what they created together in that room that morning was truly beautiful. Her passion for teaching was evident, even under the most challenging circumstances and it was extraordinary. After everything she had faced just weeks before, she was able to work magic with her class. I'd guess that this day's lesson was planned down to the minute, but I could also tell that every day was like this in her classroom, full of hard work and positive energy. It was also clear that this day, and every day after, was not just another day for her and her students. Every day was a step forward. Every lesson was progress of many kinds. And the students that left her class were leaving with a hugely positive experience.

Her energy seemingly spent after this class, she dismissed the students to their next class, and as they filed out, a parent filed in to say hello. They looked at each other and immediately hugged, strongly, tightly, and tears began to flow. There was clearly a common bond and a common understanding about what they were both going through, and I had the impression that this wasn't the first time they had checked in with each other.

I didn't see every teacher in the building that day, but I'd be willing to bet that this one anonymous teacher exemplifies the strength, professionalism, and passion of the rest of the staff of Sandy Hook School. Finally, as soon as the last student from the previous class stepped out into the hallway, the next class came in. It was time again. Time to get back up for this next group of students, to give them her all once again, with passion, energy, joy and love.

Anonymous

Bridge over Lake Zoar from Southbury to Newtown

View of Sandy Hook from bridge

Dear Newtown,

It's hard to explain how Newtown - the largest town in the state, land-wise, can feel small. There are nearly 30,000 of us. We don't all shop at the same grocery store or go to the same post office. We don't all have the same ZIP code even. Few of us would describe Newtown as bucolic or quaint or pastoral unless you were in real estate here.

But then you run into Big Y on a saturday morning, unshowered and wearing sweats, and three people stop you to chat. You sit at the traffic light near the police station and belt out a song before realizing it's your friend's dad in the car next to you. You pick up the Newtown Bee and recognize most names in the sports page (and the crime log).

When I was a kid, I hardly knew the other parts of Newtown. I had memorized every mailbox on my bus route - the same one from kindergarten to high school - but had only been to a handful of other homes outside the Head 'o Meadow lines. Then in fifth grade, we met kids who hadn't known us since we were three years old and we began to switch up our friend groups.

Together we endured a lot. Sweaty middle school classrooms. Running hills behind the NHS track. Missing homeroom because you parked at Oak View or the commuter lot. We've all been dragged to main street trick-or-treating, the christmas tree lighting and early-morning parade watching on Labor Day. Then there was the Lake Zoar rope swing, Southbury bridge jumping and campouts in our friends' backyards. We've all at least thought about sneaking into the Fairfield Hills tunnels.

My favorite town tradition is fairly new: the annual Thanksgiving capture the flag game in Rams Pasture. What started out as a much-needed break from turkey roasting and pie-rolling is now 100 people, ranging from the 5-year-olds who like to cheat to the 40-year old dads who like to cheat. If you left the field without mud stains, you weren't really playing.

I'm in my last year of college now, and for most of that time, I didn't bother telling people exactly where I was from - near Danbury about an hour from the city. You've never heard of it. My friends from dense New Jersey suburbs and the bustling outskirts of Boston were shocked when they heard about the lack of fast food and the number of farms within a two-mile radius of my house. Now my college friends know the name of my town, but they understand even less about it.

To me, Newtown has felt even smaller these last few months. We've turned inward in a way only a few other towns can understand. And there's still no place I'd rather have grown up. Thank you Newtown.

— Sarah Ferris, 144 Sugar St., Newtown.

Dear Newtown,

It's hard to explain how Newtown—the largest town in the state, land-wise, can feel small. There are nearly 30,000 of us. We don't all shop at the same grocery store or go to the same post office. We don't all have the same zip code even. Few of us would describe Newtown as bucolic or quaint or pastoral unless you were in real estate here.

But then you run into Big Y on a Sunday morning, unshowered and wearing sweats, and three people stop you to chat. You sit at the traffic light near the police station and belt out a song before realizing it's your friend's dad in the car next to you. You pick up the Newtown Bee and recognize most names in the sports page (and the crime log).

When I was a kid, I hardly knew the other parts of Newtown. I had memorized every mailbox on my bus route—the same one from kindergarten to high school—but had only been to a handful of other homes outside the Head O' Meadow lines. Then in fifth grade, we met kids who hadn't known us since we were three years old and we began to switch up our friend groups.

Together we endured a lot. Sweaty middle school classrooms. Running hills behind the NHS track. Missing homeroom because you parked at Oak View or the commuter lot. We've all been dragged to Main Street trick-or-treating, the Christmas tree lighting, and early-morning parade watching on Labor Day. Then there was the Lake Zoar rope swing, Southbury bridge jumping and campouts in our friends' backyards. We've all at least thought about sneaking into the Fairfield Hills tunnels.

My favorite town tradition is fairly new: the annual Thanksgiving capture the flag game in Rams Pasture. What started out as a much-needed break from turkey roasting and pie-rolling is now 100 people, ranging from the 5-year-olds who like to cheat to the 40-year old dads who like to cheat. If you left the field without mud stains, you weren't really playing.

I'm in my last year of college now, and for most of that time, I didn't bother telling people exactly where I was from—near Danbury about an hour from the city. You've never heard of it. My friends from dense New Jersey suburbs and the bustling outskirts of Boston were shocked when they heard about the lack of fast food and the number of farms within a two-mile radius of my house. Now my college friends know the name of my town, but they understand even less about it.

To me, Newtown has felt even smaller these last few months. We've turned inward in a way only a few other towns can understand. And there's still no place I'd rather have grown up. Thank you Newtown.

Sarah Ferris, Newtown

Many people are familiar with Newtown's Historic Main Street Flagpole. thousands of motorists pass by it every day. Some folks know some of it's history and for those that don't, I would like to share some of that with you.

The first Flagpole, with the help of volunteers, was made from a tree that grew in the Shady Rest area of Newtown. This pole was probably two sections and most likely much shorter than 100'. It was paid for from donations to the tune of $131.00. This pole was erected to celebrate the country's centennial in 1876 and named "Liberty Pole".

This pole rotted out and was replaced by a second pole in the 1890's, again with local volunteers and donations. This pole lasted until 1912 when it blew down. By this time a volunteer organization called the Men's Club, had become the unofficial custodian of the Flagpole and had made several repairs to it over the years. Now they stepped up again and raised money for a third pole which was erected in 1914, this pole was 100' tall with a gilded ball on top. The third pole lasted until 1949 when it had deteriorated to the point where it was deemed a hazard and had to be taken down.

In 1950 the Town of Newtown had the present day steel flagpole put up. This pole was made by Keake & Nelson of Bridgeport, Connecticut. It came to Newtown in two pieces and was welded together on site. A crane lifted the 100' pole and lowered it into a 21' galvanized cylinder which had been installed in concrete.

with the 16" diameter pole in place, this left
a gap around the pole and the cylinder was
filled with sand in order to make it easy
to remove if necessary. The pole was topped
with a 16" copper gold leafed ball.

Over the years the Connecticut Department
of Transportation has wanted to have the
Flag pole removed from the center of Main
Street. In 1981 State Representative Mae
Schmidle was instrumental in having a
law passed that prohibited the removal of
the landmark.

I became acquainted with the Flag pole
when I started on the Newtown Police
Department in 1967. At that time the Police
Department had an agreement with the
Town of Newtown that we would raise the
flag and lower the flag every day in exchange
the Town would pay for our uniforms.
So here I was, just fresh out of the
military and I considered this quite an
honor. Over the preceding years The Police
Department became responsible for
maintaining the flags. The cost of which
was in our budget, but there really wasn't
anything for the maintenance of the pole
itself and this fell to various volunteers
that stepped in.

By 1982 the Flagpole had deteriorated, the ball had come off the top and was damaged beyond repair and the pole had multiple coats of paint which was cracked and chipped.

I decided to try and raise funds to get it back in shape. Articles in The Newtown Bee brought many offers of money and a free crane. By 1983 I had been able to raise enough money to help have the Flagpole sand blasted, painted and a new 16" copper gold ball installed. It was looking good!

Now that I had the Flagpole in great shape I decided that needed a larger flag to fly on special occasions. The size of the flag which always had flown and paid for out of the NPD budget was 6' X 8'. I picked out a 12' X 18' flag which cost about $225. As soon as I put it up, various folks in town loved it and wanted that size flag to fly all the time and were willing to foot the bill, so that size became the standard. Now, I wanted a bigger flag for special occasions and picked out a 20 X 30' flag. It cost around $450. Again some folks now wanted this size to fly all the time and would be willing to pay. It was at this time that the 20' X 30' became the summer flag and

the 12'x18' was the standard for the winter. I had the lights that illuminate the flag installed around this time much to many folks pleasure.

I did have a problem with thieves however, who stole two 12'x18' flags soon after I started to fly them. I even had a locking mechanism installed and they climbed the pole, cut the rope and stole the flag. It was at this time that the Newtown Hook & Ladder Company came to the rescue. They agreed to raise the flag and lower it as needed and we moved the point to tie the rope off above the lights on the flagpole. No flag has been stolen since.

For the past 30 years I have facilitated the care of the flagpole with the help of various organizations and individuals from Newtown and beyond. It has been a pleasure!

Retired Newtown Police Lieutenant

David Kullgren

Many people are familiar with Newtown's Historic Main Street Flagpole; thousands of motorists pass by it every day. Some folks know some of its history and for those that don't, I would like to share some of that with you.

The first Flagpole, with the help of volunteers, was made from a tree that grew in the Shady Rest area of Newtown. This pole was probably two sections and most likely much shorter than 100'. It was paid for from donations to the tune of $131.00. This pole was erected to celebrate the country's centennial in 1876 and named "Liberty Pole".

This pole rotted out and was replaced by a second pole in the 1890's, again with local volunteers and donations. This pole lasted until 1912 when it blew down. By this time a volunteer organization called the Men's Club, had become the unofficial custodian of the Flagpole and had made several repairs to it over the years. Now they stepped up again and raised money for a third pole which was erected in 1914, this pole was 100' tall with a gilded ball on top. The third pole lasted until 1949 when it had deteriorated to the point where it was deemed a hazard and had to be taken down.

In 1950 the Town of Newtown had the present day steel flagpole put up. This pole was made by Leake & Nelson of Bridgeport, Connecticut. It came to Newtown in two pieces and was welded together on site. A crane lifted the 100' pole and lowered it into a 21" galvanized cylinder which had been installed in concrete. With the 16" diameter pole in place, this left a gap around the pole and the cylinder which was filled with sand in order to make it easy to remove if necessary. The pole was topped with a 16" copper gold leafed ball.

Over the years the Connecticut Department of Transportation has wanted to have the Flagpole removed from the center of Main Street. In 1981 State Representative Mae Schmidle was instrumental in having a law passed that prohibited the removal of the landmark.

I became acquainted with the Flagpole when I started on the Newtown Police Department in 1967. At that time the Police Department had an agreement with the Town of Newtown that we would raise the flag and lower the flag every day in exchange the Town would pay for our uniforms. So here I was, just fresh out of the military and I considered this quite an honor. Over the preceding years the Police Department became responsible for maintaining the flags. The cost of which was in our budget, but there really wasn't anything for the maintenance of the pole itself and this fell to various volunteers that stepped in.

By 1982 the Flagpole had deteriorated, the ball had come off the top and was damaged beyond repair and the pole had multiple coats of paint which was cracked and chipped.

I decided to try and raise funds to get it back in shape. Articles in The Newtown Bee brought many offers of money and a free crane. By 1983 I had been able to raise enough money to help have the Flagpole sand blasted, painted and a new 16" copper gold ball installed. It was looking good!

Now that I had the Flagpole in great shape I decided that we needed a larger flag to fly on special occasions. The size of the flag which always had flown and paid for out of the NPD budget was 6' x 8'. I picked out a 12' x 18' flag which cost about $225. As soon as I put it up, various folks in town loved it and wanted that size flag to fly all the time and were willing to foot the bill, so that size became the standard. Now, I wanted a bigger flag for special occasions and picked out a 20' x 30' flag. It cost around $450. Again some folks now wanted this size to fly all the time and would be willing to pay. It was at this time that the 20' x 30' became the summer flag and the 12' x 18' was the standard for the winter. I had the lights that illuminate the flag installed around this time much to many folks pleasure.

I did have a problem with thieves however, who stole two 12' x 18' flags soon after I started to fly them. I even had a locking mechanism installed and they climbed the pole, cut the rope and stole the flag. It was at this time that the Newtown Hook & Ladder Company came to the rescue. They agreed to raise the flag and lower it as needed and we moved the point to tie the rope off above the lights on the flagpole. No flag has been stolen since!

For the past 30 years I have facilitated the care of the Flagpole with the help of various organizations and individuals from Newtown and beyond. It has been a pleasure!

Retired Newtown Police Lieutenant
David Lydem

Flagpole in Newtown (there is a business in the open space now, so we are no longer able to see this view)

Flag being raised in Newtown

My Dear Reader,

   I met Newtown at the Flagpole, my wife
met her at the Edmond Town Hall; my
meeting was free, hers cost a two dollar
movie ticket. Twenty-five years later
it's the same price, a pretty good
old-fashion Yankee buy. I grew up in
southern Fairfield County when Trumbull
was country. My wife, Stephanie grew up
in Vermont, where it's still country.
After law school I took a job for a
law firm in Bridgeport. We moved to
Bridgeport, then Shelton, then built
a house in Oxford. Here our story begins
   "You need to cover this matter in Danbury,"
says my mentor.
   "How do you get there?" I ask.
He looks at me a little surprised.

"Take 25 North, when you see a giant flagpole in the middle of the Road you're half way there." Paul was a pretty good storyteller; it made him a good trial lawyer and a great mentor. I thought to myself, flagpole in the middle of the road... really? And then, there it was, straight-up, Smack in the middle of the Route 25 and 6 intersection, a giant flagpole pillared between two steeple churches, centering an historic district of homes and small businesses that the New York Times called 'Pristine early American elegance.'

On Thursday nights in Oxford, Stephanie and our neighbor left the young kids with the hubbies and ventured across the dam to the Edmond Town Hall for the $2.00 movie. She fell in love with historic Main Street.

Fast-forward a couple years. Good schools and a For-Sale sign in a yard on Main Street attract the attention of my wife. The schools are solid, the house not so much, it needs work. It's a good price, maybe five thousand dollars too much. I negotiate with the seller's realtor. He won't budge. We negotiate, and negotiate, and negotiate. This crusty old Yankee is giving me second thoughts. (To a then thirty-something year old, age fifty-something was old, to this old fifty-something year old guy now... fifty-something is summertime...) Two months pass. The old fifty year Yankee realtor concedes $500.00. We buy the Main Street house. The day after we move in I see him in the front yard next door.

"You selling that house, too?" I ask.

"Nope," he answers. "I live here." To paraphrase Humphrey Bogart, "that was the beginning of a beautiful friendship."

My neighbor's tall and thin, Stephanie said good-looking for an old guy. I learn he's old Yankee stock that originally settled the town. A street name has his surname. So, one day, my neighbor, Lee is smoking a cigar on his front bench.

"I guess we're pretty lucky to have Main Street," I say. We live in an 1860 CIRCA house, originally a tavern. It's one of the newer houses on the street that include Colonial Revival, Colonial Saltbox, Gothic Revival, Italianate, Victorian bracketed, and Federal architecture.

"Yup," says Lee.

"I've been thinking. A lot of other towns I see around lost their historic downtowns, developed away into strip malls."

"Sure," he nods.

"I'm thinking Main Street's still around because of this Borough we have here," I volunteer. The Borough was established in 1824, two years before John Adams and Thomas Jefferson died on the Fourth of July. It was established by Judge William Edmond, a prominent citizen, judge and U. S. Congressman. The Borough is a separate municipality, one square mile in the center of Newtown. If you live in the Borough you are a resident of both the Town and Borough. The Borough was established for preservation and business purposes. It still serves that purpose today. The Borough led the town in establishing firsts, the first fire

company, the first fire hydrants, the first
street lights and the first zoning.

"Agreed," he says. "Second Tuesday of
the month, 7:30 pm Esmond Town Hall."
I give him a puzzled look. "Board of
Burgesses meeting. Go tell them yourself."

The next month I show up at the
Board of Burgesses meeting. I'm the only
one in the audience. There's Lee sitting
at the table! Next to him a slightly younger,
silver haired woman. She's thin and
wears firm facial features. She's the Warden.
"What's he want?" she asks unconcerned
I'm but ten feet away. Lee just gives her
a slight grin. She opens the meeting.
Each member calls out their name
in roll call. There are six members of
the Board of Burgesses, a Warden, a
tax collector, a treasurer, a clerk,
and the zoning enforcement officer. Public

participation is first. I speak my piece. The red haired zoning enforcement officer is the only one to show any emotion. She nods.

"You're welcome to stay, if you really want to," says the silver haired Warden. I get it. I gestured goodbye.

Fast forward two months on a SAturday afternoon, Lee walks over. "How'd you like to be on the Board of Burgesses?" he asks. I have a lot of questions. I can ask later. I didn't want to seem too anxious. I was getting this Yankee thing.

"Sure," I said biting my tongue

"Good. You know, they thought you were okay." I didn't tell him I never would have figured so.

"Even the silver haired woman, the Warden?" I asked.

"She's my sister," he said. Joe shared a lot of Town history with me that day, including that he was the Hook and Ladder Fire Chief.

Joe learned a lot of good Yankee values over the years; the difference between frugal and cheap; to choose words carefully; disagree – yes, disagreeable – no; be cordial not intrusive; remember, Rome wasn't built in a day; and the old-timers knew what they were doing when they laid out roads and bridges, stuff like that. It has served me well as Borough Burgess, Warden, Town Board of Finance member and Town Selectman.

When my neighbor Joe retired south he left his old fire helmet to my eldest son, Jimmy. Jimmy has some of these Yankee traits. He can run or swim a marathon, repair a roof and calculate your calculus. He brings you change from the $20 dollar bill. A three time All-American swimmer in high school and recruited Division 1 college swimmer, he suffered a shoulder injury that ended his swim career. He took time off from college to participate with his older sister in the international Racing the Planet, 4 Desert Races survival run- 150 miles in six days, Atacama, Chile, Gobi Desert, China, Sahara Desert, Egypt and Antarctica. While at home training, he was elected to the Board of Finance, and joined Hook and Ladder.

On 12/14, he went on duty as a First Responder manning the Hook and Ladder fire station. Over the days that followed he was involved in ceremonies and on call fire duties. He also posted at cemeteries to keep non-local reporters and photographers out. As elected officials, together we assumed responsibilities for which we never dreamed. Old-fashioned Yankee principles were our backstop. They served us well. I think Lee would be proud. Perhaps I'll break Yankee protocol and just ask him next time he visits his sister (she's still a Burgess on the Board and a Newtown legend in her own right.) Nah, probably not.

God Bless Newtown, the Borough and Sandy Hook.

Regards,
Jim Gaston
18 Main Street

My Dear Reader,

I met Newtown at the Flagpole, my wife met her at the Edmond Town Hall; my meeting was free, hers cost a two dollar movie ticket. Twenty-five years later it's the same price, a pretty good old-fashion Yankee buy. I grew up in southern Fairfield County when Trumbull was country. My wife, Stephanie grew up in Vermont, where it's still country. After law school I took a job for a law firm in Bridgeport. We moved to Bridgeport, then Shelton, then built a house in Oxford. Here our story begins.

"You need to cover this matter in Danbury," says my mentor.

"How do you get there?" I ask. He looks at me a little surprised.

"Take 25 North, when you see a giant flagpole in the middle of the road you're half way there." Paul was a pretty good storyteller; it made him a good trial lawyer and a great mentor. I thought to myself, flagpole in the middle of the road . . . really? And then, there it was, straight-up, smack in the middle of the Route 25 and 6 intersection, a giant flagpole pillared between two steeple churches, centering an historic district of homes and small businesses that the *New York Times* called "pristine early American elegance."

On Thursday nights in Oxford, Stephanie and our neighbor left the young kids with the hubbies and ventured across the dam to the Edmond Town Hall for the $2 movie. She fell in love with historic Main Street.

Fast-forward a couple years. Good schools and a For-Sale sign in a yard on Main Street attract the attention of my wife. The schools are solid, the house not so much, it needs work. It's a good price, maybe five thousand dollars too much. I negotiate with the seller's realtor. He won't budge. We negotiate, and negotiate, and negotiate. This crusty old Yankee is giving me second thoughts. (To a then thirty-something year old, age fifty-something was old, to this old fifty something year old guy now . . . fifty-something is summer time . . .) Two months pass. The old fifty year Yankee realtor concedes $500.00. We buy the Main Street house. The day after we move in I see him in the front yard next door.

"You selling that house, too?" I ask.

"Nope," he answers. "I live here." To paraphrase Humphrey Bogart, "that was the beginning of a beautiful friendship."

My neighbor's tall and thin, Stephanie said good-looking for an old guy. I learn he's old Yankee stock that originally settled the town. A street name has his surname. So, one day, my neighbor, Lee is smoking a cigar on his front bench.

"I guess we're pretty lucky to have Main Street," I say. We live in an 1860 circa house, originally a tavern. It's one of the newer houses on the street that include Colonial Revival, Colonial Saltbox, Gothic Revival, Italianate, Victorian bracketed, and Federal architecture.

"Yup," says Lee.

"I've been thinking. A lot of other towns I see around lost their historic down towns, developed away into strip malls."

"Sure," he nods.

"I'm thinking Main Street's still around because of this Borough we have here," I volunteer. The Borough was established in 1824, two years before John Adams and Thomas Jefferson died on the Fourth of July. It was established by Judge William Edmond, a prominent citizen, judge and U.S. Congressman. The Borough is a separate municipality, one square mile in the center of Newtown. If you live in the Borough you are a resident of both the Town and Borough. The Borough was established for preservation and business purposes. It still serves that purpose today. The Borough led the town in establishing firsts, the first fire company, the first fire hydrants, the first street lights and the first zoning.

"Agreed," he says. "Second Tuesday of the month, 7:30pm Edmond Town Hall." I give him a puzzled look. "Board of Burgesses meeting. Go tell them yourself."

The next month I show up at the Board of Burgesses meeting. I'm the only one in the audience. There's Lee sitting at the table! Next to him a slightly younger silver haired woman. She's thin and wears firm facial features. She's the Warden. "What's he want?" she asks unconcerned I'm but ten feet away. Lee just gives her a slight grin. She opens the meeting. Each member calls out their name in roll call. There are six members of the Board of Burgesses, a Warden, a tax collector, a treasurer, a clerk and the zoning enforcement officer. Public participation is first. I speak my piece. The red haired zoning enforcement officer is the only one to show any emotion. She nods.

"You're welcome to stay, if you *really* want to," says the silver haired Warden. I get it. I gestured goodbye.

Fast forward two months on a Saturday afternoon, Lee walks over, "How'd you like to be on the Board of Burgesses?" he asks. I have a lot of questions. I can ask later. I didn't want to seem too anxious. I was *getting* this Yankee thing.

"Sure," I said biting my tongue.

"Good. You know, they thought you were okay." I didn't tell him I never would have figured so.

"Even the silver haired woman, the Warden?" I asked.

"She's my sister," he said. Lee shared a lot of town history with me that day, including that he was the Hook and Ladder Fire Chief.

I've learned a lot of good Yankee values over the years; the difference between frugal and cheap; to choose words carefully; disagree—yes, disagreeable—no; be cordial not intrusive; remember, Rome wasn't built in a day; and the old-timers knew what they were doing when they laid out roads and bridges, stuff like that. It has served me well as Borough Burgess, Warden, Town Board of Finance member and Town Selectman.

When my neighbor Lee retired south he left his old fire helmet to my eldest son, Jimmy. Jimmy has some of these Yankee traits. He can run or swim a marathon, repair a roof and calculate your calculus. He brings you change from the $20 dollar bill. A three time All-American swimmer in high school and recruited Division I college swimmer, he suffered a shoulder injury that ended his swim career. He took time off from college to participate with his older sister in the international *Racing the Planet, 4 Desert Races* survival run—150 miles in six days, Atacama, Chile, Gobi Desert, China, Sahara Desert, Egypt and Antarctica. While at home training, he was elected to the Board of Finance, and joined Hook and Ladder.

On 12/14 he went on duty as a First Responder manning the Hook and Ladder fire station. Over the days that followed he was involved in ceremonies and on call fire duties. He also posted at cemeteries to keep non-local reporters and photographers out. As elected officials, together we assumed responsibilities for which we never dreamed. Old-fashioned Yankee principles were our backstop. They served us well. I think Lee would be proud. Perhaps I'll break Yankee protocol and just ask him next time he visits his sister (she's still a Burgess on the Board and a Newtown legend in her own right). Nah, probably not.

God Bless Newtown, the Borough and Sandy Hook.

Regards,
Jim Gaston
18 Main Street

I long to speak of the wild flowers that grow along the pond's edge in the Ram pasture, but it has been difficult to speak. I yearn to breathe in the sweet smell of horses as they graze in the tall paddock grass on Brushy Hill, but it has been difficult to breathe. I plead for purpose, driving past the flagpole, redefining what normal will now become. Perhaps we can pretend, for just a few moments. Close your eyes... come on... we can do this! Let's close our eyes... together and imagine... What if all of us... wish hard enough? What if we all hope... long enough? Maybe just maybe we can hear the whisper of laughter breaking through the rain and in that moment, that quiet moment, discover how to take that next step. Do we stride over the deep puddles? What if we storm through them? What if.... there are endless what ifs! Who believes and understands the butterfly effect, how a seemingly small insignificant flutter of wings can have a profound ripple on the world, then why couldn't one more butterfly have taken flight early that morning? What if one more monarch glided gracefully onto the pedals of a nearby lily and changed history forever? Could that very small natural force halfway across the world have presented an altered reality of the events on that day? So many questions. Will there ever be answers?

The magnitude of the tragedy remains insurmountable.

Life became surreal... simple tasks... overwhelming and monumental. Attempts were made to process... information, intense feelings, unspeakable truths. How can it be that the sun somehow continues to rise each day? How does life simply go on? Broadcasts blare and media makes a mockery of our town on deadline. Cars are driven, horns honk, shoppers shop and many carry on. Do they all not know? Seemingly everyone who shared a common humanity across the globe knew. But this is a very different knowing. This is a knowing of interminable sorrow and grief. This is a mourning that is deepening with each day, stabbing and irreconcilable. This is an overshadowing darkness that is so difficult to share, so incomprehensible. Random thoughts and a stream of conscious explosion of emotions and heartache. "We must go where life leads, preparing for our passage and journey. All may be destined to travel these roads," they say. Who are "they" anyway? But please, not this path, not this day, not this way! Ok then, so we have two doses of denial and an ounce of anger... What were those stages again? Could we not circumnavigate another way? A less traveled route perhaps? Some paved and purposeful, or maneuvered meandering and leading nowhere kind of road. What do you think? Hey listen, what if you take the high road and I take the low road? Is this the bargaining stage? I have seen this place before. I know these colors, I know that song. Yes... yes, I can almost hear the laughter, a whisper yet so vivid, so clear. Music, there's music. How can such a precise melody fade in the distance? Listen closely, as the cellos play softly, slowly... If only for a few moments... To be able to breathe, to be able to speak. Rainbows reach past the rain... look... there... fireflies... they're everywhere! Are they flapping their wings too? Yes, yes they are and every now & then light peaks through...

Wild flowers in Ram Pasture

Horses on Brushy Hill in Newtown

I long to speak of the wild flowers that grow along the pond's edge in the Ram Pasture, but it has been difficult to speak. I yearn to breathe in the sweet smell of horses as they graze in the tall paddock grass on Brushy Hill, but it has been difficult to breathe. I plead for purpose, driving past the flagpole, redefining what normal will now become. Perhaps we can pretend, for just a few moments. Close your eyes . . . come on . . . we can do this! Let's close our eyes . . . together and imagine . . . What if all of us . . . wish hard enough? What if we all hope.. long enough? Maybe just maybe we can hear the whisper of laughter breaking through the rain and in that moment, that quiet moment, discover how to take that next step. Do we stride over the deep puddles? What if we storm through them? What if . . . there are endless what ifs! If one believes and understands the butterfly effect, how a seemingly small insignificant flutter of wings can have a profound ripple on the world, then why couldn't one more butterfly have taken flight early that morning? What if one more monarch glided gracefully onto the petals of a nearby lily and changed history forever? Could that very small natural force half way across the world have presented an altered reality of the events on that day? So many questions. Will there ever be answers?

The Magnitude of the tragedy remains insurmountable.

Life became surreal . . . simple tasks . . . overwhelming and monumental. Attempts were made to process . . . information, intense feelings, unspeakable truths. How can it be that the sun somehow continues to rise each day? How does life simply go on? Broadcasts blare and media makes a mockery of our town on deadline. Cars are driven, horns honk, shoppers shop and many carry on. Do they all not know? Seemingly everyone who shared a common humanity across the globe knew. But this is a very different knowing. This is a knowing of interminable sorrow and grief. This is a mourning that is deepening with each day, stabbing and irreconcilable. This is an overshadowing darkness that is so difficult to share, so incomprehensible. Random thoughts and a stream of conscious explosion of emotions and heart ache. "We must go where life leads, preparing for our passage and journey. All may be destined to travel these roads", they say. Who are *they*, anyway? But please, not this path, not this day, not this way! *Ok then, so we have two doses of denial and an ounce of anger . . . What were those stages again?* Could we not circumnavigate another way? A less traveled route perhaps? Some paved and purposeful, or maneuvered meandering and leading nowhere kind of road. What do you think? Hey listen, what if you take the high road and I take the low road? *Is this the bargaining stage?* I have seen this place before. I know these colors, I know that song. Yes . . . yes, I can almost hear the laughter, a whisper yet so vivid, so clear. Music, there's music. How can such a precise melody fade in the distance? Listen closely, as the cellos play softly, slowly . . . If only for a few moments . . . to be able to breath, to be able to speak. Rainbows reach past the rain . . . look . . . there . . . fireflies . . . they're everywhere! Are they flapping their wings too? Yes, yes they are and every now and then light peaks through . . .

By Phyllis Rhodes Cortese 9.6.13

I have lived in the Sandy Hook section of Newtown for 23 years; the longest I have ever resided in one area. It has been a wonderful place to raise a family and I cannot imagine ever leaving my home. Our family has belonged to Saint Rose of Lima Parish where we remain actively involved in many facets of the Church. Our children attended the school and lifelong friendships have been made here as well. There is so much to love about our town from 2 dollar movies at Edmond Town Hall to halted traffic on Route 302 as the cows cross the road. I cannot begin to count the number of delicious lunches purchased at our General Store on Main St. How many times did Don, the owner of Drug Center, deliver medicine to my home so I did not have to leave the house with a sick child? A quick stop to the grocery store turns into an hour of catching up on peoples lives. The Newtown Newcomers Club of which I had the good fortune to be President; serves as a wonderful welcoming tool for new and not so new residents.

There is a strong sense of community here and so many volunteer their time and talents for the benefit of others. While it certainly is quite the picturesque town; the caring people make it a much desired place to lay down roots. I am not able to foresee the future; however, I pray that someday my grandchildren will be able to experience for themselves the beauty of Newtown.

Respectfully submitted,
Donna M. Rahtelli

Fall scenes in Newtown

Ferris cows crossing 302

I have lived in the Sandy Hook section of Newtown for 23 years; the longest I have ever resided in one area. It has been a wonderful place to raise a family and I cannot imagine ever leaving my home. Our family has belonged to Saint Rose of Lima Parish where we remain actively involved in many facets of the Church. Our children attended the school and lifelong friendships have been made here as well. There is so much to love about our town from 2 dollar movies at Edmond Town Hall to halted traffic on Route 302 as the cows cross the road. I cannot begin to count the number of delicious lunches purchased at our General Store on Main St. How many times did Don, the owner of Drug Center, deliver medicine to my home so I did not have to leave the house with a sick child? A quick stop to the grocery store turns into an hour of catching up on people's lives. The Newtown Newcomers Club of which I had the good fortune to be President; serves as a wonderful welcoming tool for new and not so new residents.

There is a strong sense of community here and so many volunteer their time and talents for the benefit of others. While it certainly is quite the picturesque town, the caring people make it a much desired place to lay down roots. I am not able to foresee the future; however, I pray that someday my grandchildren will be able to experience for themselves the beauty of Newtown.

Respectfully submitted,
Donna M. Rahtelli

Fall scenes in Newtown

Memories of Newtown make my entire soul smile! I've always felt that somehow my guardian angel brought me here for many reasons. I've met wonderful people, my family has created lifelong friends and after twenty one years here our world revolves around this wonderful town. I remember when my son was only five and he just graduated from Trinity Day Nursery School. As a celebration for the kids a few families gathered to have a picnic at a friend's house. At the end of the evening, just before leaving, my son slipped on the grass and broke his femur bone. We were in the hospital for almost two weeks. Our house did not have any air conditioning and that was a requirement that the doctor said was a 'must have' since my son was in a total body cast. Upon arrival from the hospital there were balloons, streamers and air conditioners in the windows where my son would need them. The fridge was stocked with food. A video game console with every game a kid could want was waiting for us. That's how this town operates. Word gets out and the village comes running to help. My daughter who was two at the time was taken on trips to the town park and there were endless play dates set up for my son who was house bound for almost three months. If the weather was cool, his friends took him to the yard to play whiffle ball where someone would push him in his wheel chair to round the bases .... okay, that memory still makes me break out in a sweat but he had fun!!! It does take a village to raise a child and this town has been such a wonderful influence on my kids. My husband Bill and I have three kids. Brendan is now twenty four, Megan is twenty one and Madeline is sixteen. Newtown is our home and truly is the fabric of our lives.

Lisa Hintzen

Memories of Newtown make my entire soul smile! I've always felt that somehow my guardian angel brought me here for many reasons. I've met wonderful people, my family has created lifelong friends and after twenty one years here our world revolves around this wonderful town. I remember when my son was only five and he had just graduated from Trinity Day Nursery School. As a celebration for the kids a few families gathered to have a picnic at a friend's house. At the end of the evening, just before leaving, my son slipped on the grass and broke his femur bone. We were in the hospital for almost two weeks. Our house did not have any air conditioning and that was a requirement that the doctor said was a 'must have' since my son was in a total body cast. Upon arrival from the hospital there were balloons, streamers and air conditioners in the windows where my son would need them. The fridge was stocked with food. A video game console with every game a kid could want was waiting for us. That's how this town operates. Word gets out and the village comes running to help. My daughter who was two at the time was taken on trips to the town park and there were endless play dates set up for my son who was house bound for almost three months. If the weather was cool, his friends took him to the yard to play whiffle ball where someone would push him in his wheel chair to round the bases. . . . okay, that memory still makes me break out in a sweat but he had fun!!! It does take a village to raise a child and this town has been such a wonderful influence on my kids. My husband Bill and I have three kids. Brendan is now twenty four, Megan is twenty one and Madeline is sixteen. Newtown is our home and truly is the fabric of our lives.

Lisa Hintzen

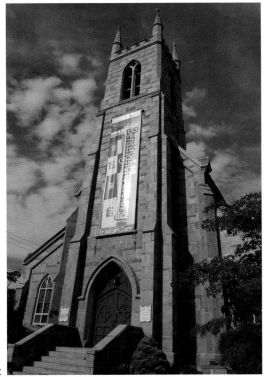

Trinity Episcopal Church on Main Street

Dear Friends,

Amid the noise and confusion of a corporate relocation a family doesn't often know what will become of them after they settle into a place. Unpacking and finding the grocery store takes precedence over discovering the true heart of a place. Little by little comes remarkable revelations that this new life, this new town, this new journey was meant to be. This has been my Newtown experience.

After the preoccupation with the move, I ventured out to find what this town held for me. Being experienced with festivals large and small and looking to get involved and meet some folks, I read in the Newtown Bee about the preparations being made for the inaugural Newtown Arts Festival scheduled for September, 2011.

Lo and behold, the committee welcomed me with open arms and I jumped in to help make that event a success. Friendships came with the hard work, the camaraderie so familiar to me in the neighborhood I'd lived in for 25 years in Atlanta emerged. Bonds were made and I started to uncover the incredible artistic talent that abounds in our community.

Now, sitting here the morning after the 2013 festival, of which I was chairman, I am filled with pride for the unbelievable display of the love for expression through art in the form of arts and crafts by moms and dads, the reading of a new play by a local equity actress, a screening of a new film by a high school junior and his 120 compatriots, a cello and violin recital, a Broadway concert featuring not only stars from the Great White Way but also the superb talent of Newtown children, a Rooster Ball, and countless artists, musicians, dancers, authors weavers, the award-winning high school marching band, the Newtown High School singers, and others. These are the people who made up the fabric of the 2013 festival. The weaving of all this into one weeklong roster was quite a task. But now I feel all the work was worth it.

The work was worth it because of the joy experienced here by virtue of the performances. A million moments allowing townspeople young and old to be taken away from the everyday. We reveled in the feeling of unity as each event unfolded, each artistic offering fated to triumph, each achievement brought something to people's lives.

"No city has ever been great without art," the actress Mary Nell Santacroce told the Atlanta City council once. I know in my heart this morning that Newtown can count itself among the great American towns because of its abundance of homegrown talent. We are rich due to our love of the arts and how our self-expressions reflect our resilience and our ability to seek the light and recognize the good. I know the cultural life of the town is in great hands. Because it's in the hands of the people themselves. They will continue the new traditions we have established. And, they will sustain, embrace and foster the arts for the well-being of a community that believes greatness is only possible by virtue of a vibrant cultural life.

Onward we go. Pushing toward enlightenment through the arts.

Terry Sagedy

Scenes from the Newtown Arts Festival, September 22, 2013

Dear Friends,

Amid the noise and confusion of a corporate relocation a family doesn't often know what will become of them after they settle into a place. Unpacking and finding the way to the grocery store and other services takes precedence over discovering the true heart of a place.

Little by little comes remarkable revelations that this new life, this new town, this new journey was meant to be. This has been my Newtown experience.

After the preoccupation with the move, I ventured out to discover what this town held for me. Being experienced with festivals large and small and looking to get involved and meet some folks, I read in The Newtown Bee about the preparations being made for the inaugural Newtown Arts Festival scheduled for September, 2012.

Lo and behold, the committee welcomed me with open arms and I jumped in to help make that event a success. Friendships came with the hard work; the camaraderie so familiar to me in the neighborhood I'd lived in for 22 years in Atlanta emerged. Bonds were made and I started to uncover the incredible artistic talent that abounds in our community.

Now, sitting here the morning after the 2013 festival, of which I was chairman, I am filled with pride for the unbelievable display of the love of expression through art in the form of arts and crafts by local moms and dads, a reading of a new play by a local equity actress, the screening of a new film by a high school junior and his 120 compatriots, a cello and violin recital, a Broadway concert featuring not only stars from the Great White Way but the superb talent of Newtown children and teens as well, a Rooster Ball, and countless artists, musicians and dancers, authors, weavers, the award-winning high school marching band, and the Newtown High School singers. These are the people who made up the fabric of the 2013 Festival. The weaving of all this into one weeklong roster of cultural programming was quite a task. But, now, I feel all the work was worth it.

The work was worth it because of the incredible joy experienced here by virtue of the performances. A million moments in time allowing townspeople young and old to be taken away from their everyday lives. We reveled in the feeling of unity as each event unfolded, each artistic offering turned into triumph, each individual achievement brought something to the audience members' lives.

"No city has ever been great without art," the actress Mary Nell Santacroce told the Atlanta City Council one evening while I was in attendance during a debate on arts funding.

I know in my heart this morning that Newtown can count itself among the great American towns because of its abundance in homegrown talent. We are rich due to our love of the arts and how our self-expressions reflect our resilience and our ability to seek the light and recognize the good.

I know the future of the cultural life of the town is in great hands because it's in the hands of the people itself. They will carry on long after I am gone. They will continue the new traditions we have established. And, they will sustain a movement to embrace and foster the arts for the well-being of a community that believes greatness is only possible by virtue of a vibrant cultural life.

Onward we go. Pushing toward enlightenment through the arts.

Terry Sagedy

Scenes from the Newtown Arts Festival, September 22, 2013

Dear America,

After the Tragic events of 12-14-12 at Sandy Hook Elementary School I want everyone to know how special our town is and how devestated we are. I live between the shooters house and the school. I seriously thought I lived in the safest place in America. Sandy Hook Elementary is a special place. I remember during the 9/11 crisis feeling grateful that my children had a school to attend that was so safe, down a long driveway with a firehouse at its entrance. Both my children attended Sandy Hook Elementary. The heroes in the school were my children's teachers. I alway knew they were heroes - now the world knows. Sandy Hook Elementary was a place of learning and laughter. Had the tragedy not happend - Sandy Hook Elementary would have been the collection site for the annual newtown Holiday Fund. newtowners adopt local families in need at Christmas and buy them gifts and food. But the tragedy did not stop our giving, instead the drop off was changed to a different school. This is the kind of community we are.

Sandy Hook Elementary is a special place, where parents devout themselves to their children. Before December 14th, one of our biggest problems was not enough field space for baseball and soccer. I look at the pictures on the television and see the baseball field at the school and think of the typical scene of parents watching their children play ball, young boys in grass stained baseball pants and their moms wiping sunscreen on the backs of their necks to protect them from the sun.

I see media at Treadwell Park where families come to swim at the local pool in the summer, play soccer in the fall and use the hills to sled on snowy days. The firehouse is normally associated with their famous town wide Lobsterfest, where families gather to eat lobster and corn on the cob and children play on the fire equipment. We are the kind of town that when we find out that someone has cancer we take up collections for their treatment, bring them casseroles and pray for them in our churches. We come together at Relay for Life and raise hundreds of thousands of dollars for cancer research. We are the kind of town that when we lose electricity in hurricanes we stick together, we open our homes and businesses to others. On Labor Day we march in the biggest parade in our state, down main street, newtown.

children ride on scooters with their schools, churches make floats on top of pick-up trucks, cancer survivors march arm in arm and politicians throw candy. On Halloween this same street turns into a magical environment of decorated homes with literally thousands of princesses, pirates and superheroes running to doors to get candy. And because our community cares about the well-being of children the "TOOTH fairy" also stands on the street passing out tooth brushes.

We are a place where kids play in their yards and mothers push strollers. One of the young lives that was lost was from my neighborhood. I use to love driving by his home to watch him, his brother and their friends playing. It brought me joy to witness their pure happiness.

This is a small town. Our lives are all intertwined. We are shaken to the core.

Please pray for our town.

Addie Sandler

Dear America,

After the tragic events of 12-14-12 at Sandy Hook Elementary School I want everyone to know how special our town is and how devastated we are. I live between the shooters house and the school. I seriously thought I lived in the safest place in America. Sandy Hook Elementary is a special place. I remember during the 9/11 crisis feeling grateful that my children had a school to attend that was so safe, down a long driveway with a firehouse at its entrance. Both my children attended Sandy Hook Elementary. The heroes in the school were my children's teachers. I always knew they were heroes— now the world knows. Sandy Hook Elementary was a place of learning and laughter. Had the tragedy not happened—Sandy Hook Elementary would have been the collection site for the annual Newtown Holiday Fund. Newtowners adopt local families in need at Christmas and buy them gifts and food. But the tragedy did not stop our giving, instead the drop off was changed to a different school. This is the kind of community we are.

Sandy Hook Elementary is a special place, where parents devout themselves to their children. Before December 14th, one of our biggest problems was not enough field space for baseball and soccer. I look at the pictures on the television and see the baseball field at the school and think of the typical scene of parents watching their children play ball, young boys in grass stained baseball pants and their moms wiping sunscreen on the backs of their necks to protect them from the sun.

I see media at Treadwell Park where families come to swim at the local pool in the summer, play soccer in the fall and use the hills to sled on snowy days. The firehouse is normally associated with their famous town wide Lobsterfest, where families gather to eat lobster and corn on the cob and children play on the fire equipment. We are the kind of town that when we find out that someone has cancer we take up collections for their treatment, bring them casseroles and pray for them in our churches. We come together at Relay for Life and raise hundreds of thousands of dollars for cancer research. We are the kind of town that when we lose electricity in hurricanes we stick together, we open our homes and businesses to others. On Labor Day we march in the biggest parade in our state, down Main Street, Newtown. Children ride on scooters with their schools, churches make floats on top of pick-up trucks, cancer survivors march arm in arm and politicians throw candy. On Halloween this same street turns into a magical environment of decorated homes with literally thousands of princesses, pirates and superheroes running to doors to get candy. And because our community cares about the well-being of children the "Tooth Fairy" also stands on the street passing out tooth brushes.

We are a place where kids play in their yards and mothers push strollers. One of the young lives that was lost was from my neighborhood. I use to love driving by his home to watch him, his brother and their friends playing. It brought me joy to witness their pure happiness.

This is a small town. Our lives are all intertwined. We are shaken to the core.

Please pray for our town.

Addie Sandler

Home

In 1978, my wife and I were happily married, and shortly thereafter were searching for our home. We both worked in Danbury and were looking for the perfect "burb" to meet our needs. We found it here in "The Hook" of Newtown.

Our home was a real "fixer upper". It was showing its wear after having been built in the forties and housing a family of six. It was needy but it became uniquely ours. Newtown became ours. It had that old world charm that we so desired. It had the Red Brick General Store for everything from basic groceries to general household needs. If they didn't have it, it was just a stones throw to A.L. Pendri's for plumbing supplies or a quick journey "uptown" to the hardware store. Wherever we

went, smiles were always the norm.
Although on a few occasions, He would
be stern with me when I failed to
solve a plumbing problem properly.
But he would always explain the
error of my ways and tell me to
go home with new parts and try
again. Then, report back to him
if his newest plan didn't work.
He had a bank of solutions!

Newtown allowed us to commune
with nature. Avid outdoors people,
it was wonderful to walk out our
door and enjoy nature's best with
all of its flora and fauna. Eagles
flying overhead, wildflowers blooming
in early spring, or even the deer
munching everything that we'd rather
they didn't; brought a smile to
our faces.

That was Newtown then. We
have more homes now. We have
more traffic lights now. We have
more cars now. But Newtown now

is the same Newtown as it was for us thirty five plus years ago. The charm is still here. Sometimes, it takes a little more time to peel back the layers to find it, but it's here. It is home.

Webster's describes "home" as a place where one likes to be. A restful or congenial place is a home. This is our community.

My wife and I have both retired from our lifelong occupations in the education field. The first question that people asked upon our leaving was "Where are you moving?" They then suggest Florida or Arizona or another milder climatic region. When we say we're going to be in Newtown, they looked puzzled. We just explain it simply with a smile on our faces. "It's Home!"

Joe Marc Jaquah
2013

Home

In 1978, my wife and I were happily married, and shortly thereafter were searching for our home. We both worked in Danbury and were looking for the perfect "burb" to meet our needs. We found it here in "The Hook" of Newtown.

Our home was a real "fixer upper". It was showing its wear after having been built in the forties and housing a family of six. It was needy but it became uniquely ours. Newtown became ours. It had that old world charm that we so desired. It had the Red Brick General Store for everything from basic groceries to general household needs. If they didn't have it, it was just a stones throw to Al Penovi's for plumbing supplies or a quick journey "uptown" to the hardware store. Wherever we went, smiles were always the norm. Although on a few occasions, Al would be stern with me when I failed to solve a plumbing problem properly. But he would always explain the error of my ways and tell me to go home with new parts and try again. Then, report back to him if his newest plan didn't work. He had a bank of solutions!

Newtown allowed us to commune with nature. Avid outdoors people, it was wonderful to walk out our door and enjoy nature's best with all of its flora and fauna. Eagles flying overhead, wildflowers blooming in early spring, or even the deer munching everything that we'd rather they didn't; brought a smile to our faces.

That was Newtown then. We have more homes now. We have more traffic lights now. We have more cars now. But Newtown now *IS* the same Newtown as it was for us thirty five plus years ago. The charm is still here. Sometimes, it takes a little more time to peel back the layers to find it, but it's here. It is home.

Webster's describes "home" as a place where one likes to be. A restful or congenial place is a home. This is our community.

My wife and I have both retired from our lifelong occupations in the education field. The first question that people asked upon our leaving was "Where are you moving?". They then suggest Florida or Arizona or another milder climatic region. When we say we're going to be in Newtown, they looked puzzled. We just explain it simply with a smile on our faces. "It's home!"

Jon Marc Jagush
2013

Waterfall by Glen Road in Sandy Hook

Katy Caulfield
12/14/2012

We're all busy. We all have schedules and agendas jam-packed with various things to do. Our days, weeks, months and years are filled with appointments, classes, paperwork, phone calls, deadlines and parties.

Sometimes we find ourselves so busy that we forget to say goodbye to our loved ones before we leave for work in the morning. Sometimes we forget to take a few minutes out of our day to send a friend a birthday text or give some affection to our dog.

However, whenever we are directly confronted with a tragedy of this magnitude, so close to home, it makes us stop dead in our tracks. We automatically call our friends and family, reach out, give a hug and kiss, and tell someone we love them.

Why must a crisis occur to remind us what is truly important in life? Why do we need to be shaken up, jerked alert to realize what really matters? I'm sure that all of the parents, siblings, relatives and friends wished they had said the words "I love you" just one more time to the sweet child they lost today.

If there's anything we can learn from the shooting at Sandy Hook School, it's that we ALL need to slow down, simplify our lives, and take the time to appreciate our loved ones each and every moment. Life is short; fragile. If we don't do it now, we may not get another chance.

Katy Caulfield
12/14/2012

We're all busy. We all have schedules and agendas jam-packed with various things to do. Our days, weeks, months and years are filled with appointments, classes, paperwork, phone calls, deadlines and parties.

Sometimes we find ourselves so busy that we forget to say goodbye to our loved ones before we leave for work in the morning. Sometimes we forget to take a few minutes out of our day to send a friend a birthday text or give some affection to our dog.

However, whenever we are directly confronted with a tragedy of this magnitude, so close to home, it makes us stop dead in our tracks. We automatically call our friends and family, reach out, give a hug and kiss, and tell someone we love them.

Why must a crisis to occur to remind us what is truly important in life? Why do we need to be shaken up, jerked alert to realize what really matters? I'm sure that all of the parents, siblings, relatives and friends wished they had said the words "I love you" just one more time to the sweet child they lost today.

If there's anything we can learn from the shooting at Sandy Hook School, it's that we ALL need to slow down, simplify our lives, and take the time to appreciate our loved ones each and every moment. Life is short; fragile. If we don't do it now, we may not get another chance.

Sabrina Style in the center of Sandy Hook

August 2013

Dear Reader,

Ah, Newtown! Forty six years of memories all beginning in September of 1967. It's hard to imagine that I've spent two-thirds of my life here. On top of that I spent 32 of those years working in the very community where I live. That began in September of 1973 at Sandy Hook School where I served as a 4th and 5th grade teacher, a lead teacher for three years and finally as the school's math/science specialist for 4 years until my retirement in 2004.

My wife and I raised two children in this town and eventually my wife established an accounting firm with her partner here. So our ties to Newtown are quite strong and certainly well established.

I have seen many changes throughout the years. But it seems the one thing that has served to keep me rooted so to speak is my years at Sandy Hook School. There were many times when I would have colleagues ask me how I could possibly stand teaching in the same community where I lived. It must be such a nuisance to have my private life scrutinized to the same extent as my professional life.

Nothing could be further from the truth.

I loved having past and present students and their parents greet me in stores, restaurants and just about anywhere else I went. The friendliness and affection shown to me was a constant source of comfort.

Make no mistake. I had my share of distractors but they were in the minority and not nearly as troublesome as you might think.

I have been retired for 9 years and while I have found plenty to do, not the least of which is frequently baby sitting for 4 grand children, I still find myself thinking of my days at Sandy Hook School — especially now.

I have many wonderful memories but one in particular involves the parent conferences we used to have twice a year. The rule was that one of those conferences had to be an evening conference to accommodate the schedules of working parents. On numerous occasions parents would use that opportunity to invite me to their houses for dinner after which we would discuss their child's progress. I don't know of many other places where something like that would happen. It served to cement relations and show the students that their education was a cooperative effort because we cared about them.

There are so many other things — the folly Green Giant fair, dozens of school bus field trips, push cart wars day, the parade of States, plays, concerts, on and on and of course the most important thing of all — the kids — many of whom have reached out to me on Facebook. It's a source of great satisfaction to see how well so many of them are doing.

There's a great deal more but I'll spare you further nostalgia. Suffice it to say these past several months have been painful beyond words — for the entire town — not just me. But at least I have all of those great memories to draw on.

And now a word about the future, my older grandson will be starting kindergarten at Sandy Hook School this year. I have already reached out to them as a volunteer so I can continue to look forward to many more good memories.

I think that's the key to getting through this good life. Dwell on the good stuff and keep moving. Simple, right? well, maybe not so simple but it's the only way. I hope you enjoyed this trip down memory lane.

Regards
George Stockwell

August 2013

Dear Reader,

Ah, Newtown! Forty six years of memories all beginning in September of 1967. It's hard to imagine that I've spent two thirds of my life here. On top of that I spent 32 of those years working in the very community where I live. That began in September of 1973 at Sandy Hook School were I served as a 4th and 5th grade teacher, a lead teacher for three years and finally as the school's math/science specialist for 4 years until my retirement in 2004.

My wife and I raised two children in this town and eventually my wife established an accounting firm with her partner here. So our ties to Newtown are quite strong and certainly well established.

I have seen many changes throughout the years. But it seems the one thing that has served to keep me rooted so to speak is my years at Sandy Hook School. There were many times when I would have colleagues ask me how I could possibly stand teaching in the same community where I lived. It must be such a nuisance to have my private life scrutinized to the same extent as my professional life.

Nothing could be further from the truth. I loved having past and present students and their parents greet me in stores, restaurants and just about anywhere else I went. The friendliness and affection shown to me was a constant source of comfort.

Make no mistake. I had my share of distractors but they were in the minority and not nearly as troublesome as you might think.

I have been retired for 9 years and while I have found plenty to do, not the least of which is frequently baby sitting for 4 grand children, I still find myself thinking of my days at Sandy Hook School—especially now.

I have many wonderful memories but one in particular involves the parent conferences we used to have twice a year. The rule was that one of those conferences had to be an evening conference to accommodate the schedules of working parents. On numerous occasions parents would use that opportunity to invite me to their houses for dinner after which we would discuss their child's progress. I don't know of many other places where something like that would happen. It served to cement relations and show the students that their education was a cooperative effort because we cared about them.

There are so many other things—the Jolly Green Giant fair, dozens of school bus field trips, Push Cart Wars Day, the Parade of States, plays, concerts, on and on and of course the most important thing of all—the kids—many of whom have reached out to me on Facebook. It's a source of great satisfaction to see how well so many of them are doing.

There's a great deal more but I'll spare you further nostalgia. Suffice it to say these past several months have been painful beyond words—for the entire town—not just me. But at least I have all those great memories to draw on.

And now a word about the future, my older grandson will be starting kindergarten at Sandy Hook School this year. I have already reached out to them as a volunteer so I can continue to look forward to many more good memories.

I think that's the key to getting through this good life. Dwell on the good stuff and keep moving. Simple, right? Well, maybe not so simple but it's the only way. I hope you enjoyed this trip down memory lane.

Regards,
George Stockwell

Alissa Silber

I am Sandy Hook, I Choose Love

I moved to Sandy Hook, Connecticut when I was just three years old. This town is where I grew up and where I continue to grow; this is my home. Having said that, I remember Sandy Hook Elementary differently than the world knows it today. I am one of the few who knows what it was like to be a part of this community before, during and after the tragedy of December 14, 2012.

To those unfamiliar with Sandy Hook beyond the tragedy, I want you to know we are so much more than that day. As a member of Sandy Hook, I can say confidently that we are a town comprised of strong, compassionate people; people that genuinely care for one another. This is a community that even if you do not know everyone by name, you treat them with the same kindness you would your family. I can tell you with confidence that it is a place parents purposefully chose to raise their children. We are a town known for our academic achievements; in fact Sandy Hook

Elementary School is recognized as a Connecticut Vanguard School, an award which recognizes high student performance and academic excellence.

When I attended Sandy Hook Elementary School in the late 90's it was a safe haven. I knew every day I walked through those hallways it was going to be a good day; a day filled with teachers who cared about each and every one of their students, a day filled giggling with friends, and a day filled with the anticipation of recess. It was not just the teachers that cared, but every faculty member, including the school nurse who would warmly welcome you even if you just needed a nap. I remember some of my favorite days at Sandy Hook Elementary School being the Jolly Green Giant fairs, Jump Rope 4 Heart, the Scholastic book fairs and the Halloween parade where everyone dressed up and marched around the courtyard. I also remember being in first grade writing in my marble notebook and telling my teacher, Mrs. Richo, that I was going to be a writer when I grew up. Currently, I am attending college pursuing my dream with a degree in professional Writing. I believe because of Sandy Hook Elementary School I am who I am today.

My memories of that happy time are now tainted. When that murderer went into my elementary school and took those 26 lives, he took more than anyone can ever fathom. He took children's futures, family's loved ones and a town's innocence. That tragedy also took my ability to look back on my childhood there without crying.

Now, I fight back tears every time I even drive down my own street. As I reach the stop sign at the end of my road, I feel the overwhelming "thank God" feeling when I look to the house on the left, where the surviving first grade girl I babysit for lives. Then I feel overcome with grief and despair as I look to the house on the right, where we lost an amazing first grade boy.

My heart aches when I pass by what were once average landmarks in town. When I reach the stop light in Sandy Hook center, my eyes transform it to when it was covered in memorials. I think about the cold days following the tragedy when it became consumed with stuffed animals, hand written cards and people from all over the world. When I drive by our police station or even just a police car, my thoughts are consumed knowing what they must have seen that day and are going through. Each time I pass by a victim's home, the memory of seeing the state trooper's vehicles in the driveway immediately comes to mind. I say a silent prayer every time I pass these homes and pray the families find peace somehow. Prayer has been a strong part of my own healing process.

I know we cannot go back and change the events that happened, but I refuse to let the memories of all these victims become more distant as time passes. Many people choose to raise their voices now on the obvious issues like gun control and mental health, but what I would like to propose is we all make sure to raise our voices to celebrate each of these innocent victim's lives.

I hope everyone will be able to take the time, even through a venue like Facebook, to learn about each of these souls lost. It is amazing what each person contributed and accomplished in their lifetimes, no matter how short their time on earth was. When you learn something wonderful about these individuals, tell someone, share who they were and do not let their memory fade.

When I think of Daniel Barden, the song "Mister Sun" comes to mind. I will never be able to hear that song without thinking of him, but along with the tears brings a smile at his sweet soul singing with his musical family.

When I think of Anna Marquez-Greene, I think of her beautiful gift of song and her great strength in her faith. Watching videos of her performing with her brother reminds me that the world has lost something very precious.

When I think of Catherine Violet Hubbard and her amazing love of all living creatures, I feel inspired by her to make a positive difference. In honor of her compassionate heart, the Animal Center is fundraising to create an animal sanctuary in Newtown in her memory. We need to foster Catherine Violet Hubbard's dreams and honor her legacy. She can no longer create new memories, but we can achieve her dreams for her.

These are just a few of the miraculous lives that will never be forgotten. In total, 26 bright futures were taken away at Sandy Hook Elementary School on December 14, 2012. They each had dreams for the future and loved ones who cared deeply about them. My hope is that we will not let their legacy be one of just loss, but also find ways to celebrate the good they brought to this world. Be part of Sandy Hook, choose love.

With love,

Alissa Silber

Alissa Silber

I am Sandy Hook, I Choose Love

I moved to Sandy Hook, Connecticut when I was just three years old. This town is where I grew up and where I continue to grow; this is my home. Having said that, I remember Sandy Hook Elementary School differently than the world knows it today. I am one of the few who knows what it was like to be part of this community before, during and after the tragedy of December 14, 2012.

To those unfamiliar with Sandy Hook beyond the tragedy, I want you to know we are so much more than that day. As a member of Sandy Hook, I can say confidently that we are a town comprised of strong, compassionate people; people that genuinely care for one another. This is a community that even if you do not know everyone by name, you treat them with the same kindness you would your family. I can tell you with confidence that it is a place parents purposefully choose to raise their children. We are a town known for our academic achievements; in fact Sandy Hook Elementary School is recognized as a Connecticut Vanguard School, an award which recognizes high student performance and academic excellence.

When I attended Sandy Hook Elementary School in the late 90's it was a safe haven. I knew every day I walked through those hallways it was going to be a good day; a day filled with teachers who cared about each and every one of their students, a day filled giggling with friends, and a day filled with the anticipation of recess. It was not just the teachers that cared, but every faculty member, including the school nurse who would warmly welcome you even if you just needed a nap. I remember some of my favorite days at Sandy Hook Elementary School being the Jolly Green Giant Fairs, Jump Rope 4 Heart, the Scholastic book fairs and the Halloween parade where everyone dressed up and marched around the courtyard. I also remember being in first grade writing in my marble notebook and telling my teacher, Mrs. Richo, that I was going to be a writer when I grew up. Currently, I am attending college pursuing my dream with a degree in Professional Writing. I believe because of Sandy Hook Elementary School I am who I am today.

My memories of that happy time are now tainted. When that murderer went into my elementary school and took those 26 lives, he took more than anyone can ever fathom. He took children's futures, family's loved ones and a town's innocence. That tragedy also took my ability to look back on my childhood there without crying.

Now, I fight back tears every time I even drive down my own street. As I reach the stop sign at the end of my road, I feel the overwhelming "thank God" feeling when I look to the house on the left, where the surviving first grade girl I babysit for lives. Then I feel overcome with grief and despair as I look to the house on the right, where we lost an amazing first grade boy.

My heart aches when I pass by what were once average landmarks in town. When I reach the stop light in Sandy Hook Center, my eyes transform it to when it was covered in memorials. I think about the cold days following the tragedy when it became consumed with stuffed animals, handwritten cards and people from all over the world. When I drive by our police station or even just a police car, my thoughts are consumed knowing what they must have seen that day and are going through.

Each time I pass by a victim's home, the memory of seeing the state trooper's vehicle in the driveway immediately comes to mind. I say a silent prayer every time I pass these homes and pray the families find peace somehow. Prayer has been a strong part of my own healing process.

I know we cannot go back and change the events that happened, but I refuse to let the memories of all these victims become more distant as time passes. Many people choose to raise their voices now on the obvious issues like gun control and mental health, but what I would like to propose is we all make sure to raise our voices to celebrate each of these innocent victim's lives.

I hope everyone will be able to take the time, even through a venue like Facebook, to learn about each of these souls lost. It is amazing what each person contributed and accomplished in their lifetimes, no matter how short their time on earth was. When you learn something wonderful about these individuals, tell someone, share who they were and do not let their memory fade.

When I think of Daniel Barden, the song "Mister Sun" comes to mind. I will never be able to hear that song without thinking of him, but along with the tears brings a smile at his sweet soul singing with his musical family.

When I think of Ana Marquez-Greene, I think of her beautiful gift of song and her great strength in her faith. Watching videos of her performing with her brother reminds me that the world has lost something very precious.

When I think of Catherine Violet Hubbard and her amazing love of all living creatures, I feel inspired by her to make a positive difference. In honor of her compassionate heart, The Animal Center is fundraising to create an animal sanctuary in Newtown in her memory. We need to foster Catherine Violet Hubbard's dreams and honor her legacy. She can no longer create new memories, but we can achieve her dreams for her.

These are just a few of the miraculous lives that will never be forgotten. In total, 26 bright futures were taken away at Sandy Hook Elementary School on December 14, 2012. They each had dreams for the future and loved ones who cared deeply about them. My hope is that we will not let their legacy be one of just loss, but also find ways to celebrate the good they brought to this world. Be part of Sandy Hook, choose love.

With love,
Alissa Silber

Center of Sandy Hook, December 17, 2012

Center of Sandy Hook, September 10, 2013

The events of December 14th changed Newtown, but there is a core that remains true. Our symbolic center is the flagpole on Main Street with its breathtaking view of the American flag waving against a backdrop of blue skies flanked on two sides by churches. However, in the heart of Newtown are its children.

When the high school marching band leads the Labor Day Parade, my eyes tear up with pride. One year, when the parade was headed by another very well known band, it just wasn't the same. They were great, but they weren't our kids.

In the spring and fall Newtowners spend their weekends at one of the football, baseball or soccer fields, sitting in lawn chairs, socializing with other parents, and watching their kids play.

The place to be on Saturday afternoons in the fall is the high school Blue and Gold Field. Newtowners don't come just to watch football. They are also supporting the colorguard, band, dance team and cheer-leaders. Some years, that combined total is 25 percent of the school population. School clubs and community organizations sell goods from cookies to seat cushions.

Young children run around on the sidelines dreaming of a time when they will be football gods or drum majorette goddesses. It's a festival of community.

The high school musical always astounds me. How talented these young people are! How well they sing and dance! What fun to watch them!

Is there something in my feelings of Garrison Keibr's Lake Wobegone, where all the women are beautiful and the children above average? You bet. And that's the thing.

In the deepest sense what happened here on December 14, 2012, struck a chord in millions. Newtown is every town. People in all places embrace the future by delighting in the prosaic accomplishments of those to whom we entrust it — our children.

Jan Lee Brookes

The events of December 14th changed Newtown, but there is a core that remains true. Our symbolic center is the flagpole on Main Street with its breathtaking view of the American flag waving against a backdrop of blue skies flanked on two sides by churches. However, in the heart of Newtown are its children.

When the high school marching band leads the Labor Day Parade, my eyes tear up with pride. One year, when the parade was headed by another very well-known band, it just wasn't the same. They were great, but they weren't our kids.

In the spring and fall Newtowners spend their weekends at one of the football, baseball or soccer fields, sitting in lawn chairs, socializing with other parents, and watching their kids play.

The place to be on Saturday afternoons in the fall is the high school Blue and Gold Field. Newtowners don't come just to watch football. They are also supporting the color guard, band, dance team and cheerleaders. Some years, that combined total is 25 percent of the school population. School clubs and community organizations sell goods from cookies to seat cushions. Young children run around on the sidelines dreaming of a time when they will be football gods or drum majorette goddesses. It's a festival of community.

The high school musical always astounds me. How talented these young people are! How well they sing and dance! What fun to watch them!

Is there something in my feelings of Garrison Keilor's Lake Wobegone, where all the women are beautiful and all the children above average? You bet. And that's the thing.

In the deepest sense what happened here on December 14, 2012, struck a chord in millions. Newtown is every town. People in all places embrace the future by delighting in the prosaic accomplishments of those to whom we entrust it—our children.

Jan Lee Brookes

Blue & Gold Stadium at Newtown High School

Dear Newtown,

Thank you for becoming my forever home. While some people are lucky enough to feel at home in the town or city they grow up in, I never really did. In suburban New York where I'm from, I was fortunate to have close access to the city, lots of culture and to live in a bustling area full of interesting people, all close to the train and the banks of the Hudson River. But I was never quite at ease there. Life just moved too fast for me and I felt like a small drop of water in a big ocean.

In my early twenties, I got married and moved with my husband to a little pre-revolutionary house in western Newtown, close to where Ferris Acres is now. In our new state and the country setting, we both felt like we'd finally come home... And we still do. The stars shine brighter in Newtown, the air smells cleaner. The open spaces and historic, New England architecture just feel comfortable and right-in a way that I never knew before I came here.

There is also a sort of New England culture that seems to value privacy, and can feel a little aloof to a transplant like me. But over the twenty years I've lived in Newtown, I have built a community of extremely close friends whom I trust, and who greatly enrich my life. Since last December-when our town was impacted by terrible tragedy, that group of friends has grown larger. And my town has truly come to feel like a family. United in pain, but also pulling together.

I'm a Newtowner now. I have spent almost my entire adult life here. We moved across town to Sandy Hook 13 years ago and brought all three of our children through the elementary school. We have watched the town evolve, grow and change. I still drive by The Pleasance and recall when that lot was an ugly, abandoned gas station. Back then, there were far fewer stores and cultural offerings, no fancy sidewalks or farmer's market.

Newtown has been around for over 300 years - and I don't think it changes much in substance. We are a town populated with surprisingly smart, talented and high-achieving people of all professions and backgrounds - who generally don't try to stand out from each other. On the contrary, people seem to choose Newtown for a quiet, family-focused, simpler life. And everyone contributes in their own unique and valuable way; whether it's running a shop, volunteering in school, showing up for town meetings, writing best-sellers, serving on a board or leading theatre productions. Whatever role or level of involvement you choose to play in this community, there's a place for you here. We're Newtowners, and that's how we do it.

Miranda Savage Pacchiana

Dear Newtown,

Thank you for becoming my forever home. While some people are lucky enough to feel at home in the town or city they grow up in, I never really did. In suburban New York where I'm from, I was fortunate to have close access to the city, lots of culture and to live in a bustling area full of interesting people, all close to the train and the banks of the Hudson River. But I was never quite at ease there. Life just moved too fast for me and I felt like a small drop of water in a big ocean.

In my early twenties, I got married and moved with my husband to a little pre-revolutionary house in western Newtown, close to where Ferris Acres is now. In our new state and the country setting, we both felt like we'd finally come home . . . and we still do. The stars shine brighter in Newtown, the air smells cleaner. The open spaces and historic, New England architecture just feel comfortable and right—in a way that I never knew before I came here.

There is also a sort of New England culture that seems to value privacy, and can feel a little aloof to a transplant like me. But over the twenty years I've lived in Newtown, I have built a community of extremely close friends whom I trust, and who greatly enrich my life. Since last December—when our town was impacted by terrible tragedy, that group of friends has grown larger. And my town has truly come to feel like a family. United in pain, but also pulling together.

I'm a Newtowner now. I have spent almost my entire adult life here. We moved across town to Sandy Hook 13 years ago and brought all three of our children through the elementary school. We have watched the town evolve, grow and change. I still drive by The Pleasance and recall when that lot was an ugly, abandoned gas station. Back then, there were far fewer stores and cultural offerings, no fancy sidewalks or farmer's market.

Newtown has been around for over 300 years—and I don't think it changes much in substance. We are a town populated with surprisingly smart, talented and high-achieving people of all professions and backgrounds—who generally don't try to stand out from each other. On the contrary, people seem to choose Newtown for a quiet, family-focused, simpler life. And everyone contributes in their own unique and valuable way; whether it's running a shop, volunteering in school, showing up for town meetings, writing best-sellers, serving on a board, or leading theatre productions. Whatever role or level of involvement you choose to play in this community, there's a place for you here. We're Newtowners, and that's how we do it.

Miranda Pacchiana

The Pleasance, Main Street, Newtown

I was very fortunate to spend 36 years as a Newtown High School teacher during its years of growth from the 1970's to the new millenium. In that time, I saw first-hand the value that Newtown parents and students placed on education, and the interest parents showed in their children's progress at teacher-parent conferences.

In the early eighties, my students in the child development sequence vocalized their interest in having a preschool built into their courses. With a lot of thought and input from other districts, especially Ridgefield, I applied for and was awarded three state grants which made the Newtown Nurtury a reality, and I am proud that the program continues to serve the community today.

The tragedy that struck Sandy Hook Elementary School on 12-14 shattered my illusion that all

citizens valued the health and
welfare of students and educators,
kindergarten through high school.
I had to pull off the road to compose
myself when I heard the awful news
on CBS radio.
To think that the precious little five-
year olds my wonderful seniors and
juniors cheerfully sent off to elementary school could be mowed
down by a former Newtown High
School student shook me to the core.
I am especially in disbelief because I know from long experience
that many kinds of professional
support are available for
students who are troubled
and in need of help.
I grieve for all the families
in Sandy Hook who have lost
their children, and the many
families all over Newtown
who have to deal with
the long-term effects of this

disaster that has touched their surviving children.

I have deep respect for the families of the six brave educators who rushed to defend their students and died trying to protect them. In their ongoing grief, they must be proud indeed that their loved ones put their lives on the line for the students they cherished. I hope I would have been brave enough to do the same. Finally, I have great appreciation for all the citizens of Newtown and Monroe who rallied to make Chalk Hill School a safe place for the children of Sandy Hook, and the teachers and staff who worked tirelessly to make it look like their familiar classrooms for children and families struggling for strength after

such an unprecedented attack.
To those who say it is time to
"get over it," I say that Sandy
Hook and Newtown have been
irreparably harmed, and have
shown great courage, compassion
and dignity in how they have
dealt with this awful blow.
With the ongoing support of
countless agencies and individuals, we will recover,
but it will be a slow journey
with many baby steps along
the way, sometimes one
step forward, and two steps
back.
Let us pray for all those
leading the way, and all
of us who follow.

Most sincerely,

Mary E. Thomas
Newtown, Connecticut

I was very fortunate to spend 36 years as a Newtown High School teacher during its years of growth from the 1970s to the new millennium. In that time, I saw first-hand the value that Newtown parents and students placed on education, and the interest parents showed in their children's progress at teacher-parent conferences.

In the early eighties, my students in the child development sequence vocalized their interest in having a preschool built into their courses. With a lot of thought and input from other districts, especially Ridgefield, I applied for and was awarded three state grants which made the Newtown Nurtury a reality, and I am proud that the program continues to serve the community today.

The tragedy that struck Sandy Hook Elementary School on 12-14 shattered my illusion that all citizens valued the health and welfare of students and educators, kindergarten through high school. I had to pull off the road to compose myself when I heard the awful news on CBS radio.

To think that the precious little five-year olds my wonderful seniors and juniors cheerfully sent off to elementary school could be mowed down by a former Newtown High School student shook me to the core. I am especially in disbelief because I know from long experience that many kinds of professional support are available for students who are troubled and in need of help.

I grieve for all the families in Sandy Hook who have lost their children, and the many families all over Newtown who have to deal with the long-term effects of this disaster that has touched their surviving children.

I have deep respect for the families of the six brave educators who rushed to defend their students and died trying to protect them. In their ongoing grief, they must be proud indeed that their loved ones put their lives on the line for the students they cherished. I hope I would have been brave enough to do the same.

Finally, I have great appreciation for all the citizens of Newtown and Monroe who rallied to make Chalk Hill School a safe place for the children of Sandy Hook, and the teachers and staff who worked tirelessly to make it look like their familiar classrooms for children and families struggling for strength after such an unprecedented attack.

To those who say it is time to "get over it," I say that Sandy Hook and Newtown have been irreparably harmed, and have shown great courage, compassion and dignity in how they have dealt with this awful blow. With the ongoing support of countless agencies and individuals, we will recover, but it will be a slow journey with many baby steps along the way, sometimes one step forward, and two steps back. Let us pray for all those leading the way, and all of us who follow.

Most sincerely,
Mary E. Thomas
Newtown, Connecticut

To Whom It May Concern,

    This is the letter I wrote, unedited since it was initially sent, to the Senate Judiciary Committee on Gun Control. This letter was placed in the binders given to legislators on the committee for them to read as testimony on this issue. It was the beginning of my efforts to move forward by taking action to change legislature and the cultural mindset surrounding gun violence, and I continue the work today as I lead the Jr. Newtown Action Alliance student group. And my views have not changed since...

February 2013:

    My name is Sarah Clements, and as your constituent; as a Sandy Hook Elementary graduate of 2006; as a daughter, a sister, and a friend; as a Newtowner; and as the daughter of a Sandy Hook School teacher, I am writing to you today to ask for your support on an issue about which I feel very strongly. On December 14, twenty of my young, beautiful neighbors had their lives abruptly ended, as did six honorable women. It is still hard for me to come to grips with this. As I write, my hands still shake. I not only can't believe it, it just doesn't make sense, and I have recently become overwhelmed with a constant, lingering fear because gun violence occurs every day. Nine other children are taken from us every day due to gun violence in the US. This goes with anywhere between 30-90 adults each day, and I physically, emotionally and mentally cannot handle it any longer. That is why when I say Newtown (including me) won't back down until something is done, I say the absolute truth.

Even before what happened in my town, I was for gun reform. That doesn't mean "taking away all the guns" or dispensing of our Second Amendment rights, as extremists would like other Americans to believe. It means we want safe towns so that parents do not have to fear sending their kids to school; so that couples can go on a normal date night to the movie theater; so that eager families can go Christmas shopping in peace and excitement; so that devoted community members may worship their religion without violence; so that there is no more emotional scarring like I and all of my fellow Newtown citizens are still recuperating from. No town should ever have to go through what mine is going through, yet every day the number of towns subject to the torment increases.

One way I am healing myself is by advocating for common sense safety measures. There is so much change that must go into this, including a change in American culture. But one step that is included in this change is one in the gun culture. There is no way anyone can say that amid this plague of gun violence, nothing has to do with guns. Everything that plays into the crimes must be addressed. Common sense. Are we going to wait until we all know someone who has lost a loved one? That is unacceptable. The unfathomable act that happened in my town — that my beautiful, strong, caring, loving, tight-knit, peaceful, quiet town — will now be known for is unacceptable. It is a national disgrace and embarrassment when compared to other first-world, industrialized, "civilized" countries. So I ask that you please help to pass common sense gun laws, as it is the _least_ we can do.

On the 26th of January, I marched on Washington. I was joined by my community members, my dad, over 6,000 Americans, and 26 of my friends lost who walked with us in spirit and in love. I marched because of my mother, because of my town, and because of the numbers killed by senseless gun violence. Because these are not just numbers; they are brothers, sisters, mothers, fathers; these are thousands of good deeds, volunteer hours, Valentine's Day cards, weddings, jobs, futures, families lost. Because I will be forever changed by that day. Marching gave me hope that my country can do better. I marched because I was surrounded (literally and figuratively) by members of the government that I know and trust (I trust you to do the right thing). I also marched with thousands of friends I will never formally meet. There were people of every age (newborn to 80+), gender, religion, ethnicity, and state. I was surrounded by a small sampling of America. We are diverse — there were mothers, daughters, sons, rabbis, fathers, grandparents, neighbors, godparents, cousins, teachers, pastors, voters, people from Newtown and people from Texas and people from Alaska — and we have coalesced around a common goal. _This_ is what America looks like. _This_ is what citizenship looks like. _This_ is what democracy looks like.

I marched, but it was just my first step, and it should just be yours, too. Please... do not let my friends pass in vain. If what happened in my town is not the turning point, I do not know what will be. This cannot continue to be the disgusting and embarrassing status quo of the U.S. Please consider reinstating the assault weapon ban, banning high-capacity ammunition magazines, require background checks for all gun purchases, enforcing a 28-day (at least) waiting period, requiring mandatory gun safety training before the purchase of a gun, outlawing bullets that literally shatter in the body, and increasing productivity of the ATF, Department of Education, and gun research.

No one needs a magazine that fires 60 bullets in a few seconds. That's for the battlefield only; that is not self-defense. The man who shot up my elementary school shot each person multiple times, literally tearing them apart. They were six and seven. The school nurse's car in the second row in the parking lot was hit by a bullet that went through the door, into a seat, and ricocheted back out. That was a car meters away... imagine what that did to my friends. This is what we are left to picture and think about. My beloved role model and third grade teacher was shot three times. It was her daughter's birthday that day. She is still recovering, and she is one of the most positive and inspirational people in my life. But, still, she was shot three times and needs countless surgeries. All the teachers I know at the school are emotionally scared. Some people in town can't sleep, some can't eat, some (like many of us) cry randomly on and off, and many are not fit to work. I am telling you the worst of the worst in my town, not because it symbolizes us at all right now, but because it proves it's not "just a gun" or "just a bullet" or "just a hobby" or "just one time". It's all of this... aftermath. Please stop letting the gun lobby bully you around. They simply want to make a profit, even if that means 30,000+ deaths a year and teachers being trained to shoot a weapon (I know My mom trained to teach, not to shoot). Just remember, as American people, we did not elect the NRA for anything. We elected you to keep us safe and to do the right thing.

There is an old Native American proverb that says, "We did not inherit the Earth from our ancestors. We are borrowing it from our children." Keep this in mind because as a senior in high school, I am between childhood and adulthood. I have heard countless stories of children in my town and all over who are scared every day because their friends died from a "bad man with a gun." Their best friends passed before they were even out of elementary school. How do you tell a child his best friend Dylan, or her best friend Olivia won't be coming back next week? Hundreds of parents had to do that last month, and thousands around the country had to explain to their kids why they were crying. Then I look to the other side. The adults, who are foolishly going back and forth with the same dialogue, going nowhere. It is upsetting.

Sure, this is a glimpse into my town and my friends and our future generation. But If I told you the incredible strength, resilience, and love that was radiating from Newtown it would not be the full truth because you have to _feel_ it. Only when you experience pain that you can literally feel, that makes you double over and scream, that makes your hands shake, that makes you have anxiety attacks, can you truly experience, truly _feel_ love. It can't be described. As Martin Luther King, Jr. said, "Darkness cannot drive out darkness only light can do that. Hate cannot drive out hate. Only love can do that." Please lead with love.

Newtown can, must, and will become a symbol of hope and change, and I hope that continues. As the Sandy Hook Promise says, we want to be remembered, "not as the town filled with grief and victims, but as the place where real change began." Please let this come true. I co-created a video called "Make Your Own Sandy Hook Promise" that is on YouTube, and I urge you to watch and share it, as it sets the tone for common sense laws and humane conversations. My principal, who is one of the strongest individuals I have ever met, who lost one of his best friends Mr. Dawn Hochsprung that day, gave us a mantra on the first day back to school that we have all memorized: Our collective strength and resilience will serve as an example for the rest of the world. I have total faith that it will. So help to make that reality.

As my town continues to heal, you must help us. We are all Newtown, and each person's son or daughter is everyone's son or daughter. When we stand together, we stand a chance. Thank You.

Sincerely,
Sarah Clements
Newtown High School Class of 2014

To Whom It May Concern,

This is the letter I wrote, unedited since it was initially sent, to the Senate Judiciary Committee on Gun Control. This letter was placed in the binders given to legislators on the committee for them to read as testimony on this issue. It was the beginning of my efforts to move forward by taking action to change legislature and the cultural mindset surrounding gun violence, and I continue the work today as I lead the Jr. Newtown Action Alliance student group. And my views have not changed since . . .

February 2013:

My name is Sarah Clements, and as your constituent; as a Sandy Hook Elementary graduate of 2006; as a daughter, a sister, and a friend; as a Newtowner; and as the daughter of a Sandy Hook School teacher, I am writing to you today to ask for your support on an issue about which I feel very strongly. On December 14, twenty of my young, beautiful neighbors had their lives abruptly ended, as did 6 honorable women. It is still hard for me to come to grips with this. As I write, my hands still shake. I not only can't believe it, it just doesn't make sense, and I have recently become overwhelmed with a constant, lingering fear because gun violence occurs every day. Nine other children are taken from us every day due to gun violence in the U.S. This goes with anywhere between 30–90 adults each day, and I physically, emotionally, and mentally cannot handle it any longer. That is why when I say Newtown (including me) won't back down until something is done, I say the absolute truth.

Even before what happened in my town, I was for gun reform. That doesn't mean "taking away all the guns" or dispensing of our Second Amendment rights, as extremists would like other Americans to believe. It means we want safe towns so that parents do not have to fear sending their kids to school; so that couples can go on a normal date night to the movie theater; so that eager families can go Christmas shopping in peace and excitement; so that devoted community members may worship their religion without violence; so that there is no more emotional scarring like I and all of my fellow Newtown citizens are still recuperating from. No town should ever have to go through what mine is going through, yet every day the number of towns subject to the torment increases.

One way I am healing myself is by advocating for common sense safety measures. There is so much change that must go into this, including a change in American culture. But one step that is included in this change is one in the *gun* culture. There is no way anyone can say that amid this plague of gun violence, nothing has to do with guns. Everything that plays into the crimes must be addressed. Common sense. Are we going to wait until we all know someone who has lost a loved one? That is unacceptable. The unfathomable act that happened in my town—that my beautiful, strong, caring, loving, tight-knit, peaceful, quiet town—will now be known for is unacceptable. It is a national disgrace and embarrassment when compared to other first-world, industrialized, "civilized" countries. So I ask that you please help to pass common sense gun laws, as it is the *least* we can do.

On the 26th of January, I marched on Washington. I was joined by my community members, my dad, over 6,000 Americans, and 26 of my friends lost who walked with us in spirit and love. I marched because of my mother, because of my town, and because of the numbers killed by senseless gun violence. Because these are not just numbers; they are brothers, sisters, mothers, fathers; these are thousands of good deeds, volunteer hours, Valentine's Day cards, weddings, jobs, futures, families lost. Because I will be forever changed by that day. Marching gave me hope that my country can do better. I marched because I was surrounded (literally and figuratively) by members of the government that I know and trust. (I trust you to do the right thing.) I also marched with thousands of friends I will never formally meet. There were people of every age (newborn to 80+), gender, religion, ethnicity, and state. I was surrounded by a small sampling of America. We are diverse—there were mothers, daughters, sons, rabbis, fathers, grandparents, neighbor, godparents, cousins, teachers, pastors, voters, people from Newtown and people from Texas and people from Alaska—and we have coalesced around a common goal. *This* is what America looks like. *This* is what citizenship looks like. *This* is what democracy looks like.

I marched, but it was just my first step, and it should just be yours, too. Please . . . do not let my friends pass in vain. If what happened in my town is not the turning point, I do not know what will be. This cannot continue to be the disgusting and embarrassing status quo of the U.S. Please consider reinstating the assault weapon ban, banning high-capacity ammunition magazines, require background checks for all gun purchases, enforcing a 28 day (at least) waiting period, requiring mandatory gun safety training before the purchase of a gun, outlawing bullets that literally shatter in the body, and increasing productivity of the ATF, Department of Education, and gun research.

No one needs a magazine that fires 60 bullets in a few seconds. That is for the battlefield only; that is not self-defense. The man who shot up my elementary school shot each person multiple times, literally tearing them apart. They were 6 and 7. The school nurse's car in the second row in the parking lot was hit by a bullet that went through the door, into a seat, and ricocheted back out. That was a car meters away . . . imagine what that did to my friends. This is what we are left to picture and think about. My beloved role model and third grade teacher was shot three times. It was her daughter's birthday that day. She is still recovering, and she is one of the most positive and inspirational people in my life. But still, she was shot three times and needs countless surgeries. All the teachers I know at the school are emotionally scarred. Some people in town can't sleep, some can't eat, some (like many of us) cry randomly on and off, and many are not fit to work. I am telling you the worst of the worst in my town, not because it symbolizes us at all right now, but because it proves it's not "just a gun" or "just a bullet" or "just a hobby" or "just one time". It's all of this . . . aftermath. Please stop letting the gun lobby bully you around. They simply want to make a profit, even if that means 30,000+ deaths a year and teachers being trained to shoot a weapon (I know *MY* mom trained to teach, not to shoot). Just remember, as American people, we did not elect the NRA for anything. We elected *you* to keep us safe and to do the right thing.

There is an old Native American proverb that says, "We did not inherit the Earth from our ancestors. We are borrowing it from our children." Keep this in mind, because as a senior in high school, I am between childhood and adulthood. I have heard countless stories of children in my town and all over who are scared every day because their friends died from a "bad man with a gun". Their best friends passed before they were even out of elementary school. How do you tell a child his best friend Dylan, or her best friend Olivia won't be coming back next week? Hundreds of parents had to do that last month, and thousands around the country had to explain to their kids why they were crying. Then, I look to the other side, the adults, who are foolishly going back and forth with the same dialogue, going nowhere. It is upsetting.

Sure, this is a glimpse into my town and my friends and our future generation. But if I told you the incredible strength, resilience, and love that was radiating from Newtown it would not be the full truth because you have to *feel* it. Only when you experience pain that you can literally feel, that makes you double over and scream, that makes your hands shake, that makes you have anxiety attacks, can you truly experience, truly *feel* love. It can't be described. As Martin Luther King Jr. said, "Darkness cannot drive out darkness only light can do that. Hate cannot drive out hate. Only love can do that." Please lead with love.

Newtown can, must, and will become a symbol of hope and change, and I hope that continues. As the Sandy Hook Promise says, we want to be remembered, "not as the town filled with grief and victims, but as the place where real change began." Please let this come true. I co-created a video called "Make Your Own Sandy Hook Promise" that is on YouTube, and I urge you to watch and share it, as it sets the tone for common sense laws and humane conversations. My principal, who is one of the strongest individuals I have ever met, who lost one of his best friends Mrs. Dawn Hocksprung that day, gave us a mantra on the first day back to school that we have *all* memorized: Our collective strength and resilience will serve as an example for the rest of the world. I have total faith that it will. So help to make that reality.

As my town continues to heal, you must help us. We are all Newtown, and each person's son or daughter is *everyone's* son or daughter. When we stand together, we stand a chance. Thank you.

Sincerely,
Sarah Clements
Newtown High School Class of 2014

I have always been proud to say that I am from Sandy Hook, Since 12/14, I am even prouder.

My husband and I have lived here since 1985. It was an adjustment at first, since we were both from Bridgeport, but we got used to living in the "woods" rather quickly. I told my mother not to worry, we do have indoor plumbing.

I remember going to see fireworks at Dickinson Park, Shopping at the Red Brick General Store, driving through Fairfield Hills when it was still a hospital and taking my Kids to the Dickinson Pool. I still love going to the Labor Day Parade and the Christmas Tree Lighting. Glad those things haven't changed.

My children had the great privilege of going to Sandy Hook School. They loved going to the Jolly Green Giant Fair, Ice Cream Social and the Sock Hop at the Fireside Inn. The Washington D.C. middle school trip, the high school football games, orchestra concerts etc. memories we will never forget.

I feel blessed to live here in Sandy Hook, and that my children graduated from Newtown High School. My Son is in college and my daughter is a Newtown First Responder. Living in the woods of Sandy Hook . . . I wouldn't change it for the world.

Gloria Miles

I have always been proud to say that I am from Sandy Hook, since 12/14, I am even prouder.

My husband and I have lived here since 1985. It was an adjustment at first, since we were both from Bridgeport, but we got used to living in the "woods" rather quickly. I told my mother not to worry, we do have indoor plumbing.

I remember going to see fireworks at Dickinson Park, shopping at the Red Brick General Store, driving through Fairfield Hills when it was still a hospital and taking my kids to the Dickinson pool. I still love going to the Labor Day Parade and the Christmas Tree Lighting. Glad those things haven't changed.

My children had the great privilege of going to Sandy Hook School. They loved going to the Jolly Green Giant Fair, Ice Cream Social and the Sock Hop at the Fireside Inn. The Washington D.C. middle school trip, the high school football games, orchestra concerts etc. Memories we will never forget.

I feel blessed to live here in Sandy Hook, and that my children graduated from Newtown High School. My son is in college and my daughter is a Newtown First Responder. Living in the woods of Sandy Hook . . . I wouldn't change it for the world.

Gloria Milas

Christmas tree lit in Ram Pasture, Newtown

As I write this, I realize that I take away all anonymity simply because of my story.

I grew up in Newtown, having moved when I was in fourth grade to Sandy Hook. I was welcomed and remain best friends with the girls that my fourth grade teacher assigned to show me around the new school. Sitting in classes in Sandy Hook I used to secretly make fun of the girls who used to say they were going to be teachers because they loved kids. I did not enjoy kids. I'm the oldest of four kids. From my perspective, my parents continued to have more kids just to torture me. I was the responsible one: I helped change diapers; I helped with feedings, naps, cleaning up and reading bedtime stories. I did not want to take care kids as a job.

Little did I know that as I graduated from High school my one goal would be to get through four years of math at the collegiate level so that I could teach math at the secondary level. Everyday I spent in a classroom was the best day, and I could share my thoughts, feelings, frustrations - all with my mother who was also going to school to finish her degree, finally, in Art Education. She finished with her master's when I was a sophomore in college. We made a big deal of it. I came home from school as a surprise and my dad took her whole family - the real family - her brothers and sisters, out to dinner.

Unfortunately she waited too long, raising the four of us instead of going out to find a job, and in 2010, there were no Art jobs. Districts were moving to hire one art teacher for two elementary schools, and mom was not about to drive away from her kids to teach other kids. She stayed at Sandy Hook working as an educational assistant. She loved her job and I loved that she was in the school because we could work together. I hated being an intern, I was a peon, and everyone treated me as such. Believe it or not, people TRIED to treat my mother as an insignificant too, not knowing she had raised four great kids, and had a full degree in education. Not to worry, my mother took nothing from anyone, and spoke her mind, putting young entitled teachers in their place. She reminded them she was there for the kids, not as a personal copier, or coffee maker.

Mom loved what she did. There were days she came home so excited that she got a full sentence out of one of her students, or she found a new way to keep the child se was working with focused on the material while expelling energy at the same time. We would spend hours walking around our neighborhood sharing thoughts, laughing at the hilarious things that students could do. I could compare the high school students that I was interning with to her fourth graders.

Days after the shooting, I walked into Newtown High School to interview for a Math position. I was treating the interview as a good experience. I could not get any of my interview materials and all my clothes were a mess. My room was covered in my mother's clothing; my dad could not handle having her clothes in the room with him. I had worn all of my interview clothes for days at her wake and her funeral. I was sick as a dog; the interview was really more of a trial run then anything else. I could feel my mother on my shoulder, making me sit up straight, keep tears at bay and smile as the interviewers realized my relationship to the shooting. I could feel her hug me as I shook hands before walking out. I could not tell you what the interviewers had asked. I got back into my car telling myself things could not get any harder than the first interview; I would have time to perfect my skills as more interviews would come.

I got a call back and had an interview with the principal of Newtown High School who seemed to be more upset about my mother's death than I was. We sat and talked for an hour and a half about how I felt about how a classroom should be run, & what was most important in the teaching world. Again I could feel my mother egging me on, smiling with each thought I shared and shaking her head at the more progressive thoughts I had. She was a modern girl but some things only had one answer according to her.

I got the job. I walked into my old high school as a teacher the day after winter break. I walked into classrooms full of students that were surprised to have a new teacher. Weeks passed, we all worked together to make the classroom comfortable and productive. In March, the first birthday of one of the children killed was celebrated throughout town with ice cream, purple ribbons on road signs and on people's shirts. This was for Dylan's birthday the little boy the media connects with my mother. The ribbons angered me. There were many other children around my mom-but only Dylan, is associated with my mom- I wanted the world to know she comforted all the children found around her. One of my classes, all sporting purple asked why I had chosen not to wear a ribbon, and for the first time, I told those students, my relationship to the shooting. The class was silent but not uncomfortable. I have the same face as my mom. I look and sound like her. There is no way I can escape any public place without someone recognizing my mother's face in me so these kids knew, they just hadn't heard it from me. We had a conversation about the ribbons. Their question was about my mom and how we, as a family, would celebrate her birthday. "What color ribbon should we be looking out for?"

My mom was an artist; there was not one color that she loved more than any other. Being a child out of the sixties, she loved tie-dye. That was what we buried her in. The conversation was fast and matter of fact. We quickly moved on to Math. Months went by and I celebrated every single day with my students. The school was my safe place. There was no media fighting for gun laws. No politician asking questions. No media contacting me. I worked hard for my students every single day. I had no time to think or get lost in any kind of negativity surrounding some families. I needed to be happy, healthy and honest with my students. Students are who my mom died trying to protect. To honor her, I protected my students with study skills, homework help, organizational skills, conversations about anything they may have needed to share and laughs we all needed to have.

The last day of classes happened to be six months after the shooting. That was a hard day. Everyone was asked to wear the black Newtown Shirts. I knew I could not do that, my mom and I LOVE color. I wore my tie-dye Newtown shirt that my mom gave me for high school graduation. I went through the first couple of periods ignoring the feelings of sadness and my personal loss. I was sad about it being the last day of school. I loved each and everyone of my students, and was nervous about the start of summer, a time of less structure and more time for thinking. I got to fourth period a little down. I heard scuffling and laughing as I walked toward the classroom. I walked in and saw everyone smiling, all wearing tie-dye shirts they had made. Some were still pulling the shirts on; others were standing ready to give me hugs. They had even made me a tie-dye shirt.

It had been almost four months since we had discussed my mom and her favorite colors. And yet every single student was wearing a tie dye shirt. Honoring me, or my mom - either way I was over come with excitement.

The thoughts and time that had gone into that one period reminded me why I still love being a teacher. There had been many days I cried going into work. I never could talk to mom about the worries I had, the stress I was under or the trouble I was having. I missed the hours of talking, sharing, laughing, and planning with her. After she died I took over her role, making dinner, cleaning the house, shopping and listening. I took it all on because it made me feel closer to her, but by June I was exhausted and wanted her back. These students in their shirts made it all worth it.

Without the shooting I would never have learned how strong I could be, and how important my family really is. I learned I could function without her just fine. The tie-dye put everything into perspective. There are people everywhere ready to love unconditionally. I want everyone to know that there are at least 15 students who graduate sometime in the next four years and are the most loving, honest, kind, carefree and comforting human beings, and my love will follow each one of them forever. The t-shirt they gave me brings so much comfort I wear it whenever possible. It makes me proud to be my mother's daughter teaching math to Newtown's most amazing citizens, and the honor will forever be mine.

As I write this, I realize that I take away all anonymity simply because of my story.

I grew up in Newtown, having moved when I was in fourth grade to Sandy Hook. I was welcomed and remain best friends with the girls that my fourth grade teacher assigned to show me around the new school. Sitting in classes in Sandy Hook I used to secretly make fun of the girls who used to say they were going to be teachers because they loved kids. I did not enjoy kids. I'm the oldest of four kids. From my perspective, my parents continued to have more kids just to torture me. I was the responsible one: I helped change diapers; I helped with feedings, naps, cleaning up and reading bedtime stories. I did not want to take care of kids as a job.

Little did I know that as I graduated from high school my one goal would be to get through four years of math at the collegiate level so that I could teach math at the secondary level. Every day I spent in a classroom was the best day, and I could share my thoughts, feelings, frustrations—all with my mother who was also going to school to finish her degree, finally, in Art Education. She finished with her master's when I was a sophomore in college. We made a big deal of it. I came home from school as a surprise and my dad took her whole family—the real family—her brothers and sisters, out to dinner.

Unfortunately she waited too long, raising the four of us instead of going out to find a job, and in 2010, there were no art jobs. Districts were moving to hire one art teacher for two elementary schools, and mom was not about to drive away from her kids to teach other kids. She stayed at Sandy Hook, working as an educational assistant. She loved her job and I loved that she was in the school because we could work together. I hated being an intern, I was a peon, and everyone treated me as such. Believe it or not, people TRIED to treat my mother as an insignificant too, not knowing she had raised four great kids, and had a full degree in education. Not to worry, my mother took nothing from anyone, and spoke her mind, putting young entitled teachers in their place. She reminded them she was there for the kids, not as a personal copier, or coffee maker.

Mom loved what she did. There were days she came home so excited that she got a full sentence out of one of her students, or she found a new way to keep the child she was working with focused on the material while expelling energy at the same time. We would spend hours walking around our neighborhood sharing thoughts, laughing at the hilarious things that students could do. I could compare the high school students that I was interning with to her fourth graders.

Days after the shooting, I walked into Newtown High School to interview for a Math position. I was treating the interview as a good experience. I could not get to any of my interview materials and all my clothes were a mess. My room was covered in my mother's clothing; my dad could not handle having her clothes in the room with him. I had worn all of my interview clothes for days at her wake and her funeral. I was sick as a dog; the interview was really more of a trial run than anything else. I could feel my mother on my shoulder, making me sit up straight, keep tears at bay and smile as the interviewers realized my relationship to the shooting. I could feel her hug me as I shook hands before walking out. I could not tell you what the interviewers had asked. I got back into my car telling myself that things could not get any harder than the first interview; I would have time to perfect my skills as more interviews would come.

I got a call back and had an interview with the principal of Newtown High School who seemed to be more upset about my mother's death than I was. We sat and talked for an hour and a half about how I felt about how a classroom should be run, & what was most important in the teaching world. Again I could feel my mother egging me on, smiling with each thought I shared, and shaking her head at the more progressive thoughts I had. She was a modern girl but some things only had one answer according to her.

I got the job. I walked into my old high school as a teacher the day after winter break. I walked into classrooms full of students that were surprised to have a new teacher. Weeks passed, we all worked together to make the classroom comfortable and productive. In March, the first birthday of one of the children killed was celebrated throughout town with ice cream, purple ribbons on road signs and on people's shirts. This was for Dylan's birthday—the little boy the media connects with my mother. The ribbons angered me. There were many other children around my mom—but only Dylan is associated with my mom—I wanted the world to know she comforted all the children found around her. One of my classes, all sporting purple asked why I had chosen not to wear a ribbon, and for the first time, I told those students, my relationship to the shooting. The class was silent but not uncomfortable. I have the same face as my mom. I look and sound like her. There is no way I can escape any public place without someone recognizing my mother's face in me so these kids knew, they just hadn't heard it from me. We had a conversation about the ribbons. Their question was about my mom and how we, as a family, would celebrate her birthday—'what color ribbon should we be looking out for?'

My mom was an artist; there was not one color that she loved more than any other. Being a child out of the sixties, she loved tie-dye. That was what we buried her in. The conversation was fast and matter of fact. We quickly moved on to math. Months went by and I celebrated every single day with my students. The school was my safe place. There was no media fighting for gun laws. No politician asking questions. No media contacting me. I worked hard for my students every single day. I had no time to think or get lost in any kind of negativity surrounding some families. I needed to be happy, healthy and honest with my students. Students are who my mom died trying to protect. To honor her, I protected my students with study skills, homework help, organizational skills, conversations about anything they may have needed to share and laughs we all needed to have.

The last day of classes happened to be six months after the shooting. That was a hard day. Everyone was asked to wear the black Newtown shirts. I knew I could not do that, my mom and I LOVE color. I wore my tie-dye Newtown shirt that my mom gave me for high school graduation. I went through the first couple of periods ignoring the feelings of sadness and my personal loss. I was sad about it being the last day of school. I loved each and every one of my students, and was nervous about the start of summer, a time of less structure and more time for thinking. I got to fourth period a little down. I heard scuffling and laughing as I walked toward the classroom. I walked in and saw everyone smiling, all wearing tie-dye shirts they had made. Some were still pulling the shirts on; others were standing ready to give me hugs. They had even made me a tie-dye shirt.

It had been almost four months since we had discussed my mom and her favorite colors. And yet every single student was wearing a tie-dye shirt. Honoring me or my mom—either way I was overcome with excitement.

The thought and time that had gone into that one period reminded me why I still love being a teacher. There had been many days I cried going into work. I never could talk to mom about the worries I had, the stress I was under or the trouble I was having. I missed the hours of talking, sharing, laughing, and planning with her. After she died I took over her role, making dinner, cleaning the house, shopping and listening. I took it all on because it made me feel closer to her, but by June I was exhausted and wanted her back. These students in their shirts made it all worth it.

Without the shooting I would never have learned how strong I could be, and how important my family really is. I learned I could function without her just fine. The tie-dye put everything into perspective. There are people everywhere ready to love unconditionally. I want everyone to know that there are at least 15 students who graduate sometime in the next four years and are the most loving, honest, kind, carefree and comforting human beings, and my love will follow each one of them forever. The t-shirt they gave me brings so much comfort I wear it whenever possible. It makes me proud to be my mother's daughter teaching math to Newtown's most amazing citizens, and the honor will forever be mine.

Fall at the Newtown Youth Academy

"Neighbors"

Dear World,

This was my school.

As I found myself in the halls of Monroe's Chalk Hill School in January of 2013, helping to prepare the building's classrooms to become the new home of Sandy Hook School after the horrific events of 12/14/12, this was one of the many thoughts that I had as I moved through the building: this was my school. There were two reasons that I had such a personal reaction: not only was I born and raised in Sandy Hook and a graduate of SHS, but I was also a teacher at Chalk Hill for nine years until it was closed in 2011 for reasons that many of my colleagues and I still have difficulty understanding. (There has been quite a lot of discussion amongst us since that December day about knowing now why Chalk Hill was fated to close when it did...) Those of us who taught at Chalk Hill know that the walls of that building are filled with love and warmth, that there is something very special about that place that made it so emotionally difficult for us to leave, and that those same qualities make us so happy that it is now embracing the students and staff of Sandy Hook with the same warmth as it serves as their second home.

In the days after 12/14, Sandy Hook School became everyone's school; the world, through letters, teddy bears, flowers, and other gifts, made it known how much it cared for and supported the students and staff there. As a teacher in the neighboring town with a personal connection to SHS, those feelings were quite intense for me. All I wanted to do was help. I didn't know what to do, or how, but I had to do something. And I wasn't alone; many of my Monroe colleagues were ready to jump at any chance to help, and that fervor grew exponentially once it was decided that Chalk Hill, which had largely been sitting fallow for two years, was going to be the new home of SHS. Let's just say that our administrators knew how anxious we were to do anything that was needed to help our now literal next-door neighbors.

In January 2013, our opportunity to help had come. Monroe teachers, especially those who had worked at Chalk Hill, were asked to help prepare the building for Sandy Hook's arrival. This was our chance to directly help our neighbors - to not feel so useless in the face of such monumental tragedy. It goes without saying that we jumped at the chance to do so. Now, if you know teachers, you know that we are all about order, expectations, and organization. We like everything in just the right place, everything just so. While the unexpected and the chaotic in the classroom can be fun sometimes, obviously that was the exact opposite of what the people coming to this building were looking for. We knew that the effort of returning to school after what had happened - and in an unfamiliar building in a different town at that - would be unimaginably difficult for the students and staff, but we knew that this was exactly what we could do to help — to in some small way, restore order. To help them put things into place, at least physically, in their new classrooms.

This, of course, was part of the game plan for those running the move to Chalk Hill. When we arrived there to get to work, our job was mainly to prepare classroom bulletin boards so that they were ready for the teachers to use. It would be one less thing for them to have to prepare themselves. The first room that I worked on was going to be a first grade classroom. As I think back now on the gravity of that, it still gives me chills, but at that time there was a job to be done. And as inappropriate as it may sound, there was also a certain positive feeling that is difficult to explain. It was the feeling of not only being helpful in a tangible way, but being back in Chalk Hill, knowing it was going to be a school again and that it would be a home away from home for a group of very special people, some of whom were the children of my childhood classmates. Maybe it was a feeling of honor.

I currently teach in a school where I can look out the window and see Sandy Hook School at Chalk Hill. Many of us have snowflakes, which were shared with us by our SHS neighbors, in our classroom windows that were sent from schools and homes all over the world, just as the Sandy Hook teachers do, to show that we (and the world) are with them. When the students arrived at their new school after the winter holiday break, we were ready to stand outside and block the media from filming them, just so they could have a slightly more "normal" return to school. (Luckily it wasn't an issue that morning.) We share the same driveway. We wave to each other as we arrive in the morning and as we leave in the evening. Just like neighbors.

So, what would I like the world to know? Whether you had the opportunity to help directly like I did, or were halfway around the world sending cards, hearts, drawings, snowflakes, or letters of support, it was proof that we are all neighbors, and that we don't have to be right next door to each other to offer our words or acts of care. Being a neighbor isn't about proximity, it's about how you treat those that are within reach. The aftermath of the horrific event that took place in my hometown revealed that we are a worldwide community that is ready to help its neighbors, however far away they may be. If you acted with kindness in the name of those who were taken from us, you have made Sandy Hook your neighbor, and SHS your school. Consciously or subconsciously, we have all tried to do our small part in making sure that those teachers and students know that they are cared for, that they are supported by their neighbors near and far, and that, as a wise young lady was known to say, "Love wins."

Sincerely, Matthew Husvar

Neighbors

Dear World,

This was my school.

As I found myself in the halls of Monroe's Chalk Hill School in January 2013, helping to prepare the building's classrooms to become the new home of Sandy Hook School after the horrific events of 12/14/12, this was one of the many thoughts that I had as I moved through the building: this was my school. There were two reasons that I had such a personal reaction: not only was I born and raised in Sandy Hook and a graduate of SHS, but I was also a teacher at Chalk Hill for nine years until it was closed in 2011 for reasons that many of my colleagues and I still have difficulty understanding. (There has been quite a lot of discussion amongst us since that December day about knowing now why Chalk Hill was fated to close when it did . . .) Those of us that taught at Chalk Hill know that the walls of that building are filled with love and warmth, that there is something very special about that place that made it so emotionally difficult for us to leave, and that those same qualities make us so happy that it is now embracing the students and staff of Sandy Hook with the same warmth as it serves as their second home.

In the days after 12/14, Sandy Hook School became everyone's school; the world, through letters, teddy bears, flowers, and other gifts, made it known how much it cared for and supported the students and staff there. As a teacher in the neighboring town with a personal connection to SHS, those feelings were quite intense for me. All I wanted to do was help. I didn't know what to do, or how, but I had to do something. And I wasn't alone; many of my Monroe colleagues were ready to jump at any chance to help, and that fervor grew exponentially once it was decided that Chalk Hill, which had largely been sitting fallow for two years, was going to be the new home of SHS. Let's just say that our administrators knew how anxious we were to do anything that was needed to help our now literal next-door neighbors.

In January 2013, our opportunity to help had come. Monroe teachers, especially those who had worked at Chalk Hill, were asked to help prepare the building for Sandy Hook's arrival. This was our chance to directly help our neighbors—to not feel so useless in the face of such monumental tragedy. It goes without saying that we jumped at the chance to do so. Now, if you know teachers, you know that we are all about order, expectations and organization. We like everything in just the right place, everything just so. While the unexpected and the chaotic in the classroom can be fun sometimes, obviously that was the exact opposite of what the people coming to this building were looking for. We knew that the effort of returning to school after what had happened—and in an unfamiliar building in a different town at that—would be unimaginably difficult for the students and staff, but we knew that this was exactly what we could do to help—to in some small way, restore order. To help them put things into place, at least physically, in their new classrooms.

This, of course, was part of the game plan for those running the move to Chalk Hill. When we arrived there to get to work, our job was mainly to prepare classroom bulletin boards so that they were ready for the teachers to use. It would be one less thing for them to have to prepare themselves. The first room that I worked on was going to be a first grade classroom. As I think back now on the gravity of that, it still gives me chills, but at that time there was a job to be done. And as inappropriate as it may sound, there was also a certain positive feeling that is difficult to explain. It was the feeling of not only being helpful in a tangible way, but being back in Chalk Hill, knowing it was going to be a school again and that it would be a home away from home for a group of very special people, some of whom were the children of my childhood classmates. Maybe it was a feeling of honor.

I currently teach in a school where I can look out the window and see Sandy Hook School at Chalk Hill. Many of us have snowflakes, which were shared with us by our SHS neighbors, in our classroom windows that were sent from schools and homes all over the world, just as the Sandy Hook teachers do, to show that we (and the world) are with them. When the students arrived at their new school after the winter holiday break, we were ready to stand outside and block the media from filming them, just so they could have a slightly more "normal" return to school. (Luckily it wasn't an issue that morning.) We share the same driveway. We wave to each other as we arrive in the morning and as we leave in the evening. Just like neighbors.

So, what would I like the world to know? Whether you had the opportunity to help directly like I did, or were halfway around the world sending cards, hearts, drawings, snowflakes or letters of support, it was proof that we are all neighbors, and that we don't have to be right next door to each other to offer our words or acts of care. Being a neighbor isn't about proximity, it's about how you treat those that are within reach. The aftermath of the horrific events that took place in my hometown revealed that we are a worldwide community that is ready to help its neighbors, however far away they may be. If you acted with kindness in the name of those who were taken from us, you have made Sandy Hook your neighbor, and SHS your school. Consciously or subconsciously, we have all tried to do our small part in making sure that those teachers and students know that they are cared for, that they are supported by their neighbors near and far, and that, as a wise young lady was known to say, "Love wins."

Sincerely, Matthew Husvar

Snowflakes from all over the world

Dearest Newtown —

I can't believe what I found at the store.

I hadn't left my house for days except for funeral after funeral: dead kid, dead mom, dead kid. Cry. Rinse. Repeat.

No surprise, we soon ran out of food & my kids were starving. Nothing but olives & cranberry sauce. Cupboards empty. Nothing. Time to go shopping.

On Queen Street, in the too bright, too cheery, too clean grocery store, it happened. I wandered aimlessly in the Newtown Fog — lost, needing groceries but not hungry. Forgetful. Hurting. Can't eat. Can't sleep. Can't breathe. Still all these days and endless days later. What was wrong with me??

But still I shopped. Milk. Toilet paper. Dog food. Barely holding it together, I noticed quiet whispers of people I knew, some by name, most by face. Friends. Neighbors.

I could not bare to talk to them. It hurt my broken heart to see them. To touch them. To hear them, huddled by the Cheerios, hugging by the avocadoes. Tiny moments of kindness and love sprinkled throughout the aisles, all while Newtown shook in the continuous aftershocks of our reality.

I first saw her in the frozen food aisle, but managed to dodge & escape. She was the first friend I had seen outside of a church or funeral line, and I did not want to talk. Not one word. Not about it. Not about anything. I just wanted to get my groceries and get out of that bright, shiney store filled with consoling neighbors — back home to my family, riddled with the guilt of how lucky I was to have a family to get home to.

But she found me. Chased me down actually, ponytail bobbing, cornering me with her shopping cart. And it was right there, near the Fritos that it happened.

She touched me gently, stripping my anonymity. "Kate?? Kate. Oh Kate — how are you?" and her arms closed around me and she pulled me in.

So I told her. And we talked. And cried. And hugged. An old friend from way back when our kids — our barely adult kids were the same ages of all those kids.

Milk. Eggs. Love.

Let the healing begin.

Kate Mayer
Newtown, Connecticut
♡

Dearest Newtown,

I can't believe what I found at the store.

I hadn't left my house for days except for funeral after funeral: dead kid, dead mom, dead kid. Cry. Rinse. Repeat.

No surprise, we soon ran out of food and my kids were starving. Nothing but olives and cranberry sauce. Cupboards empty. Nothing. Time to go shopping.

On Queen Street, in the too bright, too cheery, too clean grocery store, it happened. I wandered aimlessly in the *Newtown Fog*—lost, needing groceries but not hungry. Forgetful. Hurting. Can't eat. Can't sleep. Can't breathe. Still all these days and endless days later. What was wrong with me??

But still I shopped. Milk. Toilet paper. Dog food. Barely holding it together, I noticed quiet whispers of people I knew, some by name, most by face. Friends. Neighbors.

I could not bare to talk to them. It hurt my broken heart to see them. To touch them. To hear them, huddled by the Cheerios, hugging by the avocadoes. Tiny moments of kindness and love sprinkled throughout the aisles, all while Newtown shook in the continuous aftershocks of our reality.

I first saw her in the frozen food aisle, but managed to dodge and escape. She was the first friend I had seen outside of a church or funeral line, and I did not want to talk. Not one word. Not about it. Not about anything. I just wanted to get my groceries and get out of that bright, shiny store filled with consoling neighbors—back home to my family, riddled with the guilt of how lucky I was to have a family to get home to.

But she found me. Chased me down actually, ponytail bobbing, cornering me with her shopping cart. And it was right there, near the Fritos that it happened.

She touched me gently, stripping my anonymity. *"Kate?? Kate. Oh Kate—how are you?"* and her arms closed around me and she pulled me in.

So I told her. And we talked. And cried. And hugged. An old friend from way back when our kids— our barely adult kids were the same ages of all those kids.

Milk. Eggs. Love.

Let the healing begin.

Kate Mayer
Newtown, Connecticut

Sandy Hook Memories – 89 Years

In 1916, my father and mother, Stefan and Anna Leitner Heller, settled in Sandy Hook, Connecticut. My father yearned for country life and took a job as a caretaker for Newton M. Curtis on Curtis Hill, now Riverside Road. With a handshake and a promise, my father acquired 39 acres of woodland from Mr. Curtis where he built a 5-room house for my mother, sister Stefania and me who came along on April 6, 1924. My father was a man of his word and remained working for Mr. and Mrs. Curtis for 44 years.

In those days, Sandy Hook was the farming part of Newtown and my family was very self-sufficient. We had no electricity or running water. We raised our own vegetables, cows, chickens, hogs, had apple trees and a grapevine arbor. My mother worked hard, too. She took care of me and Stefania who was handicapped and 16 years older than me.

Besides cooking, baking and canning fruits and vegetables, she worked the farm right alongside my father. My mother was a strong woman in many ways. We never had a car until I started teaching and we walked everywhere and thought nothing of it.

In 1929 at the age of 5 years, I started first grade at Sandy Hook School which was a four-room schoolhouse located on Riverside Road; today it is where the medical office is located. There was no kindergarten in those days and I walked about a mile by myself along our tree-lined, dirt road to catch my school bus at the corner of Berkshire Road. There was no such thing as a "snow day" and many winter days, I plowed through snow above my knees. From first through high school, my bus driver was Mr. Arthur Page. My first grade teacher was Miss Bridget Kane and she was the one who dubbed me "Lucy".

My family belonged to St. Rose Church and every Friday afternoon the school bus would come to Sandy Hook School and pick up the children who attended religious education and bring us to St. Rose. When I was older and attending Hawley School, we simply walked across and down Church Hill for our religious instruction during regular school hours.

In the 1930's in addition to working for the Curtis', my father was also the caretaker for James and Althea Thurber. They were living in the former Wheeler house right next door to Newton and Blanche Curtis. One of the chapters in The Thurber Carnival is entitled, "The Black Magic of Barney Haller" and is about my father who spoke with a heavy German accent. No one who knew my father was ever fooled by the change of name in Thurber's title.

From 1935 through 1941, I attended Hawley School on Church Hill Road for grades sixth through twelfth. Upon graduation from Hawley High School in 1941, I attended Danbury State Teacher's College, now Western Connecticut State University.

World War II had a tremendous impact on all our lives. By my second year of college, all the men had left to serve in the war. In order to help with the shortage of teachers, the 19 women who remained in my class gave up our summer vacation to complete our training in 3½ years. In October 1944, I finished my training and was immediately hired by Mr. Legrow to teach sixth grade at Hawley School. Those of us who began teaching before our formal graduation in 1945 were called "Cadet teachers". Having graduated from Hawley High School, Mr. Legrow knew me well and had a lot of confidence in me.

Instead of reporting to Hawley School on my first day of work in November 1944 at the age of 20 years, I welcomed my first class at the one-room school house on Huntingtown Road, across the road from the synagogue. Huntingtown School along with several other one-room schoolhouses had been re-opened to accommodate classes while the addition was being built at Hawley School. Except for the upgrade of electricity, a telephone line and a new cloak room, the Huntingtown Schoolhouse was basically unchanged from its original years. We had an outhouse, a well with a hand-pump and a pot-bellied stove for heat. For the students and me, this was a very unique and memorable time. It was a tremendous learning experience. The sixth graders in my classes became like a close knit family. Everyone cared for and looked out for each other. They learned the importance of helping, respecting and depending on one another; they learned much more than text book lessons.

One of the greatest lessons they learned was compassion for others. Wilbur Platt was a fifteen year old young man who was confined to a wheelchair and had never attended formal school before coming into my class. Wilbur was a very, very bright young man who had perfect attendance for the two years that he was in my sixth grade class. I am pretty sure that he was the first special education student in Newtown who was mainstreamed into a regular education classroom. At lunch time, the other students would open his lunch for him and get his sandwich out. I don't think Wilbur ever knew how much he contributed to the other students in his classes. They learned that not everyone is blessed with the same gifts and how important it is to help one another.

I retired from teaching over 26 years ago and this April will be 90 years old. Sandy Hook was an idyllic place to grow up, a supportive community to work in and where growing old means being surrounded by a loving family, golden friends and helpful neighbors who check in on me. I thank God each and every day for the many blessings in my life and although some of these cherished memories may be fading, they will remain in my heart forever.

With love,

Aloise "Lucy" Heller Mulvihill
September 2013

Middle Gate School 1850 (Originally Bear Hill School District 1783)

Sandy Hook Memories—89 years

In 1916, my father and mother, Stefan and Anna Leitner Heller, settled in Sandy Hook, Connecticut. My father yearned for country life and took a job as a caretaker for Newton M. Curtis on Curtis Hill—now Riverside Road. With a handshake and a promise, my father acquired 39 acres of woodlands from Mr. Curtis (on Pole Bridge Road) where he built a 5-room house for my mother, sister Stefania and me who came along on April 6, 1924. My father was a man of his word and remained working for Mr. and Mrs. Curtis for 44 years.

In those days, Sandy Hook was the farming part of Newtown and my family was very self-sufficient. We had no electricity or running water. We raised our own vegetables, cows, chickens, hogs, had apple trees and a grapevine arbor. My mother worked hard, too. She took care of me and Stefania who was handicapped and 16 years older than me.

Besides cooking, baking and canning fruits and vegetables, she worked the farm right alongside my father. My mother was a strong woman in many ways. We never had a car until I started teaching and we walked everywhere and thought nothing of it.

In 1929 at the age of 5 years, I started first grade at Sandy Hook School which was a four-room schoolhouse located on Riverside Road; today it is where the medical office is located. There was no kindergarten in those days and I walked about a mile by myself along our tree-lined, dirt road to catch my school bus at the corner of Berkshire Road. There was no such thing as a "snow day" and many winter days, I plowed through snow above my knees. From first through high school, my bus driver was Mr. Arthur Page. My first grade teacher was Miss Bridget Kane and she was the one who dubbed me "Lucy".

My family belonged to St. Rose Church and every Friday afternoon the school bus would come to Sandy Hook School and pick up the children who attended religious education and bring us to St. Rose. When I was older and attending Hawley School, we simply walked across and down Church Hill Road for our religious instruction during regular school hours.

In the 1930's in addition to working for the Curtis', my father was also the caretaker for James and Althea Thurber. They were living in the former Wheeler house right next door to Newton and Blanche Curtis. One of the chapters in *The Thurber Carnival* is entitled, "The Black Magic of Barney Haller" and is about my father who spoke with a heavy German accent. No one who knew my father was ever fooled by the change of name in Thurber's title.

From 1935 through 1941, I attended Hawley School on Church Hill Road for grades sixth through twelfth. Upon graduation from Hawley High School in 1941, I attended Danbury State Teacher's College, now Western Connecticut State University.

WWII had a tremendous impact on all our lives. By my second year of college, all the men had left to serve in the war. In order to help with the shortage of teachers, the 19 women who remained in my class gave up our summer vacation to complete our training in 3 ½ years. In October 1944, I finished my training and was immediately hired by Mr. Legrow to teach sixth grade at Hawley School. Those of us who began teaching before our formal graduation in 1945 were called "cadet teachers". Having graduated from Hawley High School, Mr. Legrow knew me well and had a lot of confidence in me.

Instead of reporting to Hawley School on my first day of work in November 1944 at the age of 20 years, I welcomed my first class at the one-room school house on Huntingtown Road—across the road from the synagogue. Huntingtown School along with several other one-room schoolhouses had been re-opened to accommodate classes while the addition was being built at Hawley School. Except for the upgrade of electricity, a telephone line and a new cloak room, the Huntingtown schoolhouse was basically unchanged from its original years. We had an outhouse, a well with a hand-pump and a pot-bellied stove for heat. For the students and me, this was a very unique and memorable time. It was a tremendous learning experience. The sixth graders in my classes became like a close knit family. Everyone cared for and looked out for each other. They learned the importance of helping, respecting and depending on one another; they learned much more than text book lessons.

One of the greatest lessons they learned was compassion for others. Wilbur Platt was a fifteen year old young man who was confined to a wheelchair and had never attended formal school before coming into my class. Wilbur was a very, very bright young man who had perfect attendance for the two years that he was in my sixth grade class. I am pretty sure that he was the first special education student in Newtown who was mainstreamed into a regular education classroom. At lunch time, the other students would open his lunch for him and get his sandwich out. I don't think Wilbur ever knew how much he contributed to the other students in his classes. They learned that not everyone is blessed with the same gifts and how important it is to help one another.

I retired from teaching over 26 years ago and this April will be 90 years old. Sandy Hook was an idyllic place to grow up, a supportive community to work in and where growing old means being surrounded by a loving family, golden friends and helpful neighbors who check-in on me. I thank God each and every day for the many blessings in my life and although some of these cherished memories may be fading, they will remain in my heart forever.

With love,
Aloise "Lucy" Heller Mulvihill
September 2013

The Color of Newtown

Newtown is the color blue.
Every shade
for every place, event, emotion.
Every single thing we feel.

It is the navy shade to the past,
and the bright turquoise glow to the future.
It is the color of the warmth and love
we wrap our children in.
And the true blue invincible bond we share
between friends and family.

Newtown is the color blue.
The color we mourn in,
and the color that turns strangers into lifelong friends.

It is the light on a bright summer day
and the midnight blue
that covers the sky at every community hayride.
It is what keeps us united, and strong.
The color of hope, and love
that is spread every single day.

Newtown is the color blue.
The color of each candle burning bright
at Relay for Life.
The color that lines our school walls
to make them feel warm.

It is calm and peaceful at times,
but strong and powerful at others.
With much depth and stretching for forever.
It's everlasting love, hope, and strength
is apparent to all.

Newtown is the color blue.
It is the color running through my veins,
for as long as I live.

The Color of Newtown

Newtown is the color blue.
Every shade
for every place, event, emotion.
Every single thing we feel.

It is the navy shade to the past,
and the bright turquoise glow to the future.
It is the color of the warmth and love
we wrap our children in.
And the true blue invincible bond we share
between friends and family.

Newtown is the color blue.
The color we mourn in,
 and the color that turns strangers into lifelong friends.

It is the light on a bright summer day
and the midnight blue
that covers the sky at every community hayride.
It is what keeps us united, and strong.
The color of hope, and love
that is spread every single day.

Newtown is the color blue.
The color of each candle burning bright
at Relay for Life.
The color that lines our school walls
to make them feel warm.

It is calm and peaceful at times,
but strong and powerful at others.
With much depth and stretching for forever.
Its everlasting love, hope, and strength
is apparent to all.

Newtown is the color blue.
It is the color running through my veins,
for as long as I live.

The Newtown I grew up in was big and green and not full of people. There were farmers, artists and factory workers. The school bus I rode on, Bud Dayton's, was for all grades and it had one seat across the whole back of the bus. I had to walk half a mile to the bus stop in the morning and back that same distance in the afternoon. There was an Italian Community Center where I played Little League and the library was a special place to visit. Many of my friends went to Catechism on Friday afternoons and other friends belonged to a Temple - not a church.

It's the people I remember, remarkable people in my mind. Coach deGroat, Paul Cullens, Sarah mannix, State Police Officer Costello, Charley Terrell, Henry Schnackenberg, Jake Jacobi, Miss Paquin, Fred and Barbara Parr, Charley Colt, Dr. Benton Egee, Archie LeForte, Ted Carling and Fred and Fran Bresson. They are all part of the fabric of my memories of Newtown.

Our Dad was on the school board and I remember when Sandy Hook School was built. I was in the first 2nd grade class, my brother was in the first kindergarten and I learned to ride my bike in the parking lot when it was first paved. It was also the place where the First Selectman, Fenn Dickinson had been killed in an accident.

Sandy Hook was known then as "the other side of the tracks." I think because that's where the factories were, along the river. Freight trains went through and never stopped until the day some of the cars derailed right in the middle of town, right near the Boy Scout Cabin for Troop 70.

Fairfield Hills was alive with people! It made sense to me then that people might get better there because they had a job and a community. As I grew older, I had many friends that worked there and some of them settled in Newtown and made it a more diverse community. It was very sad when it closed. It was always a better place for people to be than being homeless on the street.

Bob Ohlson

Just one of many buildings at Fairfield Hills, Newtown

The Newtown I grew up in was big and green and not full of people. There were farmers, artists and factory workers. The school bus I rode on, Bud Dayton's, was for all grades and it had one seat across the whole back of the bus. I had to walk half a mile to the bus stop in the morning and back that same distance in the afternoon. There was an Italian Community Center where I played Little League and the Library was a special place to visit. Many of my friends went to Catechism on Friday afternoons and other friends belonged to a Temple—not a church.

It's the people I remember, remarkable people in my mind. Coach deGroat, Paul Cullens, Sarah Mannix, State Police Officer Costello, Charley Terrell, Henry Schnackenberg, Jake Jacobi, Miss Paquin, Fred and Barbara Parr, Charley Colt, Dr. Benton Egee, Archie LeForte, Ted Carling and Fred and Fran Bresson. They are all part of the fabric of my memories of Newtown.

Our Dad was on the school board and I remember when Sandy Hook School was built. I was in the first 2nd grade class, my brother was in the first kindergarten and I learned to ride my bike in the parking lot when it was first paved. It was also the place where the First Selectman, Fenn Dickinson had been killed in an accident.

Sandy Hook was known then as "the other side of the tracks" I think because that's where the factories were, along the river. Freight trains went through and never stopped until the day some of the cars derailed right in the middle of town, right near the Boy Scout Cabin for Troop 70.

Fairfield Hills was alive with people! It made sense to me then that people might get better there because they had a job and a community. As I grew older, I had many friends that worked there and some of them settled in Newtown and made it a more diverse community. It was very sad when it closed. It was always a better place for people to be than being homeless on the street.

Bob Osborne

Newtown United Methodist Church

92 Church Hill Road
Sandy Hook, CT 06482
203-426-9998

FAX: 203-426-0865
E-mail: newtownoffice@sbcglobal.net

Rev. Mel Kawakami, Senior Pastor
Rev. Jane3 Sibley, Pastor of Visitation and Spiritual Growth
Rev. E. Sue Klein, Deacon

July 20, 2013

This July 2013 marks the beginning of my 6th year as Senior Pastor of N.U.M.C., in the heart of Sandy Hook. Coming from Simsbury Ct, my wife Dorothy and I considered ourselves blessed to move from one beautiful town to another.

While nothing could have prepared us for the events of December 14, what continues to lift our hearts are the ways in which God has held us. Parishioners trained as Stephen Ministers arrived to sit with anyone who came to pray and grieve. Others established a "safe-zone" to gather. We hosted a Red Cross station in our basement while our Pre-School and 12 Step programs functioned as normally as possible. Other volunteers came to answer phones or catalogue gifts that poured in from everywhere.

What stands out for me was the way in which our community pulled together. What was a place of pain became a spiritual place of God's hand at work.   Mel Kawakami†

July 20, 2013

This July 2013 marks the beginning of my 6th year as Senior Pastor of N.U.M.C., in the heart of Sandy Hook. Coming from Simsbury Ct, my wife Dorothy and I considered ourselves blessed to move from one beautiful town to another.

While nothing could have prepared us for the events of December 14, what continues to lift our hearts are the ways in which God has held us. Parishioners trained as Stephen Ministers arrived to sit with anyone who came to pray and grieve. Others established a "safe-zone" to gather. We hosted a Red Cross station in our basement while our pre-school and 12 Step programs functioned as normally as possible. Other volunteers came to answer phones or catalogue gifts that poured in from everywhere.

What stands out for me was the way in which our community pulled together. What was a place of pain became a spiritual place of God's hand at work.

Mel Kawakami +

Newtown United Methodist Church, Sandy Hook

Dear Newtown —

You've told me such wondrous stories during the past twenty years that I realize I've become one of the Record Keepers, an interpreter of your life.

First as a reporter for The Newtown Bee, I roamed your 62 square miles to learn your secret triumphs, your heartbreak, your humanity. From your breath, to my ears, to newsprint. So many memorable interviews... In Al Penovi I found a kindred spirit: gregarious, innovative, and at ease in his Route 34 plumbing shop surrounded by a thousand disparate things, albeit his life was filled with used toilets, hoses, and pin-up calendars; mine overflows with books, artwork, and feathers found on hikes. Hazel Spiotti, who saw the automobile supplant the horse on your country roads, set the bar for what I aspire to be at 90 — fearlessly embracing the future, shotgun at the ready, wig askew.

Then facilitating a memoir group at the library, I heard your wisdom resonate through the stories we wrote and read to each other twice a month for six years: adventures, regrets, and ... (I'm not telling). My favorite chronicle: how a curious and kind-hearted boy from Cut Bank, Montana, travelled the world before landing in Newtown to embark on his second career, one as Probate Judge Merlin Fisk.

Next as an author, I shared your tales of horse thieves and hobos, safe crackers and arsonists in The Case Files of Detective Laszlo Briscoe: True Crime in Newtown 1889-1933. In Eleanor Mayer's History of Cherry Grove Farm, I related how three generations respected, cultivated, and conserved your land.

Then, for a full decade, as an interviewer for and editor of the oral history project Newtown Remembered, I learned about fox hunting, your Great Flood of '55, the battle for access to birth control, building a synagogue, fire department, ambulance corps. I learned how Sarah Mannix trimmed her living room in the same wood molding she cut into letter-tile racks for her employer, the developer of Scrabble. How Vern Knapp trapped muskrats along the banks of your streams. And how Doris Dickinson heard her husband died in an accident while inspecting a new construction site. This was 1955, and First Selectman A. Fenn Dickinson was your first tragedy at Sandy Hook Elementary School.

Now, as a librarian, I'm archiving your pain. Choosing, reading,

sorting and packing sorrowful
expressions of sympathy sent
to you from around the world:
letters and banners, hockey pucks,
cowboy boots, quilts, and ornaments.
Oh, the glitter! Flashy flakes that
stick to everything with a
relentless determination,
like the grief that has descended
upon you.

Your great story is unfolding
and I am swept up in it.
Twenty years gone by, scores
of stories told, a million words
written. But that's not the end
of it.

I'll still be listening, Newtown,
when I'm old and my wig's
askew.

Andrea Zimmerman
July 28, 2013

Dear Newtown,

You've told me such wondrous stories during the past twenty years that I realize I've become one of the Record Keepers, an *interpreter* of your life.

First as a reporter for *The Newtown Bee,* I roamed your 62 square miles to learn your secret triumphs, your heartbreak, your humanity. From your breath, to my ears to newsprint. So many memorable interviews . . . In Al Penovi I found a kindred spirit: gregarious, innovative, and at ease in his Route 34 plumbing shop surrounded by a thousand disparate things, albeit his life was filled with used toilets, hoses, and pin-up calendars; mine overflows with books, artwork, and feathers found on hikes. Hazel Spiotti, who saw the automobile supplant the horse on your country roads, set the bar for what I aspire to be at 90—fearlessly embracing the future, shotgun at the ready, wig askew.

Then facilitating a memoir group at the library, I heard your wisdom resonate through the stories we wrote and read to each other twice a month for six years: adventures, regrets, and . . . (*I'm not telling).* My favorite chronicle: how a curious and kind-hearted boy from Cut Bank, Montana, travelled the world before landing in Newtown to embark on his second career, one as Probate Judge Merlin Fisk.

Next as an author, I shared your tales of horse thieves and hobos, safe crackers and arsonists in *The Case Files of Detective Laszlo Briscoe: True Crime in Newtown 1889–1933.* In *Eleanor Mayer's History of Cherry Grove Farm,* I related how three generations respected, cultivated, and conserved your land.

Then, for a full decade, as an interviewer for and editor of the oral history project *Newtown Remembered,* I learned about fox hunting, your Great Flood of '55, the battle for access to birth control, building a synagogue, fire department, ambulance corps. I learned how Sarah Mannix trimmed her living room in the same wood molding she cut into letter-tile racks for her employer, the developer of Scrabble. How Vern Knapp trapped muskrats along the banks of your streams. And how Doris Dickinson heard her husband died in an accident while inspecting a new construction site. This was 1955, and First Selectman A. Fenn Dickinson was your first tragedy at Sandy Hook Elementary School.

Now, as a librarian, I'm archiving your pain. Choosing, reading, sorting and packing sorrowful expressions of sympathy sent to you from around the world: letters and banners, hockey pucks, cowboy boots, quilts, and ornaments. Oh, the *glitter!* Flashy flakes that stick to everything with a relentless determination, like the grief that has descended upon you.

Your great story is unfolding and I am swept up in it. Twenty years gone by, scores of stories told, a million words written. But that's not the end of it.

I'll still be listening, Newtown, when I'm old and my wig's askew.

Andrea Zimmermann
July 28, 2013

Newtown. I loved growing up in Newtown. I moved here the summer before seventh grade but I still feel like I did most of my growing up here. Some of my fondest memories about growing up are the ones where I developed some independence. Walking home from the middle school with a couple of friends or walking from my house to Edmond Town Hall & the General Store. We would just walk from place to place in the summer time. I love the friendly feeling & beautiful landscape — these are the things that come to mind when I think of home. I love the events the whole town participates in. Relay for Life up at Fairfield Hills or the Labor Day Parade all down Main Street.

There is a feeling of support & unity I can distinctly remember feeling when walking around during the Labor Day Parade with the high school field hockey team. We'd sell water and Gatorade to the people lining the streets.

I love the schools. I felt they were top notch academically but also the teachers are sincere. Every year and every teacher I can think of, I always felt they cared about me as a student and that they wanted me to be successful. I've felt completely prepared for college too. I had a solid foundation and a sense of confidence in myself and my academic potential party because of the support instilled by these teachers.

I've loved all my time in Newtown. I have made lasting friendships and feel forever bonded to this little town.

Kaitlin Woodard

Newtown Labor Day Parade, September 2013

Newtown. I loved growing up in Newtown. I moved here the summer before seventh grade but I still feel like I did most of my growing up here. Some of my fondest memories about growing up are the ones where I developed some independence. Walking home from the middle school with a couple of friends or walking from my house to Edmond Town Hall and the General Store. We would just walk from place to place in the summer time. I love the friendly feeling and beautiful landscape—these are the things that come to mind when I think of home. I love the events the whole town participates in. Relay for Life up at Fairfield Hills or the Labor Day Parade all down Main Street.

There is a feeling of support and unity I can distinctly remember feeling when walking around during the Labor Day Parade with the high school field hockey team. We'd sell water and Gatorade to the people lining the streets.

I love the schools. I felt they were top notch academically but also the teachers are sincere. Every year and every teacher I can think of, I always felt they cared about me as a student and that they wanted me to be successful. I've felt completely prepared for college too. I had a solid foundation and a sense of confidence in myself and my academic potential partly because of the support instilled by these teachers.

I've loved all my time in Newtown. I have made lasting friendships and feel forever bonded to this little town.

Kaitlin Woodard

1/10/13

I like our new school and how it's so big. I'm glad that we got to go to a school that was close not like Asputuck. I'm happy that I'm on the second floor because you get a good riew of the front of the school. But I would want to change that we're not in the portables because I liked the air conditioning. I'm glad that they're making a new playground because it didn't have one, I'm very thankful. I'm also glad that we get that huge soccer field to play on. I like how the gym floor was redone for us, I'm also thankful for that. Also the library, the music room, and the art room are all bigger. I'm glad that they made a new smart board for us. I'm happy that we still get to do our fraction fest. I'm glad that we got a new student and I'm glad that he's nice. I'm glad that our class didn't get affected in the tragedy and I wish the other classes weren't either. I hope that the familys that got affected are fine now.

I wish that it happened to a different school.

I'm thankful for what the Giants did for us and for what the NYA did and for what everybody else did. I'm glad that they put a huge ipad in the Library. I'm glad that we have all these police around and security cameas are around.

I really hope that because of what happened people are turning to God for help and God's in there hearts.

I wish that people are pushing this to the back of there heads and don't think about it.

A Sandy Hook School student

4-19-13

I'm doing Fine and I'm not having trouble sleeping. It is almost in the back of my mind but it will never leave it. I'm glad we get to comfort the 1st graders so we get what happened out of there minds. I'm happy that we're collecting canned goods for Monroe because they have done so much to us like providing us with policemen and with the school. I'm thankful for the Giants tickets and the Knicks tickets, the dinner, the circus tickets, and the mets tickets. When somebody talks about it it touches my heart and my eyes tear up a little but pretty much everything else is fine.

A Sandy Hook School student

1/10/13

I like our new school and how it's so big. I'm glad that we got to go to a school that was close not like Asputuck. I'm happy that I'm on the second floor because you get a good view of the front of the school. But I would want to change that we're not in the portables because I liked the air conditioning. I'm glad that they're making a new playground because it didn't have one. I'm very thankful. I'm also glad that we get that huge soccer field to play on. I like how the gym floor was redone for us, I'm also thankful for that. Also the library, the music room, and the art room are all bigger. I'm glad that they made a new smart board for us. I'm happy that we still get to do our fraction fest. I'm glad that we got a new student and I'm glad that he's nice. I'm glad that our class didn't get affected in the tragedy and I wish the other classes weren't either. I hope that the familys that got affected are fine now.

I wish that it happened to a different school.

I'm thankful for what the Giants did for us and for what the NYA did and for what everybody else did. I'm glad that they put a huge ipad in the library. I'm glad that we have all these police around and security camras are around.

I really hope that because of what happened people are turning to God for help and God's in there hearts.

I wish that people are pushing this to the back of there heads and don't think about it.

4-19-13

I'm doing fine and I'm not having trouble sleeping. It is almost in the back of my mind but it will never leave it. I'm glad we get to comfort the 1st graders so we get what happened out of there minds. I'm happy that we're collecting canned goods for Monroe because they have done so much to us like providing us with policemen and with the school. I'm thankful for the Giants tickets and the Knicks tickets, the dinner, the circus tickets, and the Mets tickets. When somebody talks about it it touches my heart and my eyes tear up a little but pretty much everything else is fine.

A Sandy Hook School student

Sandy Hook School

To anyone who would like to know about
a very special school in Newtown, Sandy Hook.

My very young family arrived in Newtown in
1972. I was totally captivated with the Newtown flag
pole on Main Street connecting roads of Church
Hill Road and West Street. I loved the ride down to
Sandy Hook. "The Hook as it was affectionately called.

My daughter, Jennifer, was 3 years old at the time
and I wanted to find a special school for her. There
were only three schools in town at the time. The Newtown
Congregational Co-Op Nursery School was located in the
church basement.

I fell in love with it immediately. The teacher was
my age and we became close friends. Back than most
of the mothers were older than me with their youngest
child in school not their first as was my case. The moms
referred to me as the "hippy mom" with an art background.
I loved the idea of a co-op and started to help out right
away with my artistic background. I loved exposing the
children to all types of media. At Thanksgiving we would
paint with turkey feathers and during our dinosaur unit
we would paint with dinosaur (chicken) bones. I loved
working with children so much that I started working
there.

I started as an assistant but, as the school grew,
I went back for my degree in early childhood and
became a full time teacher and then Director. I
actually never sought out the Directorship because my
passion was to be in the classroom with the children.

My Board agreed and I became the only teaching Director in Newtown/Sandy Hook. That allowed me to personally know all the children and parents. My parents were parents that wanted to be involved in their child's educational journey from the start. We loved having the children's parents in the classroom.

Their job was to help with the project, share their interests and/or talents but, most of all to enjoy being in our school. It was great to get to know the whole family not just the individual child. I have been privileged to have taught over 2,400 children during my career.

About 15 years ago a little child walked into my classroom with a flower in hand. I was soon to discover that I had taught her Father. I remembered him well but, it did make me feel just a little bit old. My husband, Rick, loved to tease me about it. It has happened many times since then and I embrace the good fortune that I was there to embrace my children's children. I was so blessed to have three of my grandchildren in our school.

Not only was that special for my school but, I find that in Newtown and Sandy Hook it is not unusual to have two or three generations living here. When parents would come in to observe our school, I would tell them that our parents have either lived her all their lives or for two weeks.

The local parents would embrace the new parents with ease. My parents got along so well with each other that when I still see them in town I find that they and their children have stayed in touch with each other. I even had children from preschool get married a few years ago and I heard through the grapevine that there were preschool pictures of them at the reception. Now that is special. I could go on and on but, in a nut shell—I have been blessed that the Newtown Flagpole beckoned my family here and that I was able to spend 40 years at a "job" that I truly loved and NEVER had a boring, uneventful day.

　　Today my Board and I packed up our special memories of our school and prepared the rooms to welcome Healing Newtown. I will have time now to pick up my paint brushes and continue to paint Newtown and Sandy Hook scenes. It has been a wonderful fun-filled 40 years.

　　Fondly,
　　Kathy Mundy

To anyone who would like to know about a very special school in Newtown, Sandy Hook,

My very young family arrived in Newtown in 1972. I was totally captivated with the Newtown flag pole on Main Street connecting roads of Church Hill Road and West Street. I loved the ride down to Sandy Hook. "The Hook" as it was affectionately called.

My daughter, Jennifer, was 3 years old at the time and I wanted to find a special school for her. There were only three schools in town at the time. The Newtown Congregational Co-op Nursery School was located in the church basement.

I fell in love with it immediately. The teacher was my age and we became close friends. Back then most of the mothers were older than me with their youngest child in school not their first as was my case. The moms referred to me as the "hippy Mom" with an art background. I loved the idea of a co-op and started to help out right away with my artistic background. I loved exposing the children to all types of media. At Thanksgiving we would paint with turkey feathers and during our dinosaur unit we would paint with dinosaur (chicken) bones. I loved working with children so much that I started working there.

I started as an assistant but, as the school grew, I went back for my degree in early childhood and became a full time teacher and then Director. I actually never sought out the Directorship because my passion was to be in the classroom with the children. My Board agreed and I became the only teaching Director in Newtown/Sandy Hook. That allowed me to personally know all the children and parents. My parents were parents that wanted to be involved in their child's educational journey from the start. We loved having the children's parents in the classroom.

Their job was to help with the project, share their interests and/or talents but, most of all to enjoy being in our school. It was great to get to know the whole family not just the individual child. I have been privileged to have taught over 2,400 children during my career.

About 15 years ago a little child walked into my classroom with a flower in hand. I was soon to discover that I had taught her Father. I remembered him well but, it did make me feel just a little bit old. My husband, Rich, loved to tease me about it. It has happened many times since then and I embrace the good fortune that I was there to embrace my children's children. I was so blessed to have three of my grandchildren in our school.

Not only was that special for my school but, I find that in Newtown and Sandy Hook it is not unusual to have two or three generations living here. When parents would come in to observe our school, I would tell them that our parents have either lived here all their lives or for two weeks. The local parents would embrace the new parents with ease. My parents got along so well with each other that when I still see them in town I find that they and their children have stayed in touch with each other. I even had children from preschool get married a few years ago and I heard through the grapevine that there were preschool pictures of them at the reception. Now that is special. I could go on and on but, in a nut shell—I have been blessed that the Newtown Flagpole beckoned my family here and that I was able to spend 40 years at a "job" that I truly loved and NEVER had a boring, uneventful day.

Today my Board and I packed up our special memories of our school and prepared the rooms to welcome Healing Newtown. I will have time now to pick up my paint brushes and continue to paint Newtown and Sandy Hook scenes. It has been a wonderful fun-filled 40 years.

Fondly,
Kathy Murdy

Newtown Congregation Church

KEVIN'S COMMUNITY CENTER
Free Medical Clinic

153 South Main Street • Newtown, CT 06470 • **203.426.0496** • *www.kevinscommunitycenter.org*

"One Month Later: A bereaved father's perspective".

First off, I want to extend my deepest sympathy to our bereaved families, teachers and first responders. Their lives were forever changed in an instant.

I know first hand that the death of a child is the greatest cross a parent could be asked to bear; and I know that many of us at this time are staggering under its weight.

I know how much we all want to close our eyes and wish away this horror, but for many of us now, willingly or unwillingly, we are participants in our personal Calvary.

As I reflect back on my personal experience when Kevin passed away in 2002, and for the first few weeks after his death, the shock and disbelief that his physical loss was permanent numbed me enough to allow me to keep moving on to the next thing to be done, as if I were an actor in some one' else's drama. When anguish and grief set in, weeks after his passing, I could do very little to ease the pain.

The pain was relentless and terrible, followed me everywhere; there was no place or time or circumstance to help me forget what happened, not even for one minute. Everything around me was the same, but nothing is the same. Without thinking, I started to evaluate events, people and circumstances in relationship to the day Kevin died

But I had my family to support and nurture, and I also
needed to allow myself to live a meaningful life and
honor Kevin's memory.

With the outpouring of support from friends and the help
of many Newtown residents, Kevin's Community Center
Free Clinic was born on August 7, 2003 — exactly one
year after Kevin's death. Kevin's Community Center, in
some ways, allowed me to continue to feel my son's
presence in my life in a tangible way, and gave me
the privilege of providing medical care to those less
fortunate and uninsured area residents.

I know that most Newtown residents are eager to extend
a helping hand to the bereaved families and parents, teachers
and first responders, and I know that many charities
and local organizations are doing tremendous work to take
part in the healing process, but I ask and plead with all
those intimately affected by the 12/14 tragedy to please
accept the help and seek it, and to not turn away from it.
We are all in this together, and it gives us a great sense
of purpose and community to provide it.

To that end, I would like to offer a few tips on how we
can coordinate this effort and provide long term support to
the families, teachers and first responders:

1. It is best that we build on our own resources, allowing us
   to take ownership of the problem and guide it.

KEVIN'S COMMUNITY CENTER
Free Medical Clinic

153 South Main Street • Newtown, CT 06470 • **203.426.0496** • *www.kevinscommunitycenter.org*

2. We need to stress long-term disbursement of funds, and avoid excessive spending early on since some families may not be ready for help at this early stage. Only about 10% of people needing help actually seek it, making excessive early spending unnecessary and of little benefit to those that need it the most.

3. Long-term help and support is what counts, and we need to be there for our friends and neighbors for years to come.

4. When what is private and sacred becomes so public, it prevents some bereaved families from getting and seeking the help they need.

Finally, and at the end of the day, we want to be able to look back and say we made good use of all the goodwill and resources that were made available to us, that this may in small ways help most of those that were intimately affected by this tragedy.

Z. Michael Toweh, MD
Founder/Medical Director
Kevin's Community Ctr
Free Clinic

"One Month Later: A bereaved father's perspective".

First off, I want to extend my deepest sympathy to our bereaved families, teachers and first responders. Their lives were forever changed in an instant. I know first hand that the death of a child is the greatest cross a parent could be asked to bear; and I know that many of us at this time are staggering under its weight. I know how much we all want to close our eyes and wish away this horror, but for many of us now, willingly or unwillingly, we are participants in our personal Calvary.

As I reflect back on my personal experience when Kevin passed away in 2002, and for the first few weeks after his death, the shock and disbelief that his physical loss was permanent numbed me enough to allow me to keep moving on to the next thing to be done, as if I were an actor in someone else's drama. When anguish and grief set in, weeks after his passing, I could do very little to ease the pain. The pain was relentless and terrible, followed me everywhere; there was no place or time or circumstance to help me forget what happened, not even for one minute. Everything around me was the same, but nothing is the same. Without thinking, I started to evaluate events, people and circumstances in relationship to the day Kevin died. But I had my family to support and nurture, and I also needed to allow myself to live a meaningful life and honor Kevin's memory. With the outpouring of support from friends and the help of many Newtown residents, Kevin's Community Center Free Clinic was born on August 07, 2003—exactly one year after Kevin's death. Kevin's Community Center, in some ways, allowed me to continue to feel my son's presence in my life in a tangible way, and gave me the privilege of providing medical care to those less fortunate and uninsured area residents.

I know that most Newtown residents are eager to extend a helping hand to the bereaved families and parents, teachers and first responders, and I know that many charities and local organizations are doing tremendous work to take part in the healing process, but I ask and plead with all those intimately affected by the 12/14 Tragedy to please accept the help and seek it, and to not turn away from it. We are all in this together, and it gives us a great sense of purpose and community to provide it. To that end, I would like to offer a few tips on how we can coordinate this effort and provide long term support to the families, teachers and first responders:

1. It is best that we build on our own resources, allowing us to take ownership of the problem and guide it.
2. We need to stress long-term disbursement of funds, and avoid excessive spending early on since some families may not be ready for help at this early stage. Only about 10% of people needing help actually seek it, making excessive early spending unnecessary and of little benefit to those that need it the most.
3. Long-term help and support is what counts, and we need to be there for our friends and neighbors for years to come.
4. When what is private and sacred becomes so public, it prevents some bereaved families from getting and seeking the help they need.

Finally, and at the end of the day, we want to be able to look back and say we made good use of all the goodwill and resources that were made available to us, that this may in small ways help most of those that were intimately affected by this tragedy.

Z. Michael Taweh, MD
Founder/Medical Director
Kevin's Community Center Free Clinic

They Say "Home is where the heart is", Sandy Hook / Newtown has been our home for the last 28 years, where memories have been made, dreams realized, hearts broken and tears cried. We have been happy and proud to call Sandy Hook home.

Coming to Sandy Hook from the midwest was a major change. Our realtor had taken us to Danbury, Bethel, Monroe and many surrounding towns - but there was a feeling in Newtown that this was where we should be. The town with the flagpole in the middle of the road! The view from Castle Hill, the sprawling campus of Fairfield Hills and even working farms. All this and only a hour from New York and two from Boston.

Driving up the driveway to Sandy Hook School where she said our son would be attending Kindergarten, we pass the welcoming foot prints of the Green Giant! (Our eldest son did not attend Sandy Hook, but Hawley, which was a wonderful experience under the direction of Doris Bushaw.)

Redistricting brought our youngest son to Sandy Hook for two years, which was a great experience, but Hawley was still the best in our family!

How does one begin to talk about a town that is like no other?

Where we didn't have family in the northeast, but our friends became the family we chose. They invited us into their lives to share holidays, birthdays and celebrations. Sharing to loss of spouses, parents, friends and yes, even the heart breaking loss of some of our children long before their time should be.

Where you went to the ice cream shop to treat the team after a baseball game and knew everyone there and of course you probably had your picture on the wall. And you went to Andrea's Bakery for the best donuts in town and took your kids to my Place for a hamburger and a milk shake and to Boyd's Toy Store when your kids needed a gift for a birthday party. We still have 100 Church Hill and now we have the Toy Chest.

Where everyone has marched in the Labor Day Parade at least once! And Ascro's haunted yard went from a small yard to a town wide, highly anticipated event for kids of all ages.

Where the town pulled together to purchase a playground for Dickerson Park with pennies, pennies and more pennies.

Where children can ride bikes to the neighbors and also have to be driven 30 minutes across town to play with a friend. Where you can walk down the street for a chat with a friend and know there is always someone to listen.

Where we have made friends and sadly buried friends.

Yes Sandy Hook/Newtown is home, Sandy Hook/Newtown is love!

They say "Home is where the heart is", Sandy Hook/Newtown has been our home for the last 28 years, where memories have been made, dreams realized, hearts broken and tears cried. We have been happy and proud to call Sandy Hook home.

Coming to Sandy Hook from the Midwest was a major change. Our realtor had taken us to Danbury, Bethel, Monroe and many surrounding towns—but there was a feeling in Newtown that this was where we should be. The town with the flagpole in the middle of the road! The view from Castle Hill, the sprawling campus of Fairfield Hills and even working farms, all this and only an hour from New York and two from Boston.

Driving up the driveway to Sandy Hook School, where she said our son would be attending kindergarten, we had the welcoming foot prints of the Green Giant! (Our eldest son did not attend Sandy Hook, but Hawley, which was a wonderful experience under the direction of Doris Bushaw.) Redistricting brought our youngest son to Sandy Hook for two years, which was a great experience, but Hawley was still the best in our family!

How does one begin to talk about a Town that is like no other?

Where we didn't have family in the northeast, but our friends became the family we choose. They invited us into their lives to share holidays, birthdays and celebrations. Sharing the loss of spouses, parents, friends and yes, even the heart breaking loss of some of our children long before their time should be.

Where you went to the Ice Cream Shop to treat the team after a baseball game and knew everyone there and of course you probably had your picture on the wall. And you went to Andreas Bakery for the best donuts in town and took your kids to My Place for a hamburger and a milk shake and to Boyds toy store when your kids needed a gift for a birthday party. We still have 100 Church Hill and now we have the Toy Chest.

Where everyone has marched in the Labor Day parade at least once! And Socko's Haunted Yard went from a small yard to a town wide highly anticipated event for kids of all ages.

Where the town pulled together to purchase a playground for Dickinson Park with pennies, pennies, and more pennies.

Where children can ride bikes to the neighbors and also have to be driven 30 minutes across town to play with a friend. Where you can walk down the street for a chat with a friend and know there is always someone to listen.

Where we have made friends and sadly buried friends.

Yes, Sandy Hook/ Newtown is home, Sandy Hook/Newtown is love!

Playground at Dickinson Park in Newtown

Snow in Sandy Hook

The Inn at Newtown

Fall view from Castle Hill of Newtown

Dickinson Park leapfrog statues

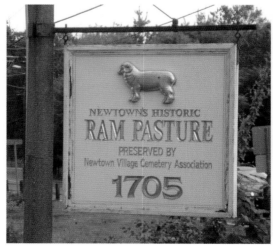

Ram Pasture sign

Newtown Cemetery

The Pleasance

Snow scene in Sandy Hook

Inside the movie theater

Dickinson Park sign

Edmond Town Hall

Castle Hill Farm

The nation's flag at the Labor Day Parade 2013

C.H. Booth Library

C.H. Booth Library Genealogy Room

Walnut Tree Village

Newtown Flag on Main Street

Ducks ready for the Great Duck Race

Ram Pasture

Bridge behind Sabrina Style

Let me introduce myself. I am Maureen Crick Owen. I am 11th generation in Newtown on my Mother's side. My Mother is Joan Glover Crick. My father was James W. Crick, Jr. I was raised in a red house on Glover Avenue. In fact my mother still lives in the same house where my two brothers and I grew up.

What is my legacy? It goes very far back. But I'll start when I was growing up on Glover Avenue. You see Glover Avenue — the entire street — was land that at one time was owned by my great-great grandfather William H. Glover, then by my great grandfather William B. Glover. I went to Hawley School. My grandfather Walter L. Glover was the Chairman of the Building Committee for Hawley School. I went to the Newtown Middle School. My grandfather was the Town Supervisor for the building of the Newtown High School now the Newtown Middle School. My great grandfather and grand father were involved in many other ways in Newtown.

My Mother is on the Borough Board of

-1-

Burgesses and has been for 33 years. 20 of those years were as Borough Warden. For 42 years my father worked at the Newtown Post Office. Everyone knew Jim Crick. He was also on the Borough's Zoning Board of Appeals and a trustee of Newtown Savings Bank. While those positions were very important to him his biggest passion was Newtown Village Cemetery. He was on the board for many years and loved caring for Ram Pasture and made sure the Cemetery was in pristine condition. He is buried there along with my nephew, my grandparents (Crick and Glover) and many other family members.

After moving out of my parents' house on Glover Avenue I lived in the surrounding communities. Then I had the brainstorm that I wanted to move to Hilton Head Island, South Carolina (one of my brothers live there). It wasn't such a great brainstorm! I did not like it and decided to move back to Connecticut. But more importantly is that I wanted to move back to Newtown. Why you ask? I don't know. It was just what I wanted to do.

-2-

Moving back was the start of it. I was following in my parents' and ancestors' first steps. It's a thread I have. I am the clerk to the Borough's zoning commission and zoning Board of appeals. I am a member of the Newtown Parks and recreation commission. While these are important, just like my father my biggest passion is Newtown Village Cemetery. I have been a board member since the late 1990's and president for about the past eight years. And yes it was my father that got me involved in the cemetery. It's hard to describe why this too is my passion... there's that thread again.

Who would have imagined that this picturesque, New England town would be deep within the veins of the Glover/Crick families for so many generations. I don't know exactly what the pull is. It may be a sense of tradition and heritage. Or it may be that Newtown has somehow become part of me, my blood and my life. I just know Newtown is home to me and where I belong. And, now to go full circle, I hope to live

-3-

on Glover Avenue again – Land
that was owned by my great-
great grandfather and my great
grandfather. Where my grandfather
and mother grew up, and where
I grew up.

Maureen Crick Owen
08.11.2013

Let me introduce myself. I am Maureen Crick Owen. I am 11th generation in Newtown on my mother's side. My mother is Joan Glover Crick. My father was James W. Crick, Jr. I was raised in a red house on Glover Avenue. In fact my mother still lives in the same house where my two brothers and I grew up.

What is my legacy? It goes very far back. But I'll start when I was growing up on Glover Avenue. You see Glover Avenue—the entire street—was land that at one time was owned by my great-great grandfather, William H. Glover, then by my great grandfather, William B. Glover. I went to Hawley School. My grandfather, Walter L. Glover, was the chairman of the Building Committee for Hawley School. I went to the Newtown Middle School. My grandfather was the Town Supervisor for the building of the Newtown High School now the Newtown Middle School My great grandfather and grandfather were involved in many other ways in Newtown.

My mother is on the Borough Board of Burgesses and has been for 33 years, 20 of those years were as Borough Warden. For 42 years, my father worked at the Newtown Post Office. Everyone knew Jim Crick. He was also on the Borough's Zoning Board of Appeals and a trustee of Newtown Savings Bank. While those positions were very important to him, his biggest passion was Newtown Village Cemetery. He was on the board for many years and loved caring for Ram Pasture and made sure the cemetery was in pristine condition. He is buried there along with my nephew, my grandparents (Crick and Glover) and many other family members.

After moving out of my parents' house on Glover Avenue, I lived in the surrounding communities. Then I had the brain storm that I wanted to move to Hilton Head Island, South Carolina (one of my brothers live there). It wasn't such a great brain storm! I did not like it and decided to move back to Connecticut. But more importantly is that I wanted to move back to Newtown. Why you ask? I don't know. It was just what I wanted to do.

Moving back was the start of it. I was following in my parents and ancestors' footsteps. It's a thread I have. I am the clerk to the Borough's Zoning Commission and Zoning Board of Appeals. I am a member of the Newtown Parks and Recreation Commission. While these are important, just like my father, my biggest passion is Newtown Village Cemetery. I have been a board member since the late 1990's and president for about the past eight years. And yes, it was my father that got me involved in the cemetery. It's hard to describe why this too is my passion . . . there's that thread again.

Who would have imagined that this picturesque New England town would be deep within the veins of the Glover/Crick families for so many generations. I don't know exactly what the pull is. It may be a sense of tradition and heritage. Or it may be that Newtown has somehow become part of me, my blood and my life. I just know Newtown is home to me and where I belong. And, now to go full circle, I hope to live on Glover Avenue again—land that was owned by my great-great grandfather and my great grandfather, where my grandfather and mother grew up, and where I grew up.

Maureen Crick Owen
08.11.2013

I never would have thought I would be writing this letter in regards to my memories of Sandy Hook School. Those memories have always been tucked in the back of my mind. They are the memories that have brought me to where I am today. Being born and raised in Sandy Hook, Connecticut, I have grown up in this wonderful community. Growing up, I always felt safe in Sandy Hook and knew I would always call and know this place as home. On December 14, 2012, I remember every moment of learning the news. Before the details came out, I immediately called my family and my best friend from Newtown. All agreed, this was unbelievable. I was attending college in Rhode Island and immediately ran home to my roommates. I was glued to the television all day with my nine other housemates by my side, consoling and crying with me. People told me to take a break from the news, but I knew I had to watch until I actually believed that such a horrific event occurred in my beautiful hometown. That same weekend I came home for winter break and as I entered Sandy Hook via Route 34, I could not breathe. What was going to happen? What is my town doing to help? How could I possibly help the grieving families and scarred teachers and students? Is my town forever changed? I still do not know the answers to those questions, but I do know that my town is forever going to be a town I am proud to say I am from and a town that is defined by hope, faith and love. Now, the only thing left for me to do is share those fond memories of a school that shaped me to be the person I am today.

During the summer, kindergarteners had a mock

first day of school and I met my bus driver, who drove me to school for the next 12 years. I met my first friends that would last for years. Once school started, I knew school was the place and the future for me. I loved exploring the different stations in the classroom like the sand table, library and house play set. I remember our Halloween parade into the courtyard in front of all the parents, singing "You are my Sunshine." I remember St. Patrick's Day where we had to search the school for the leprechauns. Lastly, in Kindergarten, I remember how my teacher and the school allowed my father dressed as a dog mascot to enter my classroom and read a story to my class. As mortified as I was, kindergarten was a great year.

Besides having one of my favorite teachers, first grade was a time to grow. I started new friendships with people who just moved to the town. My fondest memory of first grade was Valentine's Day Week. My teacher set the classroom up into eight different streets and each day we wrote letters to everyone in the class. Each day we would rotate who the mailmen were. In second grade, I still remember having a unit on sea turtles and loving every minute of discovering a world underneath the ocean water. I also remember ringing the bell of the Meeting House during our Tour of Newtown. Third grade was another year that influenced me to this day. We partnered up and each created a suitcase and brochure on a New England state. I even modified this idea to bring to my own classroom during student teaching at college.

In fourth grade, I was lucky enough to have my favorite teacher of all time who ultimately influenced me into going into the teaching field. My class was placed in the portables in our own little world and it was perfect. We put on a play about a Japanese exchange student to our fellow peers and parents. It was my first role as an actress and most likely my last, but a successful play nonetheless. Not only did

I create some of my best friendships in this fourth grade class but witnessed a great act of love. My teacher was proposed to during class and each and every student in her class were involved in the proposal. We even attended the wedding! My last year at Sandy Hook was a momentous one. We were the last class to experience a full year of fifth grade at SHS. Some students, including myself, had the privilege of signing the beam in the new Reed Intermediate School. As fifth graders, we were the role models to the younger grades and the leaders. As fifth graders, we had the esteemed privilege of calling out bus names and numbers during dismissal. The most coveted event in fifth grade was Push Cart Day. Groups of students built a pushcart and sold knick knacks to the younger grades and we had the time of our lives.

Those six years attending SHS were more than just those few memories. We had Jump Rope for Heart events Field Days and the Jolly Green Giant Fair. I learned how to ride my bike on two wheels in the soccer field and it was the meeting place for the first time I met my new puppy. Sandy Hook taught me about reading, writing, math, etc., but more importantly SHS taught me how to be a good human being. The day the tragic events occurred, the first instinct was to drive home to be with my community and my family and a wave of compassion fell over me. To those parents, families, and friends grieving over losing one of those 26 beautiful angels, you are my heroes for making it through another day. Just know that the memories live on and will never be forgotten. Those 26 will never be forgotten. Sandy Hook is full of memories and still has wonderful memories to be created. One act of evil cannot hurt such a strong community. We are still here, we are Sandy Hook Strong, and we are here to stay to share the hope, faith and love those 26 angels showed in their short, beautiful lives.

Thank you,
Danielle Norris

I never would have thought I would be writing this letter in regards to my memories of Sandy Hook School. Those memories have always been tucked in the back of my mind. They are the memories that have brought me to where I am today. Being born and raised in Sandy Hook, Connecticut, I have grown up in this wonderful community. Growing up, I always felt safe in Sandy Hook and knew I would always call and know this place as home. On December 14, 2012, I remember every moment of learning the news. Before the details came out, I immediately called my family and my best friend from Newtown. All agreed, this was unbelievable. I was attending college in Rhode Island and immediately ran home to my roommates. I was glued to the television all day with my nine other house mates by my side, consoling and crying with me. People told me to take a break from the news, but I knew I had to watch until I actually believed that such a horrific event occurred in my beautiful hometown. That same weekend I came home for winter break and as I entered Sandy Hook via Route 34, I could not breathe. What was going to happen? What is my town doing to help? How could I possibly help the grieving families and scarred teachers and students? Is my town forever changed? I still do not know the answers to those questions, but I do know that my town is forever going to be a town I am proud to say I am from and a town that is defined by hope, faith and love. Now, the only thing left for me to do is share those fond memories of a school that shaped me to be the person I am today.

During the summer, kindergarteners had a mock first day of school and I met my bus driver, who drove me to school for the next 12 years. I met my first friends that would last for years. Once school started, I knew school was the place and the future for me. I loved exploring the different stations in the classroom like the sand table, library and house play set. I remember our Halloween parade into the courtyard in front of all the parents, singing "You are my Sunshine." I remember St. Patrick's Day where we had to search the school for the leprechauns. Lastly, in kindergarten, I remember how my teacher and the school allowed my father dressed as a dog mascot to enter my classroom and read a story to my class. As mortified as I was, kindergarten was a great year.

Besides having one of my favorite teachers, first grade was a time to grow. I started new friendships with people who just moved to the town. My fondest memory of first grade was Valentine's Day Week. My teacher set the classroom up into eight different streets and each day we wrote letters to everyone in the class. Each day we would rotate who the mailmen were. In second grade, I still remember having a unit on sea turtles and loving every minute of discovering a world underneath the ocean water. I also remember ringing the bell of the Meeting House during our Tour of Newtown. Third grade was another year that influenced me to this day. We partnered up and each created a suitcase and brochure on a New England state. I even modified this idea to bring to my own classroom during student teaching at college.

In fourth grade, I was lucky enough to have my favorite teacher of all time who ultimately influenced me into going into the teaching field. My class was placed in the portables in our own little world and it was perfect. We put on a play about a Japanese exchange student to our fellow peers and parents. It was my first role as an actress and most likely my last, but a successful play nonetheless. Not only did I create some of my best friendships in this fourth grade class but witnessed a great act of love. My teacher was proposed to during class and each and every student in her class were involved in the proposal. We even attended the wedding! My last year at Sandy Hook was a momentous one.

We were the last class to experience a full year of fifth grade at SHS. Some students, including myself, had the privilege of signing the beam in the new Reed Intermediate School. As fifth graders, we were the role models to the younger grades and the leaders. As fifth graders, we had the esteemed privilege of calling out bus names and numbers during dismissal. The most coveted event in fifth grade was Push Cart Day. Groups of students built a pushcart and sold knick knacks to the younger grades and we had the time of our lives.

Those six years attending SHS were more than just those few memories. We had Jump Rope for Heart events, Field Days and the Jolly Green Giant Fair. I learned how to ride my bike on two wheels in the soccer field and it was the meeting place for the first time I met my new puppy. Sandy Hook taught me about reading, writing, math, etc., but more importantly SHS taught me how to be a good human being. The day the tragic events occurred, the first instinct was to drive home to be with my community and my family and a wave of compassion fell over me. To those parents, families, and friends grieving over losing one of those 26 beautiful angels, you are my heroes for making it through another day. Just know that the memories live on and will never be forgotten. Those 26 will never be forgotten. Sandy Hook is full of memories and still has wonderful memories to be created. One act of evil cannot hurt such a strong community. We are still here, we are Sandy Hook Strong, and we are here to stay to share the hope, faith and love those 26 angels showed in their short, beautiful lives.

Thank you,
Danielle Norris

Welcome to Sandy Hook sign on Church Hill Road in Sandy Hook Center

St. John's Episcopal Church, Sandy Hook

— My Memory of Newtown —

Newtown is not my birth town and for a while it was just the place in which my home was. My family drove many times throughout the years to the bright lights and cheery companionship of our New York roots. New York was where was where my heart was; where I belonged, until my father was diagnosed with cancer. At first I didn't tell many people. This was my father's fight and it was not my place to tell others who need not know. However; when I needed to help at home more, when my mother needed help bringing my siblings to play dates so she could be at all his chemotherapy treatments, some people found out.

My single memory that remains with me is from the day of the funeral for my father. My family sat in the front and listened to the mass and my family making speeches about how my father was such a wonderful man. Nothing stuck out to me until the mass of people were allowed to file to the front and slowly go past to the coffin. to say their respects and prayers. I barely paid attention, uncaring of others but my mother and my siblings, until I saw a collection of tiny navy blue tops and skirts. all of my father's middle school girls lacrosse team dressed in their Newtown uniforms. I had no clue that these middle school girls and their amazing parents were so kind to come and dress as if ready to play another game. By coming down in their Newtown emblazoned uniforms, they made me realize not only how much my father meant to those girls, but how much this town cared about my small family.

This small gesture of respect meant everything to me; it made me look back at the other people that filled St. Rose's Church. It made me see how many of my friends were right there, behind my family and I, never jumping up and enforming us they were there. They were all there to hold us up and to keep us strong. From that day until the present, the wonderful people of Newtown have been there.

~ Lisa

~ My Memory of Newtown ~

Newtown is not my birth town and for a while it was just the place in which my home was. My family drove many times throughout the years to the bright lights and cheery companionship of our New York roots. New York was where my heart was; where I belonged, until my father was diagnosed with cancer. At first I didn't tell many people. This was my father's fight and it was not my place to tell others who need not know. However; when I needed to help at home more, when my mother needed help bringing my siblings to play dates so she could be at all his chemotherapy treatments, some people found out.

My single memory that remains with me is from the day of the funeral for my father. My family sat in the front and listened to the mass and my family making speeches about how my father was such a wonderful man. Nothing stuck out to me until the mass of people were allowed to file to the front and slowly go past the coffin to say their respects and prayers. I barely paid attention, uncaring of others but my mother and my siblings, until I saw a collection of tiny navy blue tops and skirts. All of my father's middle school girl's lacrosse team dressed in their Newtown uniforms. I had no clue that these middle school girls and their amazing parents were so kind to come and dress as if ready to play another game. By coming down in their Newtown emblazoned uniforms, they made me realize not only how much my father meant to those girls, but how much this town cared about my small family.

This small gesture of respect meant everything to me; it made me look back at the other people that filled St. Rose's Church. It made me see how many of my friends were right there, behind my family and I, never jumping up and informing us they were there. They were all there to hold us up and to keep us strong. From that day until the present, the wonderful people of Newtown have been there.

~ Lisa

Saint Rose of Lima Church, Church Hill Road, Newtown

SANDY HOOK - THERE'S NO BETTER PLACE!!!

Sandy Hook (Newtown) has come to be the most important and memorable place that has shaped my entire life.

Way back in late 1990, my wife Amy and I began our journey to become the best possible parents that could be imagined. Our 1st born, Nicole, joined us in December of 1990. Our journey was underway. Michael, our son, joined us in November of 1993. These two little treasures brought along great responsibilities as well as many great challenges involved in the ever changing times.

It was an easy decision for us, that to achieve the best possible result, we would set our roots in an area away from the hustle and bustle of the bigger cities of Southern Fairfield / Westchester Counties. After just over a year of searching and saving, we found ourselves checking out the Newtown / Sandy Hook area. We must have looked at over 60 homes and finally, in June of 1991 we moved into OUR new home in Sandy Hook.

This turned out to be the BEST move that could EVER have happened for our young family.

Since the first time we traveled north on Route 25 into NEWTOWN we felt as if we had crossed into ANOTHER WORLD. Coming from the busy, congested area of Stamford, NEWTOWN seemed totally different. A feel for the old New England charm was noticed as you approached the town center, passing Ram Pasture and Climbing Main Street with dozens of homes from the 1700's and 1800's along both sides, and then having to navigate safely around the 100 foot tall flagpole right in the middle of the road. There's no place like Newtown.

It did not take long to learn the real challenges found here. First was getting use to the slow pace of life. When driving around town you would notice that the motoring public in this area actually have manners. At intersections it would be a fight over who could be more courteous. While in town shopping at

ANY of the local MERCHANTS (SuperMarKET, hardware, Drug STore or POST OFFICE) IT DID NOT take long to get USE to the Friendly / courteous NATure OF EveryONE. EVEN the MEN AT A local gas station helped US OUT WHEN WE ACCIDENTAlly locked our Keys iN our CAR. The only charge For their help WAS A thank you. Another EXAMPle that took NO getting USE to, the FAct that there WERE NO FAST FOOD RESTAURANTS iN town (the only ONE Closed up Shortly AFTER WE Arrived). AND iF you were interested iN the large Chain StoreS (FOOD, CloTHES, ETC.) you WOULDN't FIND them here. NoPE - you could FiND them ANyWHEre NEARby - OUTSIDE OF NEWTOWN.

All these EXAMPleS AND I have yet To mention our top Notch School System. It would be impossible to ACHIEVE our WISHES OF RAISING OUR CHilDrEN withOUT the Support AND EXPERIENCE OF these WONDErFUl AND CArING EDUCATORS. OVER the years WE WEre privileged to have Shared our Kid's EDUCATIONAl joURNEY WITH Them. OUR FIRST STOP CAME WHEN bOTH OUR KidS ATTENDED the NEWTOWN CONGREGATIONAl NURSEry School lED by MrS MURDY AND MrS. M. The KIDS SPENT Their FIRST

Two years on their educational journey forming the foundations that they would need as they moved along. Several long time friendships for both our kids and ourselves were formed in these very early days.

Our most memorable times were during their early years attending the Sandy Hook School. The bonds / friendships and memories that both we and the kids formed during these years, in many, many cases still live on today. Our school days while at SHS always started out on the happiest note, right there at our bus stop awaiting the arrival of Bus #13 - Mr. Carroll. As parents, we would always feel quite comfortable having Mr. Carroll (Phil) navigate our children to and from the SHS. Every morning and afternoon upon Bus #13's arrival, we were always greeted by Mr. Carroll's infectious personality. The kids absolutely loved the experience of riding to and from school on his bus. To this day - Mr. Carroll is often in our thoughts and quite often while around town, we pass and share both old and new stories.

During our kids school journey, the Newtown School System had a wonderful and trustworthy Owner/Operator School Transportation System. As young parents, this was a VERY, VERY important factor in allowing us to know that we always knew our Bus Drivers and were able to rest assured that our kids were in the best of hands. In our opinion, Mr. Carroll was the best that there ever could have been.

Our teachers at Sandy Hook were also second to none. A great deal of credit goes to them for helping to mold our kids into the great adults that they have become today. Looking back over the years, I truly believe that the decisions that we made way back in the begining of our journey have totally paid off and that our neighbors and friends from all around Sandy Hook and the great Town of Newtown have been some of the largest contributing factors leading to these results. Given all that occurs in the world these days, both here in Newtown/Sandy Hook and abroad, I know that I would make the same choice again without a second thought.

I'm proud to be a Sandy Hooker and to have raised our family in this great Town of Newtown – Connecticut!

Michael J. Reyen

Porco's Karate Academy

Sandy Hook—there's no better place!!!

Sandy Hook (Newtown) has come to be the most important and memorable place that has shaped my entire life.

Way back in late 1990, my wife Amy and I began our journey to become the best possible parents that could be imagined. Our 1st born, Nicole, joined us in December of 1990. Our journey was underway. Michael, our son, joined us in November of 1993. These two little treasures brought along great responsibilities as well as many great challenges involved in the ever changing times.

It was an easy decision for us, that to achieve the best possible result, we would set our roots in an area away from the hussle and bussle of the bigger cities of southern Fairfield / Westchester Counties. After just over a year of searching and saving, we found ourselves checking out the Newtown / Sandy Hook area. We must have looked at over 60 homes and finally, in June of 1991 we moved into OUR new home in Sandy Hook. This has turned out to be the best move that could ever have happened for our young family.

Since the first time we traveled north on Route 25 into Newtown we felt as if we had crossed into another world. Coming from the busy, congested area of Stamford, Newtown seemed totally different. A feel for the old New England charm was noticed as you approached the town center, passing Ram Pasture and climbing Main Street with dozens of homes from the 1700's and 1800's along both sides, and then having to navigate safely around the 100 foot tall flagpole right in the middle of the road. There's no place like Newtown.

It did not take long to learn the real challenges found here. First was getting use to the slow pace of life. When driving around town you would notice that the motoring public in this area actually have manners. At intersection's it would be a fight over who could be more courteous. While in town shopping at any of the local merchant's (supermarket, hardware, drug store or post office) it did not take long to get use to the friendly / courteous nature of everyone. Even the men at a local gas station helped us out when we accidentally locked our keys in our car. The only charge for their help was a thank you. Another example that took no getting use to, the fact that there were no fast food restaurants in town (the only one closed up shortly after we arrived). And if you were interested in the large chain store's (food, clothes, etc.) you wouldn't find them here. Nope—you could find them anywhere nearby—outside of Newtown.

All these examples and I have yet to mention our top notch school system. It would be impossible to achieve our wishes of raising our children without the support and experience of these wonderful and caring educators. Over the years we were privileged to have shared our kid's educational journey with them. Our first stop came when both our kids attended the Newtown Congregational Nursery School led by Mrs. Murdy and Mrs. M. The kids spent their first two years on their educational journey forming the foundations that they would need as they moved along. Several long time friendships for both our kids and ourselves were formed in these very early days.

Our most memorable times were during their early years attending the Sandy Hook School. The bonds / friendships and memories that both we and the kids formed during these years, in many, many cases still live on today. Our school days while at SHS always started out on the happiest note, right there at our bus stop awaiting the arrival of Bus #13—Mr. Carroll. As parent's, we would always feel quite comfortable having Mr. Carroll (Phil) navigate our children to and from the SHS. Every morning and afternoon upon Bus #13's arrival, we were always greeted by Mr. Carroll's infectious personality. The kids absolutely loved the experience of riding to and from school on his bus. To this day—Mr. Carroll is often in our thoughts and quite often while around town, we pass and share both old and new stories.

During our kid's school journey, the Newtown School System had a wonderful and trustworthy owner / operator School Transportation System. As young parent's, this was a very, very important factor in allowing us to know that we always knew our bus drivers and were able to rest assured that our kids were in the best of hands. In our opinion, Mr. Carroll was the best that there ever could have been.

Our teacher's at Sandy Hook were also second to none. A great deal of credit goes to them for helping to mold our kids into the great adult's that they have become today. Looking back over the years, I truly believe that the decisions that we made way back in the beginning of our journey have totally paid off and that our neighbors and friends from all around Sandy Hook and the great town of Newtown have been some of the largest contributing factors leading to these results. Given all that occurs in the world these days, both here in Newtown / Sandy Hook and abroad, I know that I would make the same choice again without a second thought.

I'm proud to be a Sandy Hooker and to have raised our family in this great Town of Newtown—Connecticut!

Michael J. Reyen

View from the bridge in Sandy Hook Center

Dear Friend,

I'd like to tell you a little about the amazing town
that I've grown up in. A town that I will always
love, no matter where life takes me.

Back in 1977, my family moved from Huntington
to Sandy Hook. I was 10 years old and really hated
the idea of leaving my friends behind, even though
they were only a few towns away. I couldn't understand
why my parents wanted to leave our perfect house,
with pretty floors and perfect rooms for an old one,
with big wide floor boards that you could see through
and cracks in the ceiling. Even the rooms in the
house had strange names, birthing rooms, servants' quarters,
even a carriage house. The huge brick fireplace
with the oven that looked like a beehive didn't
even impress me. All I kept asking was, Why?
The fact that my dad was an executive during the
week, but on weekends would be out with my mom
enjoying their favorite hobby together, which was
antiquing, didn't even connect to the house in my mind.

As a new student as Sandy Hook School, I was a little
nervous, but by the end of the first week, I loved it. From
the first day I was there, until the last day of 5th
grade, I was in love with that school. I loved my
teachers and loved making new friends. To many, it
was just a brick building that held kids and
teachers, but as I got older and had children
of my own attend the school, I realized the

reason I loved that building so much wasn't
represented all that was good about being a
child in Sandy Hook and enjoying everything life
had to offer. It was always filled with laughter,
joy, and fun celebrations.

Sandy Hook School had this amazing fair every
year called the "Jolly Green Giant Fair". I looked forward to
the fair every year. When the time was approaching
for the fair, I'd look out the front windows of the school
Bus at the big Green Giant footprints. I remember vividly
riding in the car to the fair with my parents, Rod
Stewart singing on the car radio as we got to the
school. The fair was held on the back playground,
which is now the courtyard. There were so many
great games and activities. So many friends
would be there and we would have such a
great time.

I have so many great memories of growing up
in Sandy Hook.

Our summers were spent playing on the farm
next to our house and teasing the one-horned
goat named Clancy. We would all play
"King of the Hill", which was a great game we all
loved. We would get Clancy so worked up, he'd
chase all of us, and we would have to run like
crazy to get to "base", which was the top ring
of the fence, before his one horn would hook us.

We'd always end up laughing like crazy when the one person who didn't run quick enough ended up being the target of that evil ham.

As soon as the sun went down, the neighborhood would gather just on the edge of the corn field to determine who would be "it," meaning the seeker and the rest of us would be the hiders. It was always fun and games running and hiding in those fields, trying to be as quiet as possible so we didn't get found.

In the winter, we had just as many entertaining things to do as we did in the summer. We always hoped for lots of cold and snow... if it was cold enough, we would play on the frozen pond across the street for hours, or at least until our fingers and toes were so numb, we could barely feel them. If we had gotten a lot of snow, we would walk up the big hill and sled down the middle of the road, not worrying about any cars because most people didn't have SUV's or 4 wheel drives. Not sure if they even made them back then. We also had some nice big hills in our backyard, but you had to be really good at steering the sled through the obstacle course of trees.

We would often take trips into the "Hook" with my mother to purchase dad's newspaper and cigarettes at a small store we referred to as "Helens."

Helens carried some of the basics, canned and boxed foods, candy, gum and ice cream. Helen was an elderly woman who sat behind the old wooden counter. She had long black and gray hair, and my brothers and I thought she was a witch in disguise. I remember her knuckles were so swollen and she would slide the change across the counter into her drawer because she couldn't pick it up. When we asked my mother what was wrong with her hands, she told us she had very bad arthritis. At that time, we had no idea what that was, but we certainly didn't want that.

I remember being at the laundromat, which was on Glen Road along the river, helping my mother do laundry. After we would put the clothes into the dryer, we would walk next door to the Red Brick General Store to pick up a few groceries and chat with the store owners.

As a teenager, we'd still stop in at Helen's, but the store next to it was much more appealing to the teens in the area. The store was called Putnam's Place and they sold an array of different things, from tie dyed wall hangings and shirts, to posters, stickers and lots of other interesting things that were in the counter by the register.

Fast forward 35 years and I'm still a "Sandy Hooker", married to a Newtowner, living in the same house I grew up in, but now raising my own two children.

Growing up in this house, I have so many memories and I have the unique opportunity to share those memories with my children. They were able to attend my elementary and middle school, and one has already graduated from NHS and the other is on her way there.

A lot has changed throughout the decades in Sandy Hook. Helens is now a toy store, the Red Brick General Store is a restaurant and the Old Laundromat by the river is a coffee shop. Where the barns and fields once were, McMansions now stand.

Even with these changes, I still feel pride and love for my community. I have always and will always be proud to be part of this small town.

On December 14, 2012, things changed within this community. Twenty Six precious lives were taken from us in the most horrific way, in a building that represented love and happiness. How could this happen? In our community? In our beloved Sandy Hook School? How could this happen at all? So many questions, many that could be asked in anger, but quickly we realized there was no time for anger, it was a wasted energy and we needed as much positive energy as we could muster.

We needed an energy that would help this community pull even closer and _____ we could to help the grieving families and our fellow neighbors... it was LOVE. Love came pouring into our ~~too~~ community from all over the world. People brought it with them, they mailed it, they wrote it in letters and poems, they left it as a token, they built memorials with it, they hugged us with it and their tears were filled with it and all these months later, the sadness still weigh heavily on our hearts, but we know we are not alone.

So begins the story of Hearts of Hope. On February 2013, after one of the worst snowstorms of the season, volunteers came from New York and New Jersey to pay our community a surprise visit, leaving behind thousands of beautiful, hand painted hearts hanging throughout town for residents to find. These hearts, hung against the backdrop of white snow, were beautiful, hanging on branches, signs, fence posts and telephone poles. They brought brightness into a community that was still struggling with the horrific event ~~from two months prior~~. Each heart came with a card that contained information about the painter, including a note of comfort. Mine was painted by a 1st grader from New Jersey and when I saw it, I thought, wow, here's more love and it's from a 6 year old child!

After the Boston tragedy, letters and calls went out to Hearts of Hope's main office and it was decided that hearts would be created here to send to Boston. Events were set up throughout the town, in people's homes, senior center and a local church. From there over 1600 hearts were hand delivered by volunteers, including two families from Sandy Hook. So many residents enjoyed creating these hearts and paying it forward that a few of us decided to see if we could do something on a more permanent basis. After speaking with the founder of the program, we felt even more certain that this community needed to have this therapeutic program on a permanent basis. After the second painting event for Oklahoma, we were asked if we would like to become an official Chapter of Hearts of Hope, the first chapter, as well.

There wasn't any way we could turn down such a wonderful honor, after all, witnessing first hand how this program was helping so many was confirmation enough that it was meant to be.

What is so astounding to me, is that people in the community who are still grieving and hurting from our own tragedy, are able to think about others who are hurting in their own way, by creating such beautiful keepsakes.

These hearts have truly become "tangible prayers" for those who receive them. A teacher from Sandy Hook School told me that she enjoys the painting events, because for those few hours, the heaviest thing on her mind is what color and design to put on her hearts. This statement in itself tells me that we are helping our community and will continue to for many years to come. To date, over 2,500 hearts have been created and distributed by the Newtown Chapter, and we plan on continuing for many years to come.

As I watched my oldest child graduate from NHS this past June, I realized just how blessed and wonderful my life has been, living in my beautiful hometown of Sandy Hook.

Sue (Taylor) Shaw

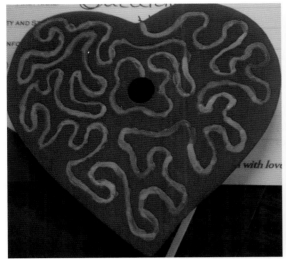

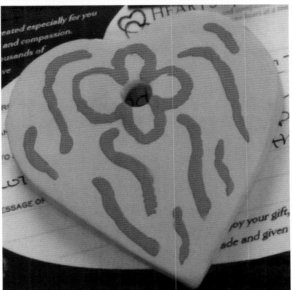

Hearts for Hope hearts from Newtown

Dear Friend,

I'd like to tell you a little about the amazing town that I've grown up in. A town that I will always love, no matter where life takes me.

Back in 1977, my family moved from Huntington to Sandy Hook. I was 10 years old and really hated the idea of leaving my friends behind, even though they were only a few towns away. I couldn't understand why my parents wanted to leave our perfect house, with pretty floors and perfect rooms for an old one with big wide floor boards that you could see through and cracks in the ceiling. Even the rooms in the house had strange names, birthing rooms, servants' quarters, even a carriage house. The huge brick fireplace with the oven that looked like a beehive didn't even impress me. All I kept asking was, why? The fact that my dad was an executive during the week, but on weekends would be out with my mom enjoying their favorite hobby together, which was antiquing, didn't even connect to the house in my mind.

As a new student at Sandy Hook School, I was a little nervous, but by the end of the first week, I loved it. From the first day I was there, until the last day of 5th grade, I was in love with that school. I loved my teachers and loved making new friends. To many, it was just a brick building that held kids and teachers, but as I got older and had children of my own attend the school, I realized the reason I loved that building so much was it represented all that was good about being a child in Sandy Hook and enjoying everything life had to offer. It was always filled with laughter, joy, and fun celebrations.

Sandy Hook School had this amazing fair every year called the "Jolly Green Giant Fair". I looked forward to the fair every year. When the time was approaching for the fair, I'd look out the front windows of the school bus at the big Green Giant footprints. I remember vividly riding in the car to the fair with my parents, Rod Stewart singing on the car radio as we got to the school. The fair was held on the back playground, which is now the courtyard. There were so many great games and activities. So many friends would be there and we would have such a great time.

I have so many great memories of growing up in Sandy Hook.

Our summers were spent playing on the farm next to our house and teasing the one-horned goat named Clancy. We would all play "King of the Hill", which was a great game we all loved. We would get Clancy so worked up, he'd chase all of us, and we would have to run like crazy to get to "base", which was the top rung of the fence, before his one horn would hook us. We'd always end up laughing like crazy when the one person who didn't run quick enough ended up being the target of that evil horn.

As soon as the sun went down, the neighborhood would gather just on the edge of the corn field to determine who would be "it", meaning the seeker and the rest of us would be the hiders. It was always fun and games running and hiding in those fields, trying to be as quiet as possible so we didn't get found.

In the winter, we had just as many entertaining things to do as we did in the summer. We always hoped for lots of cold and snow . . . if it was cold enough, we would play on the frozen pond across the street for hours, or at least until our fingers and toes were so numb, we could barely feel them. If we had gotten a lot of snow, we would walk up the big hill and sled down the middle of the road, not worrying about any cars because most people didn't have SUV's or 4 wheel drives. Not sure if they even made them back then. We also had some nice big hills in our backyard, but you had to be really good at steering the sled through the obstacle course of trees.

We would often take trips into the "Hook" with my mother to purchase dad's newspaper and cigarettes at a small store we referred to as "Helens". Helens carried some of the basics, canned and boxed foods, candy, gum and ice cream. Helen was an elderly woman who sat behind the old wooden counter. She had long black and gray hair, and my brothers and I thought she was a witch in disguise. I remember her knuckles were so swollen and she would slide the change across the counter into her drawer because she couldn't pick it up. When we asked my mother what was wrong with her hands, she told us she had very bad arthritis. At that time, we had no idea what that was, but we certainly didn't want that.

I remember being at the Laundromat, which was on Glen Road along the river, helping my mother do laundry. After we would put the clothes into the dryer, we would walk next door to the Red Brick General Store to pick up a few groceries and chat with the store owners.

As a teenager, we'd still stop in at Helens, but the store next to it was much more appealing to the teens in the area. The store was called Putnam's Place and they sold an array of different things, from tie dyed wall hangings and shirts, to posters, stickers and lots of other interesting things that were in the counter by the register.

Fast forward 35 years and I'm still a "Sandy Hooker", married to a Newtowner, living in the same house that I grew up in, but now raising my own two children.

Growing up in this house, I have so many memories and I have the unique opportunity to share those memories with my children. They were able to attend my elementary and middle school, one has already graduated from NHS and the other is on her way there.

A lot has changed throughout the decades in Sandy Hook, Helens is now a toy store, the Red Brick General Store is a restaurant and the old laundromat by the river is a coffee shop. Where the barns and fields once were, McMansions now stand.

Even with these changes, I still feel pride and love for my community. I have always and will always be proud to be part of this small town.

On December 14, 2012, things changed within this community. Twenty six precious lives were taken from us in the most horrific way, in a building that represented love and happiness. How could this happen? In our community? In our beloved Sandy Hook School? How could this happen at all? So many questions, many that could be asked in anger, but quickly realized there was no time for anger, it was a wasted energy and we needed as much positive energy as we could muster.

We needed an energy that would help this community pull even closer and we could to help the grieving families and our fellow neighbors . . . it was LOVE. Love came pouring into our community from all over the world. People brought it with them, they mailed it, they wrote it in letters and poems, they left it as a token, they built memorials with it, they hugged us with it and their tears were filled with it, and all these months later, the sadness still weighs heavily on our hearts, but we know we are not alone.

So begins the story of Hearts of Hope. In February 2013, after one of the worst snowstorms of the season, volunteers came from New York and New Jersey to pay our community a surprise visit, leaving behind thousands of beautiful hand painted hearts hanging throughout town for residents to find. These hearts, hung against the backdrop of white snow, were beautiful, hanging on branches, signs, fence posts and telephone poles. They brought brightness into a community that was still struggling with the horrific event from two months prior. Each heart came with a card that contained information about the painter, including a note of comfort. Mine was painted by a 1st grader from New Jersey and when I saw it, I thought, wow, here's more love and it's from a 6 year old child!

After the Boston tragedy, letters and calls went out to Hearts of Hope's main office and it was decided that hearts would be created here to send to Boston. Events were set up throughout the town, in people's homes, senior center and a local church. From there over 1600 hearts were hand delivered by volunteers, including two families from Sandy Hook. So many residents enjoyed creating these hearts and paying it forward that a few of us decided to see if we could do something on a more permanent basis. After speaking with the founder of the program, we felt even more certain that this community needed to have this therapeutic program on a permanent basis. After the second painting event for Oklahoma, we were asked if we would like to become an official Chapter of Hearts of Hope, the first chapter, as well.

There wasn't any way we could turn down such a wonderful honor, after all, witnessing first hand how this program was helping so many was confirmation enough that it was meant to be.

What is so astounding to me, is that people in the community who are still grieving and hurting from our own tragedy, are able to think about others who are hurting in their own way by creating such beautiful keepsakes.

These hearts have truly become "tangible prayers" for those who receive them. A teacher from Sandy Hook School told me that she enjoys the painting events because for those few hours, the heaviest thing on her mind is what color and design to put on her hearts. This statement in itself tells me that we are helping our community and will continue to for many years to come. To date, over 2,500 hearts have been created and distributed by the Newtown Chapter, and we plan on continuing for many years to come.

As I watched my oldest child graduate from NHS this past June, I realized just how blessed and wonderful my life has been, living in my beautiful hometown of Sandy Hook.

Sue (Taylor) Shaw

Center of Sandy Hook (formerly the Red Brick Grocery Store)

I was born in Russia, adopted and moved to Sandy Hook when I was four years old. There are countless memories of an amazing childhood in that town. The friends I made were ones I will never forget and still see to this day. I made a lot of friends in school or during after school sports. The families in this town are so kind and it is that kindness that makes each individual so memorable.

No matter where you go you will always see someone you know. A popular spot to see old friends is at the General Store on Main Street. Even though it is a small place, with a few tables you are guaranteed to run into an old friend. There is always a sense of connection with the people who live here.

One of my favorite annual festivities is the Labor Day Parade. There is another place to see anyone and everyone in town. I may only be 23 years old but it's parades like this that make me feel like our town is one big family. I run into old friends, old families I used to babysit or petsit for, town officials and even old neighbors that have moved to other towns. There is always a sense of unity you feel with the people who live here.

I no longer live in Sandy Hook because my family moved into Newtown. It didn't mean anything to me at the time and I still feel like they are one in the same. Families that lived in

Sandy Hook sent their kids to Newtown Middle School and Newtown High School. It didnt matter that there was a line.

When I went off to colkge in another town in Connecticut, I had immediately noticed that I was no longer in Newtown, and I had to deal with the fact that I had to adjust to the newness around me. I would always enjoy venturing back home for the weekends because there is a sense of warmth that you feel that comes from the people who live here.

No matter what happens in this town, I will always feel a sense of connection, unity and warmth from the families that live here with me. I am very thankful for this town.

Marina

Newtown Labor Day Parade, 2013

I was born in Russia, adopted and moved to Sandy Hook when I was four years old. There are countless memories of an amazing childhood in that town. The friends I made were ones I will never forget and still see to this day. I made a lot of friends in school or during after school sports. The families in this town are so kind and it is that kindness that makes each individual so memorable.

No matter where you go you will always see someone you know. A popular spot to see old friends is at the General Store on Main Street. Even though it is a small place with a few tables you are guaranteed to run into an old friend. There is always a sense of connection with the people who live here.

One of my favorite annual festivities is the Labor Day Parade. There is another place to see anyone and everyone in town. I may only be 23 years old but its' parades like this that make me feel like our town is one big family. I run into old friends, old families I used to babysit or pet sit for, town officials and even old neighbors that have moved to other towns. There is always a sense of unity you feel with the people who live here.

I no longer live in Sandy Hook because my family moved into Newtown. It didn't mean anything to me at the time and I still feel like they are one in the same. Families that lived in Sandy Hook sent their kids to Newtown Middle School and Newtown High School. It didn't matter that there was a line.

When I went off to college in another town in Connecticut, I had immediately noticed that I was no longer in Newtown, and I had to deal with the fact that I had to adjust to the newness around me. I would always enjoy venturing back home for the weekends because there is a sense of warmth that you feel that comes from the people who live here.

No matter what happens in this town, I will always feel a sense of connection, unity and warmth from the families that live here with me. I am very thankful for this town.

Marina

I spent some time the other day sitting on the bench at the top of Castle Hill looking across the landscape to the east dotted with my favorite Newtown images of church steeples and the flagpole. This is a place of reverie for me. A place of quiet where I can rein in my thoughts, slow my pace and give my mind freedom to travel the highways and byways of the past and explore some imaginings of our future. My forty-plus years living in this community have gone by quickly, too quickly. I long for some of that time to return. There are perhaps different choices to be made had I known then what I know now about life, about parenting, about community, about friendship, about me. Absent the luxury of a redo of time spent, I commit myself to looking at today and tomorrow armed with the knowledge that time is indeed fleeting.

I fully imagine that all of my remaining years will be spent in this community I have come to care for so deeply. It is not just that I came here as a young parent of three children; that my kids grew up here, were schooled here, played all team sports, made lasting friendships and more. It is not even that my middle child, my Sharon, is buried here that ensures my remaining forever. It is that somehow this town has become part of me in a way that draws me ever closer. It truly is my home and I reach for that closeness evermore.

The Newtown I see today is both the same and different than the one I first came to in the '70's. We are larger in population, more affluent and busier. In some ways, too, we are less connected to each other — maybe in part because of those three attributes. There is continuity, though, a sameness with past decades that evidences the constancy that is Newtown. We are a place of families and neighbors- as now and have always been. Families live at the very core of our identity. Not just families with young kids, but families with persons of all ages, interests, resources and life styles. That is what first drew me and my husband Bob to our neighborhood of Sandy Hook. We continue to see that communally-held value as foundational to much of what drives our town's development. Our quest for excellence in education, for safe streets, for leisure and recreational opportunities for all ages, for open spaces that please the eye and soothe the soul, for housing diversity to meet the needs of all, for enough commerce to help mitigate taxes - all of these things are pursued because they help create a place where people can live in comfort and thrive.

We are also a community of significant strength of character and capacity to prevail in the face of horrendous circumstances. Nothing, ever, in our long 300 year history has hurt us more than the shooting at Sandy Hook Elementary School. That act of violence damaged us in ways that are almost indescribable. But we are working hard to bandage those wounds, and tease out some future goodness from that horror. I think often that we are different because of that violence ... how our focus on kindness and compassion has strengthened. I recognize, too, that the path forward for many individuals and maybe even the community as a whole is uneven and sometimes tortuous. We are regaining our footing, reestablishing confidence, but are not yet at that point where the events of a day cannot rock us and knock us back down a bit.

The final chapters of this story have not been written and we can only speculate on what is to come. But as I sit on that bench on Castle Hill, I see a bright and positive future for Newtown. I am confident for our people. I see their strength and their commitment, and their goodness.

Pat Llodra

August 2013

View of Newtown from Castle Hill

I spent some time the other day sitting on the bench at the top of Castle Hill looking across the landscape to the east dotted with my favorite Newtown images of church steeples and the flagpole. This is a place of reverie for me. A place of quiet where I can rein in my thoughts, slow my pace and give my mind freedom to travel the highways and byways of the past and explore some imaginings of our future. My forty-plus years living in this community have gone by quickly, too quickly. I long for some of that time to return. There are perhaps different choices to be made had I known then what I know now about life, about parenting, about community, about friendship, about me. Absent the luxury of a redo of time spent, I commit myself to looking at today and tomorrow armed with the knowledge that time is indeed fleeting.

I fully imagine that all of my remaining years will be spent in this community I have come to care for so deeply. It is not just that I came here as a young parent of three children; that my kids grew up here, were schooled here, played all team sports, made lasting friendships and more. It is not even that my middle child, my Sharon, is buried here that ensures my remaining forever. It is that somehow this town has become part of me in a way that draws me ever closer. It truly is my home and I reach for that closeness evermore.

The Newtown I see today is both the same and different than the one I first came to in the 70's. We are larger in population, more affluent and busier. In some ways, too, we are less connected to each other—maybe in part because of those three attributes. There is continuity, though, a sameness with past decades that evidences the constancy that is Newtown. We are a place of families and neighbors—are now and have always been. Families lie at the very core of our identity. Not just families with young kids, but families with persons of all ages, interests, resources and lifestyles. That is what first drew me and my husband Bob to our neighborhood of Sandy Hook. We continue to see that communally-held value as foundational to much of what drives our town's development. Our quest for excellence in education, for safe streets, for leisure and recreational opportunities for all ages, for open spaces that please the eye and soothe the soul, for housing diversity to meet the needs of all, for enough commerce to help mitigate taxes—all of these things are pursued because they help create a place where people can live in comfort and thrive.

We are also a community of significant strength of character and capacity to prevail in the face of horrendous circumstances. Nothing, ever, in our long 300 year history has hurt us more than the shooting at Sandy Hook Elementary School. That act of violence damaged us in ways that are almost indescribable. But we are working hard to bandage those wounds, and tease out some future goodness from that horror. I think often that we are different because of that violence . . . how our focus on kindness and compassion has strengthened. I recognize, too, that the path forward for many individuals and maybe even the community as a whole is uneven and sometimes tortuous. We are regaining our footing, reestablishing confidence, but are not yet at that point where the events of a day cannot rock us and knock us back down a bit.

The final chapters of this story have not been written and we can only speculate on what is to come. But as I sit on that bench on Castle Hill, I see a bright and positive future for Newtown. I am confident for our people. I see their strength and their commitment, and their goodness.

Pat Llodra
August 2013

Petunia the Silly Goose and
How She Laid the Golden Egg

Have you ever read "Petunia the Silly Goose?" Well, I have, maybe a gazillion times. Petunia was my daughter Daryl's most favorite book when she was very little and, as most parents know, once a child hears something they love, they want to hear it read to them over and over and over. We moved to Sandy Hook from NYC in 1973 when Daryl was two and Petunia of course moved with us. Our son, Edward, was born here in 1974 (sorry to my kids that I'm giving away their ages). Since Daryl loved to be read to, we soon found the library on Main Street. I thought that some new books were needed to give me a break from Petunia. The children's section at the library was very small at the time and all the books were Very well read. The library didn't have much of a budget back then, because it was existing on the income from the Hawley trust fund. At the time Maureen, one of the staff, was selling the library's discards for maybe 10 cents each in the front vestibule. Hmmm, I thought that I could do better than that!! I could make some extra cash and maybe the library could buy some brand new children's books and Petunia could get a rest.

Thus began the journey. The staff saved up the books

to be discarded. On Labor Day, 1975, with my son safely tucked into his "snuggly" and with Mary as a helper, the book sale opened with two tables of books near the sidewalk on Main Street. It was great fun with the parade going by and lots of people coming to buy books!!! Success!!! We sold out and made a whopping $35. The staff was very happy and so was I. The book sale grew from two tables that year to a few more the next. After many years and much help the sale needed three tents to fill the parking lot at the library. We were growing by leaps and bounds. The library underwent an expansion in the late 1990's and had to close down. We were fortunate enough to be able to move into a building that stood where Dunkin' Donuts is now. That was a hard year. We almost got blown away by a hurricane. The next year we moved the sale to Fairfield Hills into Shelton House that could accommodate both the library and sale. Again an interesting year. The following year we finally got Bridgeport Hall on the FFH campus. The huge dining halls and kitchens were great spaces, but came with leaking ceilings, peeling paint and no water. The sale always took place on Labor Day weekend and I missed seeing the parade on Main Street, but the people always came after the parade in their costumes and band uniforms. Finally, the Town decided to renovate Bridgeport Hall and use it as Newtown's new Municipal

Center. We were homeless once again. Now, the sale takes place in the Reed School with all its amenities of air conditioning, bathrooms and large open spaces.

Many odd and interesting things have happened over the years. One year we got a very large collection of books on chess; it filled at least two tables. Mr. Chang slept in his car on Main Street and was the first one into the sale. He ran for the chess books and threw himself spread eagle over all those chess books yelling "Sold." He went away very happy, but there were a lot of disappointed chess players who left with no books. Once we had a two-volume set of mathematics books. Well, each book was picked up separately by two different men. They argued and argued over who should get the set. They never agreed and each of them left with one book, both unhappy. One year we were awaiting the tables to go into the tents behind the library. We were to open at noon and it was 11 o'clock and still no tables. As we were deciding to just put the boxes on the ground and let the people go through them that way, the tables arrived. The book sale never got put up so fast as that year.

I decided to resign my chairpersonship of the book sale in 2004. From the time that it made $35 the first year, it had earned more than $1,000,000 by 2004. The book sale could never have taken place and become successful without the very generous donations of books from Newtowners. Newtown Loves to read!!! I continue to work at the booksale and now my grandson, Fritz, helps me set up the books for the sale. I am so glad that the love of reading has passed down to him, he is a true Newtowner!! The sale now is in the very capable hands of Denise and a very loyal band of volunteers. Denise takes care of the children's books and sometimes comes across "Petunia." So, if you should find "Petunia" at the book sale give her a smile and a wink and thank her for bringing the book sale to Newtown.

Sincerely,

Joanne E. Zang
(and Petunia, too!)

Petunia the Silly Goose and How She Laid the Golden Egg

Have you ever read "Petunia The Silly Goose?" Well, I have, maybe a gazillion times. Petunia was my daughter Daryl's most favorite book when she was very little and, as most parents know, once a child hears something they love, they want to hear it read to them over and over and over. We moved to Sandy Hook from NYC in 1973 when Daryl was two and Petunia of course moved with us. Our son, Edward, was born here in 1974 (sorry to my kids that I'm giving away their ages). Since Daryl loved to be read to, we soon found the library on Main Street. I thought that some new books were needed to give me a break from Petunia. The children's section at the library was very small at the time and all the books were *Very* well read. The library didn't have much of a budget back then, because it was existing on the income from the Hawley trust fund. At the time, Maureen, one of the staff, was selling the library's discards for maybe 10 cents each in the front vestibule. Hmmm, I thought that I could do better than that!! I could make some extra cash and maybe the library could buy some brand new children's books and Petunia could get a rest.

Thus began the journey. The staff saved up the books to be discarded. On Labor Day, 1975, with my son safely tucked into his "snuggly" and with Mary as a helper, the book sale opened with two tables of books near the sidewalk on Main Street. It was great fun with the parade going by and lots of people coming to buy books!!! Success!!! We sold out and made a whopping $35. The staff was very happy and so was I. The book sale grew from two tables that year to a few more the next. After many years and much help, the sale needed three tents to fill the parking lot at the library. We were growing by leaps and bounds. The library underwent an expansion in the late 1990s and had to close down. We were fortunate enough to be able to move into a building that stood where Dunkin' Donuts is now. That was a hard year. We almost got blown away by a hurricane. The next year we moved the sale to Fairfield Hills into Shelton House that could accommodate both the library and sale. Again an interesting year. The following year, we finally got Bridgeport Hall on the FFH campus. The huge dining halls and kitchens were great spaces, but came with leaking ceilings, peeling paint and no water. The sale always took place on Labor Day weekend and I missed seeing the parade on Main Street, but the people always came after the parade in their costumes and band uniforms. Finally, the Town decided to renovate Bridgeport Hall and use it as Newtown's new Municipal Center. We were homeless once again. Now, the sale takes place in the Reed School with all its amenities of air conditioning, bathrooms and large open spaces.

Many odd and interesting things have happened over the years. One year we got a very large collection of books on chess; it filled at least two tables. Mr. Chang slept in his car on Main Street and was the first one into the sale. He ran for the chess books and threw himself spread eagle over all those chess books yelling "SOLD." He went away very happy, but there were a lot of disappointed chess players who left with no books. Once we had a two-volume set of mathematics books. Well, each book was picked up separately by two different men. They argued and argued over who should get the set. They never agreed and each of them left with one book, both unhappy. One year we were awaiting the tables to go into the tents behind the library. We were to open at noon and it was 11 o'clock and still no tables. As we were deciding to just put the boxes on the ground and let the people go through them that way, the tables arrived. The book sale never got put up so fast as that year.

I decided to resign my chairpersonship of the book sale in 2004. From the time that it made $35 the first year, it had earned more than $1,000,000 by 2004. The book sale could never have taken place and become successful without the very generous donations of books from Newtowners. Newtown LOVES to read!!! I continue to work at the book sale and now my grandson, Fritz, helps me set up the books for the sale. I am so glad that the love of reading has passed down to him, he is a true Newtowner!! The sale now is in the very capable hands of Denise and a very loyal band of volunteers. Denise takes care of the children's books and sometimes comes across "Petunia." So, if you should find "Petunia" at the book sale give her a smile and a wink and thank her for bringing the book sale to Newtown.

Sincerely,
Joanne E. Zang
(and Petunia, too!)

Main Street in the fall

Halloween on Main Street

It's pretty safe to assume Halloween wouldn't rise too high on any person's top holiday list. As a kid, its appeal lies mostly in the fact that Kit Kats and Reese's are subsituted for dinner, while you pretend to be your favorite cartoon character or superhero. And in the eyes of a teenager, Halloween still means you can dress up, only now the costume has a little less fabric than it used to, and the high school parties are usually a chance to get caught up in a little mischief. Although this is all speculative seeing as I never really had the traditional Halloween experience. Sure I've Trick-or-Treated, dressed up in matching costumes with friends, eaten enough Twix in one night to make me sick, and even found myself at a Halloween party or two. Yet, the Halloweens I can remember most were the ones I spent at home, willingly I might add. They were the Halloweens where planning began a year in advance, and I am not talking about for the costume. So what is it exactly that makes teenage siblings and their friends find it more fun to stay at home on Halloween instead of partaking in the typical holiday traditions? That's simple. I grew up in an old house on the rumored-to-be-haunted Main Street in Newtown, CT.

Halloween on Main Street isn't just a convenient spot for townspeople, and even those from neighboring towns, to bring their kids and hit up the greatest number of houses over the least amount of time. Halloween on Main Street is a game; it's an unspoken contest amongst neighbors asto who can generate the most "talk of the town". Whose house was the most well decorated? Who gave out the best candy (although we all know there is no competing with the Shepard's super-sized candy bars)? Whose theme walked the closest line to being the most politically incorrect? A neighbor had a ten foot mechanical spider that climbed up and down the three stories of their historic house.

I was a freshman in high school when the art of putting together a well-crafted, front-yard Halloween display became a family hobby. I can still remember the very first scene. An old car Mercedes crashed into one of our great sugar maple trees on the Main Street tree line. Skeleton operator and front seat passenger hang out the open car doors, martini glasses in hand. An arm hangs out of the closed trunk and from inside a voice calls out, "Excuse me, excuse me, could someone let me out of here?!" Ghostly shrieks, witches cackling, glass windows shattering, spooky footsteps, evil laughter, and for the few lucky ones, an occasional Monster Mash, plays via cassette in the background. And the only way to the cauldron of candy is through a dark, cornhusk pathway decorated with scary masks and bats. Looking back now, that was mere child's play compared to the themes that transpired thereafter.

A family favorite was when our house became the prison for all evil Halloween characters. We had Jason, Freddy Krueger, Chucky, the Grim Reaper, and even Jaws locked up in cages and chains on the front lawn, while my family played the police officers. Well everyone except my father who spent the entire night on the grass in the mouth of Jaws, only to pop up and start yelling for help when kids walked past. This might not seem too much of a feat, but Halloween on Main Street starts at 4 p.m. for the youngsters, and can end as late as 11:00 P.M. If you ask me, that's a long time to be lying around in a shark's mouth.

Another classic involved the lost tunnels of Fairfield Hills. (Remember that politically incorrect line I mentioned earlier). After receiving their candy, a nice looking friendly nurse led the Trick-or-Treaters to the Bilco doors on the side of the house. On the way, they passed a patient lying on a bed, motionless, as a doctor prepared to operate. "Take a closer look," smiled the nurse reassuringly. What happened next, I assure you was not the first or last time we waited for phone calls. As the Trick-or-Treaters inched their way closer to the patient, the patient lurched forward screaming and reaching for them. And for those who got a little too close, a pull of their shirt, or grabbing of their hand would certainly teach them to keep a safe distance next time. I would say our dearest patient still holds the Main Street Academy Award for "Most Animated in a Halloween Picture", because she sent more than one Trick-or-Treater back to their parents. The best part, the patient's number one fans were the parents of the children. I guess that just goes to show the power of Halloween on Main Street.

And perhaps the most enjoyable time was when we dragged an old, big screen TV outside and set up a movie theatre for our goblins, skeletons, and scarecrows (dummies of course). They were feasting on worms and eyeball infested popcorn, while kicking back to the movie, Children of the Corn. That was until after the first blood and gore scene, when we realized that might be too much, so we switched over to the classic Rocky Horror Picture Film. We ended up having our longest Halloween ever, lasting well past 11 PM, as teens and adults decided to stay and watch the show. Although by 10 PM it is almost guaranteed that the thousands of pieces of candy, sometimes replaced with pennies and dimes, are exhausted. So, as to compensation to running out of candy that night, we sent our visitors over to sneak some popcorn and candy when our R.I.P. guests weren't looking. Now some of you may still be stuck on the word "thousands," but this is no exaggeration. Can you say

Over 3500 Trick-or-Treaters? In fact, every year we are grateful to receive bags of candy from various town organizations and anonymous donors, because even on top of all the candy we buy ourselves, it never seems to be enough!

When I began writing this Halloween memoir I was hoping to be able to fill a page, if I was lucky. It turns out Halloween for a Main Street resident isn't something that begins and ends on October 31st. It lives within us, whether as a happy childhood memory, or an idea in the back of our minds for next year's theme. Maybe my family takes an extreme point of view, exemplified by a Parent's Weekend college visit turned into the search for Gettysburg battle attire to wear during that year's Civil War theme. Or how a spring break family vacation to Key West ended up costing as much as it did to ship back home the boxes of life-like ghost and ghoul characters we found. I exaggerate a little, but you get the idea. Halloween on Main Street is something

I always find myself describing to others, but in its finest cliché form, you really must see it to believe it. So to wrap this up, despite Halloween being cancelled one year due to a hurricane, I warn everyone to be prepared ... a zombie apocalypse is in the forecast.

Tora Gostan
18 Main Street

Halloween on Main Street, Newtown

Halloween on Main Street

It's pretty safe to assume Halloween wouldn't rise too high on any person's top holiday list. As a kid, its appeal lies mostly in the fact that Kit Kats and Reese's are substituted for dinner, while you pretend to be your favorite cartoon character or superhero. And in the eyes of a teenager, Halloween still means you can dress up, only now the costume has a little less fabric than it used to, and the high school parties are usually a chance to get caught up in a little mischief. Although this is all speculative seeing as I never really had the traditional Halloween experience. Sure I've Trick-or-Treated, dressed up in matching costumes with friends, eaten enough Twix in one night to make me sick, and even found myself at a Halloween party or two. Yet, the Halloweens I can remember most were the ones I spent at home, willingly I might add. They were the Halloweens where planning began a year in advance, and I am not talking about for the costume. So what is it exactly that makes teenage siblings and their friends find it more fun to stay at home on Halloween instead of partaking in the typical holiday traditions? That's simple. I grew up in an old house on the rumored-to-be-haunted Main Street in Newtown, CT.

Halloween on Main Street isn't just a convenient spot for townspeople, and even those from neighboring towns, to bring their kids and hit up the greatest number of houses over the least amount of time. Halloween on Main Street is a game; it's an unspoken contest amongst neighbors as to who can generate the most "talk of the town." Whose house was most well decorated? Who gave out the best candy (although we all know there is no competing with the Shepard's super-sized candy bars)? Whose theme walked the closest line to being the most politically incorrect? A neighbor had a ten foot mechanical spider that climbed up and down the three stories of their historic house.

I was a freshman in high school when the art of putting together a well-crafted, front-yard Halloween display became a family hobby. I can still remember the very first scene. An old car Mercedes crashed into one of our great sugar maple trees on the Main Street tree line. Skeleton operator and front seat passenger hang out the open car doors, martini glasses in hand. An arm hangs out of the closed trunk and from inside a voice calls out, "Excuse me, excuse me, could someone let me out of here?!" Ghastly shrieks, witches cackling, glass windows shattering, spooky footsteps, evil laughter, and for the few lucky ones, an occasional Monster Mash, plays via cassette in the background. And the only way to the cauldron of candy is through a dark, cornhusk pathway decorated with scary masks and bats. Looking back now, that was mere child's play compared to the themes that transpired thereafter.

A family favorite was when our house became the prison for all evil Halloween characters. We had Jason, Freddy Krueger, Chucky, the Grim Reaper, and even Jaws locked up in cages and chains on the front lawn, while my family played the police officers. Well everyone except my father who spent the entire night on the grass in the mouth of Jaws, only to pop up and start yelling for help when kids walked past. This might not seem too much of a feat, but Halloween on Main Street starts at 4PM for the youngsters and can end as late as 11:00PM. If you ask me, that's a long time to be lying around in a shark's mouth.

Another classic involved the lost tunnels of Fairfield Hills. (Remember that politically incorrect line I mentioned earlier.) After receiving their candy, a nice looking friendly nurse led the Trick-or-Treaters to the Bilco doors on the side of the house. On the way, they passed a patient lying on a bed, motionless, as a doctor prepared to operate. "Take a closer look," smiled the nurse reassuringly. What happened next, I assure you was not the first or last time we waited for phone calls. As the Trick-or-Treaters inched their way closer to the patient, the patient lurched forward screaming and reaching for them. And for those who got a little too close, a pull of their shirt, or grabbing of their hand would certainly teach them to keep a safe distance next time. I would say our dearest patient still holds the Main Street Academy Award for "Most Animated in a Halloween Picture," because she sent more than one Trick-or-Treater back to their parents. The best part, the patient's number one fans were the parents of the children. I guess that just goes to show the power of Halloween on Main Street.

And perhaps the most enjoyable theme was when we dragged an old, big screen TV outside and set up a movie theatre for our goblins, skeletons, and scarecrows (dummies of course). They were feasting on worms and eyeball infested popcorn, while kicking back to the movie, Children of the Corn. That was until after the first blood and gore scene, when we realized that might be too much, so we switched over to the classic Rocky Horror Picture Film. We ended up having our longest Halloween ever, lasting well past 11PM, as teens and adults decided to stay and watch the show. Although by 10PM it is almost guaranteed that the thousands of pieces of candy, sometimes replaced with pennies and dimes, are exhausted. So, as to compensation to running out of candy that night, we sent our visitors over to sneak some popcorn and candy when our R.I.P. guests weren't looking. Now some of you may still be stuck on the word "thousands," but this is no exaggeration. Can you say over 3500 Trick-or-Treaters? In fact, every year we are grateful to receive bags of candy from various town organizations and anonymous donors, because even on top of all the candy we buy ourselves, it never seems to be enough!

When I began writing this Halloween memoir I was hoping to be able to fill a page, if I was lucky. It turns out Halloween for a Main Street resident isn't something that begins and ends on October 31st. It lives within us, whether as a happy childhood memory, or an idea in the back of our minds for next year's theme. Maybe my family takes an extreme point of view, exemplified by a Parent's Weekend college visit turned into the search for Gettysburg battle attire to wear during that year's Civil War theme. Or how a spring break family vacation to Key West ended up costing as much as it did to ship back home the boxes of life-like ghost and ghoul characters we found. I exaggerate a little, but you get the idea. Halloween on Main Street is something I always find myself describing to others, but in its finest cliché form, you really must see it to believe it. So to wrap this up, despite Halloween being cancelled one year due to a hurricane, I warn everyone to be prepared . . . a zombie apocalypse is in the forecast.

Tara Gaston
18 Main Street

Halloween on Main Street, Newtown

Dear World,

It's a well-known fact that I love to talk. My husband and sons- not so much. It got to the point that it was a game- Let's see if Mom can get of the store without stopping to talk to anyone. I don't think I ever won that game! Or if I did - it was so few times that its almost not worth mentioning. That is one of things I love (or hate if I haven't showered, my hair is not having a good day and I just need one gallon of milk - that is in the farthest corner of the store) - you always see someone you know. And that is also what makes our town just like thousands of other small towns ... you always see someone you know! Don't you do that? Don't you run into the grocery store for just one thing and forty-five minutes later (the ice cream half melted in your bag) you finally walk out. But you walk out feeling good because you connected with someone you hadn't seen in a while. "A while" could mean last week or two years ago when your kids were both on the same baseball team! But it doesn't matter. You catch up in the first two minutes and then continue your conversation like you just spoke yesterday. It's what life is like in a small town. In a town where the woman that owns the bagel place asks about your kids by name ... where the kid cutting your deli meat went to school with your son ... where the physical therapist who works on your shoulder is good friends with your husband (so no trashing your husband while you are laying on the table next to the woman whose daughter is close friends with your son and he was just over their house the other day)... this is my town.

My town is not that glimpse that the world saw. We are not just that moment. Although that moment is forever etched upon our hearts along with a great portion of the rest of the world - as many people have stated before (and will state over and over again) December 14, 2012 does not define us. You might think it did. Some of us here in town might even think it did.

But I don't. It made some of us change our lives. We think about some things differently now. I cringe a bit everytime I hear a siren. My soft whisper under my breath of "be safe" everytime I heard the sirens now means something different. Now my wish for safety includes those first responders as well. Because now I realize that the call they are going on, can be just as dangerous for them as for the people they are going to help.

When I first started this project, I thought 90% of the letters would state "everybody knows everybody" in our community but that didn't happen. Maybe because it's a given, we don't even have to say it. We all know each other. And now, we all share something that could either rip our community apart or bring us together. When you are as small a community as we are - you can't just go on with your life without making some changes after the tragedy of December 14, 2012. People can step up or they can check out. Or they can try to go on as they did before. The rest of the world may have moved on - because that is how life happens. But yet, I know I can't go on as I did before. I've made changes in my life and I will continue to make more. I hope what our town has experienced will be a catalyst for others to make changes in their lives. To realize what is important to them. We were brought to our knees in pain and anguish. But I am SANDY HOOK STRONG! And will continue to be so!

With love
Suzanne Davenport

Sandy Hook Firehouse

Ram Pasture

Dear World,

It's a well-known fact that I love to talk. My husband and sons—not so much. It got to the point that it was a game—let's see if Mom can get in and out of the store without stopping to talk to anyone. I don't think I ever won that game! Or if I did—it was so few times that it's almost not worth mentioning. That is one of the things I love (or hate if I haven't showered, my hair is not having a good day and I just need one gallon of milk—that is in the farthest corner of the store)—you always see someone you know. And that is also what makes our town just like thousands of other small towns . . . you always see someone you know! Don't you do that? Don't you run into the grocery store for just one thing and forty five minutes later (the ice cream half melted in your bag) you finally walk out. But you walk out feeling good because you connected with someone you haven't seen in a while. "A while" could mean last week or two years ago when your kids were both on the same baseball team! But it doesn't matter. You catch up in the first two minutes and then continue your conversation like you just spoke yesterday. It's what life is like in a small town. In a town where the woman that owns the bagel place asks about your kids by name . . . where the kid cutting your deli meat went to school with your son . . . where the physical therapist who works on your shoulder is good friends with your husband (so no trashing your husband while you are laying on the table next to the woman whose daughter is close friends with your son and he was just over their house the other day) . . . this is my town.

My town is not that glimpse that the world saw. We are not just that moment. Although that moment is forever etched upon our hearts along with a great portion of the rest of the world—as many people have stated before (and will state over and over again) December 14, 2012 does not define us. You might think it did. Some of us here in town might even think it did. But I don't. It made some of us change our lives. We think about some things differently now. I cringe a bit every time I hear a siren. My soft whisper under my breath of "be safe" every time I heard the sirens now means something different. Now my wish for safety includes those first responders as well. Because now I realize that the call they are going on, can be just as dangerous for them as for the people they are going to help.

When I first started this project, I thought 90% of the letters would state "everybody knows everybody" in our community but that didn't happen. Maybe because it's a given, we don't even have to say it. We all know each other. And now, we all share something that could either rip our community apart or bring us together. When you are as small a community as we are—you can't just go on with your life without making some changes after the tragedy of December 14, 2012. People can step up or they can check out. Or they can try to go on as they did before. The rest of the world may have moved on—because that is how life happens. But yet, I know I can't go on as I did before. I've made changes in my life and I will continue to make more. I hope what our town has experienced will be a catalyst for others to make changes in their lives. To realize what is important to them. We were brought to our knees in pain and anguish. But I am SANDY HOOK STRONG! And will continue to be so!

With love,
Suzanne Davenport

While not born in Sandy Hook, I moved there when I was five and it is the place I call home. I started kindergarten at Hawley School and graduated from Newtown Middle and High School.

As a child, I could not think of a better place to grow up - in a nice house with a large lawn and in a neighborhood with lots (more than 20) of kids within three or four years of me to play with. We rode the bus together from our half-days of kindergarten to the last days in High School, before we started driving. We would spend summers playing baseball, football, soccer, basketball, anything we could in our front yards or in the ball field at the end of the street and the hardest decision we would make was whose house we would go to for lunch or dinner.

During my later years (high school and college) I used to look at Sandy Hook and tell my parents how I hated growing up here because there was nothing to do and nothing exciting ever happened (this was a common theme among my friends and brother). After graduating college, I lived at home while I commuted to Manhattan for my first job still not understanding how people could choose to live in this town and commute so long every day for a town that did not have much to offer.

As I write this letter, I have not lived in Sandy Hook for over nine years (my parents and some friends still live there), and I am more happy and proud to have grown up in Sandy Hook than I ever thought I would be. While Sandy Hook is a very simple town it has everything you need: fields and parks for kids to play on, a general store where you can buy a breakfast sandwich for $1.25, a movie theater where every kid in town has been to on a first date and of course a flag pole in the middle of Main Street.

Looking back on it now, Sandy Hook is the only kind of place for a kid to grow up in. Sandy Hook is a place that encourages you to be who you are, that accepts anybody and everybody and a place where nine years later they still recognize me in Bagel Delight. It's a place where parents move to so their kids can ride bikes at night and play outside after dark without having to worry.

Sandy Hook is a place, even after the horrific events of 12/14/12, I am proud to call home. I am even more proud to call it home now, because I know this tragedy will not define the town but the people and their strength will. My only hope is that other kids (hopefully for generations to come) will get to experience the same victories and defeats that I did on the athletic fields, the same love and loss that I did in the halls of the schools, the same joy and heartache that came from rooting for the Nighthawks (although I still consider myself an Indian), the same excitement and quaintness that only a little town can provide and of course the flag pole.

For the rest of my life I can proudly say that I grew up in Sandy Hook. It has made me the person I am today and I would not trade it for any place else.

Justin Gaines
Newtown High School Class of 1998

Walnut Tree baseball field in Sandy Hook

While not born in Sandy Hook, I moved there when I was five and it is the place I call home. I started kindergarten at Hawley School and graduated from Newtown Middle and High School.

As a child, I could not think of a better place to grow up—in a nice house with a large lawn and in a neighborhood with lots (more than 20) of kids within three or four years of me to play with. We rode the bus together from our half-days of kindergarten to the last days in high school, before we started driving. We would spend summers playing baseball, football, soccer, basketball, anything we could in our front yards or in the ball field at the end of the street and the hardest decision we would make was whose house we would go to for lunch or dinner.

During my later years (high school and college) I used to look at Sandy Hook and tell my parents how I hated growing up here because there was nothing to do and nothing exciting ever happened (this was a common theme among my friends and brother). After graduating college, I lived at home while I commuted to Manhattan for my first job still not understanding how people could choose to live in this town and commute so long every day for a town that did not have much to offer.

As I write this letter, I have not lived in Sandy Hook for over nine years (my parents and some friends still live there), and I am more happy and proud to have grown up in Sandy Hook than I ever thought I would be. While Sandy Hook is a very simple town it has everything you need: fields and parks for kids to play on, a general store where you can buy a breakfast sandwich for $1.25, a movie theater where every kid in town has been to on a first date and of course a flag pole in the middle of Main Street.

Looking back on it now, Sandy Hook is the only kind of place for a kid to grow up in. Sandy Hook is a place that encourages you to be who you are, that accepts anybody and everybody and a place where nine years later they still recognize me in Bagel Delight. It's a place where parents move to so their kids can ride bikes at night and play outside after dark without having to worry.

Sandy Hook is a place, even after the horrific events of 12/14/12, I am proud to call home. I am even more proud to call it home now, because I know this tragedy will not define the town but the people and their strength will. My only hope is that other kids (hopefully for generations to come) will get to experience the same victories and defeats that I did on the athletic fields, the same love and loss that I did in the halls of the schools, the same joy and heartache that came from rooting for the Nighthawks (although I still consider myself an Indian), the same excitement and quaintness that only a little town can provide and of course the flag pole.

For the rest of my life I can proudly say that I grew up in Sandy Hook. It has made me the person I am today and I would not trade it for anyplace else.

Justin Gaines, Newtown High School Class of 1998

My name is Lynn Kovack. I have lived in Newtown/Sandy Hook for over 25 years. My 2 children attended Sandy Hook School. I started off working for our local Town Doctor for almost 10 years and then got hired by the Town of Newtown Building Department. I have been the Administrative Assistant there for almost 10 years now. My husband has worked for the Newtown BOE Department for over three years now. Our daughter, Mindy, worked in the Newtown Assessor office for over nine years and just became the Town of Monroe Town Appraiser. Our son, Billy, is an Electrical Apprentice for a local electrician in Newtown. Mindy has given us a beautiful granddaughter, Briana, who just completed her first year of Kindergarten. We also have two Rottweilers who are Certified Therapy dogs and have been doing a reading program with 2nd graders throughout the school year for over three years now. They are also Champion Show dogs.

We moved to Newtown because we fell in love with the town immediately. The beautiful Main Street with the flagpole. The annual Labor Day Parade, many small businesses owned by local Newtown people. You can still see a movie for $2.00 in Newtown. People know your name at local stores, delis, salons, etc.

December 14th changed everything for my family. We went from feeling safe and secure to having all we can do to send Briana to school after that. We pulled together to help each other each day with any issues we were dealing with and helped each other get through it. I have a hard time feeling safe and secure anymore personally. Briana knew somebody who passed away and she misses him dearly.

She wants to know when she can play with him again and I don't know what to say to her as an adult to make her feel okay. I have gotten to know each and every person through all the mail I have opened since Dec 20th. I have opened so many packages and envelopes from all over the world. With the internet these days it is beyond touching to me the time so many people are taking to send us something personally. I can specifically remember several stuffed animals that came. They came with letters stating that the bear helped them through a very difficult time and now it was time for the bear to help us through our difficult times. We have seen everything from scarves, stuffed animals, angels, socks and even pajamas that have been opened and distributed to the families. I have seen each and every one of my coworkers looking at life a little differently these days.

We are coming upon the six month Anniversary and it still seems like yesterday. I find myself thinking about each and every person every single day and find it hard to focus sometimes. I think it was so hard on us town employees because we had to look at each and every item that came in. If we didn't open it we would see it on a table, shelf or even on the floor in the hall up until March when the displays were finally removed. We had to try and get some normalcy for the town employees so we can perform our every day jobs.

We will be in Newtown for many more years to come. I couldn't imagine living anywhere else. Newtown has always been a beautiful place to me and I have been very proud to be part of this community for so long. There is beautiful scenery everywhere you look. The people in town are so pleasent. I am very proud to say I am from Newtown. I just want people to stop saying to me when they find out I am from Newtown. "Oh that Town" (because of the tragedy) Yes that town - that is a beautiful town to bring up a family and just a beautiful place in general. That is the town I want to be known as.

I am still trying to figure out what my NEW NORMAL is!!!!

Newtown Municipal Center

My name is Lynn Kovack. I have lived in Newtown/Sandy Hook for over 25 years. My 2 children attended Sandy Hook School. I started off working for our local Town Doctor for almost 10 years and then got hired by the Town of Newtown Building Department. I have been the Administrative Assistant there for almost 10 years now. My husband has worked for the Newtown BOE Department for over three years now. Our daughter, Mindy, worked in the Newtown Assessor Office for over nine years and just became the Town of Monroe Town Appraiser. Our son, Billy, is an Electrical Apprentice for a local electrician in Newtown. Mindy has given us a beautiful granddaughter, Briana, who just completed her first year of Kindergarten. We also have two Rottweilers who are Certified Therapy dogs and have been doing a reading program with 2nd graders throughout the school year for over three years now. They are also champion show dogs.

We moved to Newtown because we fell in love with the town immediately. The beautiful Main Street with the Flagpole. The annual Labor Day Parade. Many small businesses owned by local Newtown people. You can still see a movie for $2.00 in Newtown. People know your name at local stores, delis, salons, etc.

December 14th changed everything for my family. We went from feeling safe and secure to having all we can do to send Briana to school after that. We pulled together to help each other each day with any issues we were dealing with and helped each other get through it. I have a hard time feeling safe and secure anymore personally. Briana knew somebody who passed away and she misses him dearly. She wants to know when she can play with him again and I don't know what to say to her as an adult to make her feel okay. I have gotten to know each and every person through all the mail I have opened since Dec 20th. I have opened so many packages and envelopes from all over the world. With the internet these days it is beyond touching to me the time so many people are taking to send us something personally. I can specifically remember several stuffed animals that came. They came with letters stating that the bear helped them through a very difficult time and now it was time for the bear to help us through our difficult times. We have seen everything from scarves, stuffed animals, angels, socks and even pajamas that have been opened and distributed to the families. I have seen each and every one of my coworkers looking at life a little differently these days. We are coming upon the six month Anniversary and it still seems like yesterday. I find myself thinking about each and every person every single day and find it hard to focus sometimes. I think it was so hard on us town employees because we had to look at each and every item that came in. If we didn't open it we would see it on a table, shelf or even on the floor in the hall up until March when the displays were finally removed. We had to try and get some normalcy for the town employees so we can perform our every day jobs.

We will be in Newtown for many more years to come. I couldn't imagine living anywhere else. Newtown has always been a beautiful place to me and I have been very proud to be part of this community for so long. There is beautiful scenery everywhere you look. The people in town are so pleasant. I am very proud to say I am from Newtown. I just want people to stop saying to me when they find out I am from Newtown—"Oh that town" (because of the tragedy). Yes that town—that is a beautiful town to bring up a family and just a beautiful place in general. That is the town I want to be known as.

I am still trying to figure out what my new Normal is!!!!

Walking trail at Fairfield Hills

The Pleasance Fountain, Main Street, Newtown

Newtown-Through My Eyes

My husband and I moved to Newtown in 1996, the year our oldest daughter was born. We were both born and raised in Bridgeport, Connecticut and felt that we wanted a more quiet, country setting to raise our children. It was a big adjustment, the quiet was deafening. When my daughter was born I became a stay at home Mom. My husband commuted to Darien but didn't mind because we both loved our new home in Newtown.

I felt a bit isolated living in a new town and not working but that didn't last long. I enrolled my daughter at the Mr. Turtle School in a Mommy and Me program. It was a wonderful experience for her and a great way for me to meet other parents in town who had children the same age. We also joined another program that helped me get to know Newtown people called KidsFit. The coordinator took great care in helping the parents and kids get to know each other. It was then that I started to feel a part of the Newtown community.

We became members of Trinity Episcopal Church and were welcomed with open arms into the church community. Pastor Kathie Adams-Shepherd is truly a blessing to Newtown and our church community. So, when it came time for pre-school, Trinity Day School was the logical choice for us. The teachers were amazing! Trinity had the right balance of learning and socializing. I met so many great parents at Trinity Day School that are my closest friends today.

My girls have gone through Hawley, Reed, St. Rose, Newtown Middle School and now Newtown

High School. The teachers they have
had over the years have truly
been amazing, quality teachers.
There have been a handful of
teachers and coaches who went
above and beyond to make a
lasting impression on my girls.
To them I am very grateful and
will never forget what they did
for my children. But none have
had such an impact as Mr.
Dumais, the principal at Newtown
High School. I have never met
him but plan to before my kids
graduate from the high school.
I have to personally thank him
for everything he and the staff
at Newtown High School did during
and after the Sandy Hook
tragedy. His inspiring words
and presence at the high school
made us as parents feel safe
to let our kids go back to school.
We knew they were in good hands –

he reassured us of that. I will always have a special place in my heart for him. I could only imagine how hard it must have been to be the one everyone was looking to for guidance. He is a true leader and a wonderful role model for our children.

For 13 years now, I have been a member of the Newtown Junior Women's Club and I couldn't imagine my life without these wonderful ladies. It is through the NJWC that I have seen the generosity of the Newtown community. We head the back to school backpack program, Tag a Gift during the holidays and a free day of science for the children of Newtown. I have seen members of the community fill a child's holiday wish list above and beyond what the child asked for. I have seen a young child donate her favorite toy to a child in need because they couldn't find a new one to buy. Just recently, a woman from Washington contacted our club to deliver handmade quilts, one for every 12/14 family, one for the first responders, one for the twin left behind, one for the boyfriend of a teacher lost. I was so touched by the love for one human being for another.

Another Newtown event that has touched my life is the Newtown Relay for Life. I have been involved in Newtown's Relay for Life since it was brought to Newtown 10 years ago. My Relay for Life team is filled with the beautiful people I have met in Newtown. Everyone is touched by cancer sometime in their life so I never have trouble getting people involved in Relay for

Life. What an amazing event! I suggest everyone experience Newtown's Relay for Life at least once. It's a fun filled day of fundraising and then at night the evening turns into a beautiful tribute to those we have lost or those still fighting. The luminaria ceremony is one of the most beautiful, touching events I have ever seen. The survivor lap is also very moving and so symbolic. Those fighting this horrible disease are on the track with their caregivers and surrounding them is the rest of the community, as if to say we are here for you, whatever you need. That's my Newtown, a caring community.

I have seen people throw together a tag sale to help a family pay for huge medical bills. I have seen time and time again meal schedules for others to cook for the families of those undergoing treatment. I have seen everyone clean their closets out to donate their clothes for families who have lost everything in a fire. Whenever there is a tragedy in Newtown, and we have had our share before 12/14, I have seen people go into action. I don't know if it is like this in other towns. I tend to think our town is special.

Now, in the wake of 12/14 I have had the privilege to help with the My Sandy Hook Family Fund. Again, I have seen first-hand how Newtown people spring into action after a tragedy. This group has given so much of their time and energy to the families to help ease their pain. I am so grateful that there are such caring people out there in my community who always rise to the occasion.

Newtown is such a beautiful, picturesque town. I love the old, country feel you get being at the Labor Day Parade. The sense of pride we felt when we celebrated the 300th year birthday. The sense of love we feel at Relay for Life. The sense of community you feel at the Duck Race, Rooster Run or Newtown Road race. And the sense of love and humanity I have felt at every vigil for 12/14.

This is my town, my community, my Newtown. IN Newtown ... Love Wins

Sincerely,

Charlene Calandro

Newtown—Through My Eyes

My husband and I moved to Newtown in 1996, the year our oldest daughter was born. We were both born and raised in Bridgeport, Connecticut and felt that we wanted a more quiet, country setting to raise our children. It was a big adjustment, the quiet was deafening. When my daughter was born I became a stay at home Mom. My husband commuted to Darien but didn't mind because we both loved our new home in Newtown.

I felt a bit isolated living in a new town and not working but that didn't last long. I enrolled my daughter at the Mr. Turtle School in a Mommy and Me program. It was a wonderful experience for her and a great way for me to meet other parents in town who had children the same age. We also joined another program that helped me get to know Newtown people called KidsFit. The coordinator took great care in helping the parents and kids get to know each other. It was then that I started to feel a part of the Newtown community.

We became members of Trinity Episcopal Church and were welcomed with open arms into the church community. Pastor Kathie Adams-Shepherd is truly a blessing to Newtown and our church community. So, when it came time for pre-school, Trinity Day School was the logical choice for us. The teachers were amazing! Trinity had the right balance of learning and socializing. I met so many great parents at Trinity Day School that are my closest friends today.

My girls have gone through Hawley, Reed, St. Rose, Newtown Middle School and now Newtown High School. The teachers they have had over the years have truly been amazing, quality teachers. There have been a handful of teachers and coaches who went above and beyond to make a lasting impression on my girls. To them I am very grateful and will never forget what they did for my children. But none have had such an impact as Mr. Damais, the principal at Newtown High School. I have never met him but plan to before my kids graduate from the high school. I have to personally thank him for everything he and the staff at Newtown High School did during and after the Sandy Hook tragedy. His inspiring words and presence at the high school made us as parents feel safe to let our kids go back to school. We knew they were in good hands—he reassured us of that. I will always have a special place in my heart for him. I could only imagine how hard it must have been to be the one everyone was looking to for guidance. He is a true leader and a wonderful role model for our children.

For 13 years now, I have been a member of the Newtown Junior Women's Club and I couldn't imagine my life without these wonderful ladies. It is through the NJWC that I have seen the generosity of the Newtown community. We head the back to school backpack program, Tag a Gift during the holidays and a free day of science for the children of Newtown. I have seen members of the community fill a child's holiday wish list above and beyond what the child asked for. I have seen a young child donate her favorite toy to a child in need because they couldn't find a new one to buy. Just recently, a woman from Washington contacted our club to deliver handmade quilts, one for every 12/14 family, one for the first responders, one for the twin left behind, one for the boyfriend of a teacher lost. I was so touched by the love for one human being for another.

Another Newtown event that has touched my life is the Newtown Relay for Life. I have been involved in Newtown's Relay for Life since it was brought to Newtown 10 years ago. My Relay for Life team is filled with the beautiful people I have met in Newtown. Everyone is touched by cancer sometime in their life so I never have trouble getting people involved in Relay for Life. What an amazing event! I suggest everyone experience Newtown's Relay for Life at least once. It's a fun filled day of fundraising and then at night the evening turns into a beautiful tribute to those we have lost or those still fighting. The luminaria ceremony is one of the most beautiful, touching events I have ever seen. The survivor lap is also very moving and so symbolic. Those fighting this horrible disease are on the track with their caregivers and surrounding them is the rest of the community, as if to say we are here for you, whatever you need. That's my Newtown, a caring community.

I have seen people throw together a tag sale to help a family pay for huge medical bills. I have seen time and time again meal schedules for others to cook for the families of those undergoing treatment. I have seen everyone clean their closets out to donate their clothes for families who have lost everything in a fire. Whenever there is a tragedy in Newtown, and we have had our share before 12/14, I have seen people go into action. I don't know if it is like this in other towns, I tend to think our town is special.

Now, in the wake of 12/14 I have had the privilege to help with the My Sandy Hook Family Fund. Again, I have seen firsthand how Newtown people spring into action after a tragedy. This group has given so much of their time and energy to the families to help ease their pain. I am so grateful that there are such caring people out there in my community who always rise to the occasion.

Newtown is such a beautiful, picturesque town. I love the old, country feel you get being at the Labor Day Parade. The sense of pride we felt when we celebrated the 300th year birthday. The sense of love we feel at Relay for Life. The sense of community you feel at the Duck Race, Rooster Run or Newtown Road race. And the sense of love and humanity I have felt at every vigil for 12/14.

This is my town, my community, my Newtown. In Newtown . . . Love Wins

Sincerely,
Charlene Calandro

Relay for Life at Blue & Gold Stadium at Newtown High School, 2004

One of my greatest accomplishments in my short life thus far was to become a volunteer firefighter in Sandy Hook. What started out as a childhood dream has showed me one of the greatest community services a person can preform. Nothing makes me feel better than returning from a call knowing that I was there when I was needed most, and did everything possible to help. However, our local fire departments do so much more than respond to emergencies. We perform fire prevention activities in the local schools, hold food drives for our local food pantries, and provide open houses for residents to see how we turn their donations into life saving training and equipment. One of our biggest fundraising events, 'Lobsterfest,' provides customers with steak or lobster dinners. For weeks we plan and prepare for this event, eventually transforming our firehouse into a restaurant, bar and dance floor. Families from across the town come in for a good meal and a great night out. While the kids climb through the fire trucks, the adults enjoy a live band each night and the company of hundreds of other visitors. It is an enormous feat to provide meals for around 1500 people in two nights, but we have perfected the event to go on without a flaw. Whether they've

Been to every one of our 26 events to date, or it's their first time, everyone enjoys the company of one another while doing what we do best - Supporting each other.

Ryan Clark

Losterfest at the Sandy Hook Fire Department

One of my greatest accomplishments in my short life thus far was to become a volunteer firefighter in Sandy Hook. What started out as a childhood dream has showed me one of the greatest community services a person can perform. Nothing makes me feel better than returning from a call knowing that I was there when I was needed most, and did everything possible to help. However, our local fire departments do so much more than respond to emergencies. We perform fire prevention activities in the local schools, hold food drives for our local food pantries, and provide open houses for residents to see how we turn their donations into life saving training and equipment. One of our biggest fundraising events, 'Lobsterfest' provides customers with steak or lobster dinners. For weeks we plan and prepare for this event, eventually transforming our firehouse into a restaurant, bar and dance floor. Families from across the town come in for a good meal and a great night out. While the kids climb through the fire trucks, the adults enjoy a live band each night and the company of hundreds of other visitors. It is an enormous feat to provide meals for around 1500 people in two nights, but we have perfected the event to go on without a flaw. Whether they've been to every one of our 26 events to date, or it's their first time, everyone enjoys the company of one another while doing what we do best—supporting each other.

Ryan Clark

Losterfest at the Sandy Hook Fire Department

Dear CNN Correspondant,

Please forgive me for not remembering your name, but I do remember you. We stood in the hall outside the concession stand at Edmond Town Hall on a cold December night. While various news crews filmed outside, we talked about the weather, our families, — everything except the events that brought you to our town. At one point I asked you to share the warmest, happiest story you had covered in your travels. You smiled sadly and said, "I don't get to cover those."

You moved on a few days later; images of stuffed animals, flowers and votive candles and other symbols of a wounded community etched in your memory. And that, to me, is a tragedy - that you left not knowing why so many of us moved to Newtown. That you departed before learning the secret of how we will move forward on a path no one expected to travel. So please, accept this letter — this post script to your visit. A simple story to warm you and lighten your burden.

Sincerely,
Larry

Fifteen years ago, as new residents of Sandy Hook, our family participated in our first Christmas Tree Lighting at Rams Pasture. The snow was deep that year and our sons were bundled like the characters in A Christmas Story. Both boys carried their favorite stuffed animals - Our oldest carried Clifford the Big Red Dog and our youngest clung to White Tiger as we joined the throng who had already gathered around the tree and Santa's sleigh.

After the carols were sung, the tree lit, and Santa informed of Christmas wishes, we made our way to a friend's house for hot chocolate. Buckling my son in his seat we made a horrible discovery; Clifford was gone! Grateful it was Clifford and not White Tiger that had been dropped in the snow, we made our way back to Rams Pasture. There was no sign of Clifford. Tucking my son into bed that night, I assured him Clifford had been found by someone who knew he was loved. Clifford was safe and warm.

The next day I went to the police station and asked if anyone had turned in a stuffed red dog. No one had. As I turned to leave, the officer suggest I try the library because some of the staff were involved in planning the event. I thanked the officer and left. Logic told me Clifford was gone. My heart hoped he would find his way back home to my son, who held Clifford closer since the death of his own dog.

A soft spoken woman answered the phone at Booth Library. I shared how we had lost Clifford and desperately hoped to find him. Could she help? Yes - she could. Clifford was at her house. As the volunteers began cleaning up the remnants of hot chocolate, donuts, and cookies after the tree lighting, someone spied Clifford near Santa's sleigh. Clifford was given to the librarian who took him home, bathed and fluffed him - knowing that somewhere a child was longing to be reunited with their friend. And they were.

Safe at home, my son and I marveled at how Clifford had grown during his adventure. For, just like in the stories, Clifford had been loved by someone with a heart as big as all outdoors.

The adventures of Clifford on that first Christmas Tree Lighting has become a family favorite. When friends and relatives express their amazement that "we got Clifford back" we simply smile and say, "That's why we moved to Newtown."

Fifteen years later, Clifford sits on a shelf in the room of the boy who loved him.— the boy — now nineteen — who spent his first two weeks of winter break setting up tables and chairs at Edmond Town Hall for fire fighter, police, and other first responders attending funerals for children who sat in his former classroom. The boy — now young man — who placed teddy bears on chairs and behind stage curtains so

Children could find them and claim a new friend, as Clifford had been his. The boy who upon hearing his elementary teachers were at Town Hall, sought them out so he could hug them – hold them close – and tell them he loved them still.

From his shelf Clifford reminds me why we have stayed in Sandy Hook all these years: because even in the coldest, darkest night, when all seems lost – one person can make the difference to a child and the parents who want to reassure him –

All will be well – in time – with love and hope.

Dear CNN Correspondent,

Please forgive me for not remembering your name, but I do remember you. We stood in the hall outside the concession stand at Edmond Town Hall on a cold December night. While various news crews filmed outside, we talked about the weather, our families—everything except the events that brought you to our town. At one point I asked you to share the warmest, happiest story you had covered in your travels. You smiled sadly and said, "I don't get to cover those."

You moved on a few days later; images of stuffed animals, flowers and votive candles and other symbols of a wounded community etched in your memory. And that, to me, is a tragedy—that you left not knowing why so many of us moved to Newtown. That you departed before learning the secret of how we will move forward on a path no one expected to travel. So please, accept this letter—this postscript to your visit. A simple story to warm you and lighten your burden.

Sincerely, Karen

Fifteen years ago, as new residents of Sandy Hook, our family participated in our first Christmas tree lighting at Rams Pasture. The snow was deep that year and our sons were bundled like the characters in *A Christmas Story*. Both boys carried their favorite stuffed animals—Our oldest carried Clifford the Big Red Dog and our youngest clung to White Tiger, as we joined the throng who had already gathered around the tree and Santa's sleigh.

After the carols were sung, the tree lit, and Santa informed of Christmas wishes, we made our way to a friend's house for hot chocolate. Buckling my son in his seat we made a horrible discovery: Clifford was gone! Grateful that it was Clifford and not White Tiger that had been dropped in the snow, we made our way back to Rams Pasture. There was no sign of Clifford. Tucking my son into bed that night, I assured him Clifford had been found by someone who knew he was loved. Clifford was safe and warm.

The next day I went to the police station and asked if anyone had turned in a stuffed red dog. No one had. As I turned to leave, the officer suggested I try the library because some of the staff were involved in planning the event. I thanked the officer and left. Logic told me Clifford was gone. My heart hoped he would find his way back home to my son, who held Clifford closer since the death of his own dog.

A soft spoken woman answered the phone at Booth Library. I shared how we had lost Clifford and desperately hoped to find him. Could she help? Yes—she could. Clifford was at her house. As the volunteers began cleaning up the remnants of hot chocolate, donuts, and cookies after the tree lighting ceremony, someone spied Clifford near Santa's Sleigh. Clifford was given to the librarian who took him home, bathed and fluffed him—knowing that somewhere a child was longing to be reunited with their friend. And they were.

Safe at home, my son and I marveled at how Clifford had grown during his adventure. For, just like in the stories, Clifford had been loved by someone with a heart as big as all outdoors.

The adventures of Clifford on that first Christmas Tree Lighting has become a family favorite. When friends and relatives express their amazement that "we got Clifford back" we simply smile and said, "That's why we moved to Newtown."

Fifteen years later, Clifford sits on a shelf in the room of the boy who loved him—the boy—now nineteen—who spent his first two weeks of winter break setting up tables and chairs at Edmond Town Hall for fire fighter, police and other first responders attending funerals for children who sat in his former classroom. The boy—now a young man—who placed teddy bears on chairs and behind stage curtains so children could find them and claim a new friend, as Clifford had been his. The boy who upon hearing his elementary teachers were at Town Hall, sought them out so he could hug them—hold them close—and tell them he loved them still.

From his shelf, Clifford reminds me why we have stayed in Sandy Hook all these years: because even in the coldest, darkest night, when all seems lost—one person can make the difference to a child and the parents who want to reassure him—

All will be well—in time—with love and hope.

Edmond Town Hall, 2005, during the Tercentennial in Newtown

12/21/2012

I grew up in a town with a flagpole placed awkwardly in the middle of Main Street, where the loudest sound was the high school marching band at the Friday night football game and the worst worry was forgetting a book in your locker after school. I read my name in the local paper when I made the honor roll, greeted my neighbors by name at the Starbucks where I held my first job, ordered my chocolate-banana-peanut-butter ice cream from the town creamery - a place so fresh you can smell manure from the cows on the premises while you eat. At Sandy Hook School, I sat on the floor in Mr. Ballerini's fourth grade class while he read Harry Potter aloud, and I performed an original song about Jacques Cousteau on Explorer Day. Here, I learned important things about the world, like what kind of tea they serve in Japan and to where the Frilled Lizard is an indigenous animal. I made lifelong friends rehearsing for the class musical.

I grew up fearing ghosts and monsters and boogie men, the kind that children and children alone fear; the kind you grow up and get over by convincing yourself that the world is a good place, where extraterrestrials don't haunt you in your sleep and bad guys don't lurk in your closet, waiting for you to least expect them.

In the years since I left this town, I've returned to a place where I look forward to fresh apples in the fall and a used book sale in the summer. A place where I now put on mascara when I go into town, because the drug store can be an impromptu high school reunion. A place where I often drive the longest route possible, just so I can see the beauty of the old houses and winding streets in the place that is my truest home.

Last weekend, I returned to the same town, but to a very different place.

A place overflowing with reporters and cameras and teddy bears and handmade ribbons and tears and empty words of reassurance, a place of heartbreak beyond all reasonable measure. I returned to a place where 20 innocent children, 6 heroes, and 1 mother have made history in the worst way possible. To a place where 27 lives have become pictures and candles and names on a list read by the President of the United States of America.

I do not know what to do with this sadness. I do not know where to place my sorrow for these families, my numbness, my overwhelming sense of loss, my feeling that a piece of my own foundation has been ripped out from under me.

I cannot convince myself that these ghosts will not haunt me, nor that the bad guys won't find me in my simple little town. When I wake up in the middle of the night in fear, I can't crawl into my parents' room with a blanket until morning proves the evil is just pretend. I have to turn on the TV, think of something else, and hope I fall asleep in spite of it all.

My solace comes when I tell myself that we are not alone. That though I know the route to Treadwell Park with my eyes closed, though I accepted my first boyfriend over science-class rockets on the playground of Sandy Hook School, though money from this school's scholarship fund helped me pay for college, I share my grief with the world. With every parent, every teacher, every student who ever went to any elementary school, anywhere.

The issues behind this tragedy are complex and painful. But to ever recover from this horror, this both surreal and vivid nightmare, we have to do something to keep this from happening again. Nothing will make the cost these families must bear worthwhile, but we can try to stop others from the same suffering.

The people of Newtown can organize, whether to run a gift-wrap fundraiser, host a rubber-duck race in the local creek, or create meaningful and necessary change in the world. I hope you stay with us because with your help, we will do great things.

With sorrow and hope,

Tony

I grew up in a town with a flagpole placed awkwardly in the middle of Main Street, where the loudest sound was the high school marching band at the Friday night football game and the worst worry was forgetting a book in your locker after school. I read my name in the local paper when I made the honor roll, greeted my neighbors by name at the Starbucks where I held my first job, ordered my chocolate-banana-peanut-butter ice cream from the town creamery—a place so fresh you can smell manure from the cows on the premises while you eat. At Sandy Hook School, I sat on the floor in Mr. Ballerini's fourth grade class while he read Harry Potter aloud, and I performed an original song about Jacques Cousteau on Explorer Day. Here, I learned important things about the world, like what kind of tea they serve in Japan and to where the Frilled Lizard is an indigenous animal. I made lifelong friends rehearsing for the class musical.

I grew up fearing ghosts and monsters and boogie men, the kind that children and children alone fear; the kind you grow up and get over by convincing yourself that the world is a good place, where extraterrestrials don't haunt you in your sleep and bad guys don't lurk in your closet, waiting for you to least expect them.

In the years since I left this town, I've returned to a place where I look forward to fresh apples in the fall and a used book sale in the summer. A place where I now put on mascara when I go into town, because the drug store can be an impromptu high school reunion. A place where I often drive the longest route possible, just so I can see the beauty of the old houses and winding streets in the place that is my truest home.

Last weekend, I returned to the same town, but to a very different place. A place overflowing with reporters and cameras and teddy bears and handmade ribbons and tears and empty words of reassurance, a place of heartbreak beyond all reasonable measure. I returned to a place where 20 innocent children, 6 heroes, and 1 mother have made history in the worst way possible. To a place where 27 lives have become pictures and candles and names on a list read by the President of the United States of America.

I do not know what to do with this sadness. I do not know where to place my sorrow for these families, my numbness, my overwhelming sense of loss, my feeling that a piece of my own foundation has been ripped out from under me.

I cannot convince myself that these ghosts will not haunt me, nor that the bad guys won't find me in my simple little town. When I wake up in the middle of the night in fear, I can't crawl into my parents' room with a blanket until morning proves the evil is just pretend. I have to turn on the TV, think of something else, and hope I fall asleep in spite of it all.

My solace comes when I tell myself that we are not alone. That though I know the route to Treadwell Park with my eyes closed, though I accepted my first boyfriend over science-class rockets on the playground of Sandy Hook School, though money from this school's scholarship fund helped me pay for college, I share my grief with the world. With every parent, every teacher, every student who ever went to any elementary school, anywhere.

The issues behind this tragedy are complex and painful. But to ever recover from this horror, this both surreal and vivid nightmare, we have to do something to keep this from happening again. Nothing will make the cost these families must bear worthwhile, but we can try to stop others from the same suffering.

The people of Newtown can organize, whether to run a gift-wrap fundraiser, host a rubber-duck race in the local creek, or create meaningful and necessary change in the world. I hope you stay with us, because with your help, we will do great things.

With sorrow and hope,
Tory

Flagpole at the intersection of Main Street and Church Hill Road

July 4th 2013

Dear Reader,

Newtown is a place that we have called home since 2000. We live in Newtown because we wanted to remain in a small northern Town even after the company I work for was sold and relocated to South Florida. I was fortunate to be able to stay where I wanted since my job involves travel and being near an airport is the main requirement. We chose to stay right here. We love the change of seasons, our friends, the wonderful recreation leagues for the kids and the excellent education all three of our sons received. I have lived and worked in many cities across the United States but I believe this area of Connecticut to be a place with the perfect combination of all the necessary ingredients to enjoy life

However, the Town has not been immune to the effects of a terrible economy, and we remain concerned that the state of Connecticut is losing out to other states where the tax burden is not nearly a high. It was partially for that reason that I decided to run for election as a member of the Newtown Board of Finance where I have served for 10 years, the past two as Vice Chairman.

Concurrent with the Board of Finance service, I was an active member for 5 years and currently serve as an associate member of the 2nd Company Governor's Horseguard located right here in Newtown. I discovered that stable duty (which naturally included shoveling a lot of horse manure) was a good preparation for serving as an elected official, even in an unpaid voluntary position. The 2nd Company Governor's Horseguard is one of the oldest active cavalry units in the United States, having been chartered in 1808. The duties now are all ceremonial in nature but in many previous wars, including WWI, the unit was activated and served with distinction. I learned to play the bugle while in the guard and had the honor of representing the state by riding a fine horse named Trav'ler in the Presidential Inaugural parade in 2004 through the streets of Washington, D.C.

2

In that parade, our horses wore ribbons representing the soldiers from Connecticut who lost their lives in the Iraq and Afghanistan wars. My horse had the ribbon of a courageous young Marine from Connecticut named Kemaphoom "Ahn" Chanawongse who died in Iraq in 2003.

He has a headstone in the now infamous section 60 at Arlington National Cemetery, where he is in good company, along with many other brave soldiers of those wars. I stop by his grave every time I am in Washington DC to visit my own late father's gravesite in Section 65 at Arlington.

Both sections are in sight of where the hijacked passenger jet smashed into the Pentagon on Sept 11, 2001. I believe that anyone who sees the young ages on the headstones of our soldiers buried in Arlington, or any other National Cemeteries, can't help but feel the true impact of the terrible price we pay, and have always paid from the day our nation was founded, for the price of freedom. We can never repay them and their loved ones for their sacrifice, except through our eternal respect and gratitude.

The road + Newtown has been quite an experience on many levels. It's where my wife Azian, our youngest son Torin and I still reside, and a place that I would have remembered as a simple, classic New England community. Sadly, December 14, 2012 changed the way our Town will be viewed by the world due to the Tragic events of "that day". My hope and belief is that we will be measured in the future on how we dealt with the aftermath and how we honored, and continue to honor the innocent victims and the heroes of Sandy Hook Elementary School.

While we are not certain that we will remain in Newtown forever, we do know that living here has been among the best, if not the best years of our lives.

Sincerely,

Joe Kearney

4

July 4, 2013

Dear Reader,

Newtown is a place that we have called home since 2000.

We live in Newtown because we wanted to remain in a small northern town even after the company I work for was sold and relocated to South Florida. I was fortunate to be able to stay where I wanted since my job involves travel and being near an airport is the main requirement. We chose to stay right here. We love the change of seasons, our friends, the wonderful recreation leagues for the kids and the excellent education all three of our sons received. I have lived and worked in many cities across the United States but I believe this area of Connecticut to be a place with the perfect combination of all the necessary ingredients to enjoy life.

However, the town has not been immune to the effects of a terrible economy, and we remain concerned that the State of Connecticut is losing out to other states where the tax burden is not nearly as high. It was partially for that reason that I decided to run for election as a member of the Newtown Board of Finance where I have served for 10 years, the past two as Vice Chairman.

Concurrent with the Board of Finance service, I was an active member for 5 years and currently serve as an associate member of the 2nd Company Governors Horseguard located right here in Newtown. I discovered that stable duty (which naturally included shoveling a lot of horse manure) was a good preparation for serving as an elected official, even in an unpaid voluntary position. The 2nd Company Governor's Horseguard is one of the oldest active cavalry units in the United States, having been chartered in 1808. The duties now are all ceremonial in nature but in many previous wars, including WW1, the unit was activated and served with distinction. I learned to play the bugle while in the guard and had the honor of representing the state by riding a fine horse named Trav'ler in the Presidential Inaugural parade in 2004 through the streets of Washington DC. In that parade, our horses wore ribbons representing the soldiers from Connecticut who lost their lives in the Iraq and Afghanistan wars. My horse had the ribbon of a courageous young marine from Connecticut named Kemaphoom "Ahn" Chanawongse who died in Iraq in 2003. He has a headstone in the now infamous section 60 at Arlington National Cemetery, where he is in good company, along with many other brave soldiers of those wars. I stop by his grave every time I am in Washington DC to visit my own late father's gravesite in section 65 at Arlington.

Both sections are in sight of where the hijacked passenger jet smashed into the Pentagon on September 11, 2001. I believe that anyone who sees the young ages on the headstones of our soldiers buried in Arlington, or any other National Cemeteries, can't help but feel the true impact of the terrible price we pay, and have always paid from the day our nation was founded, for the price of freedom. We can never repay them and their loved ones for their sacrifice, except through our eternal respect and gratitude.

The road to Newtown has been quite an experience on many levels. It's where my wife Azian, our youngest son Torin and I still reside and a place that I would have remembered as a simple, classic New England community. Sadly, December 14, 2012 changed the way our town will be viewed by the world due to the tragic events of "that day." My hope and belief is that we will be measured in the future on how we dealt with the aftermath and how we honored, and continue to honor the innocent victims and the heroes of Sandy Hook Elementary School.

While we are not certain that we will remain in Newtown forever, we do know that living here has been among the best, if not the best years of our lives.

Sincerely,
Joe Kearney

2nd Company Governor's Horseguard

Dear Friends,

When my family and I moved to Newtown 19 years ago, we were able to find land and build a house for a reasonable price. Unable to afford to live in lower Fairfield County, we thought this would be a great place to raise a family and to commute to Norwalk where we both work. Right away when we moved in people came to greet us. One organization that reached out to us was the Newtown Bridle and Saddle. We became official members of this organization by agreeing to let the horses cut across our property. It was exciting for us to see these people riding horses. My children would run from window to window waving at them as they walked by. Periodically they would stop and let the boys pet their horses. It was a great way to build community in our neighborhood. In my opinion there aren't nicer people than the "horse" community. We felt and still feel privileged that they cut through our yard anytime they need to.

Being a public school teacher I felt strongly that my children would attend a public school. Newtown was noted high (and still is) for its public school system. My children were part of the public school from preschool on. Two of my sons attended the reverse mainstream preschool where they have "typical" students along with special needs students. This experience has made these boys caring, empathetic and fair young men. One son who is a junior in high school volunteered to be a "buddy" to two special needs students in his chemistry class this year. When nobody else wanted to work with these students my son volunteered and showed the other students that it is pretty cool to accept everyone. All the schools are open and welcoming to parents and their concerns. We have had a great experience in the public school system here in town.

An organization that we joined right away upon moving to town was St. Rose of Lima Roman Catholic church. We became involved in the church right away. I helped out at Youth Group (being a former Youth Minister at another church) and our second and third sons were baptized there. Close to 60% of Newtown is Catholic. That is pretty amazing to me. Along with that it has a Catholic school. I had the preconceived notion that when there was a Catholic school at a church the public school children were second class citizens. This is not the case at St. Rose. We have never felt anything but welcomed and wanted in the church. I believe that there are 1,600 public school students in the Religious Education Program. What a group to organize! Being a teacher already I was asked to teach for the Religious Education Program. I volunteered for 14 years teaching Catechism.

Finally another big event in Newtown is St. Rose Carnival. Somebody came up to the pulpit one Sunday 14 years ago and asked for help in the food booth. I volunteered to help them out. Fourteen years later I'm still running the food booth. I love it! I love seeing people who come and volunteer to work in the food booth. They come year after year. We run a clean carnival and follow the health inspector's regulations, where we always get a great rating. It is a lot of work but it is worth it. We try and keep the prices reasonable so anyone can come to feed their families for a fair price. Many of the restaurants in town donate the food that we serve. Year after year they are giving us pulled pork, sausage and peppers, eggplant, meatballs, pizza and pasta to serve. These restaurants are asked for donations from every organization in town, yet they still give us a large tray of something every year. They are amazing!

The feeling I get when working with people in town is a warm feeling. We are in it for the right reasons. We are a loving, generous and caring community that I am so proud to be a part of.

Mary Jo Pecora-Runkle
Newtown Resident

Horses in Fall

Dear Friends,

When my family and I moved to Newtown 19 years ago, we were able to find land and build a house for a reasonable price. Unable to afford to live in lower Fairfield County, we thought this would be a great place to raise a family and to commute to Norwalk where we both work. Right away when we moved in people came to greet us. One organization that reached out to us was the Newtown Bridle and Saddle. We became official members of this organization by agreeing to let the horses cut across our property. It was exciting for us to see these people riding horses. My children would run from window to window waving at them as they walked by. Periodically they would stop and let the boys pet their horses. It was a great way to build community in our neighborhood. In my opinion there aren't nicer people than the "horse" community. We felt and still feel privileged that they cut through our yard anytime they need to.

Being a public school teacher I felt strongly that my children would attend a public school. Newtown was noted high (and still is) for its public school system. My children were part of the public school from preschool on. Two of my sons attended the reverse mainstream preschool where they have "typical" students along with special needs students. This experience has made these boys caring, empathetic and fair young men. One son who is a junior in high school volunteered to be a "buddy" to two special need students in his chemistry class this year. When nobody else wanted to work with these students my son volunteered and showed the other students that it is pretty cool to accept everyone. All the schools are open and welcoming to parents and their concerns. We have had a great experience in the public school system here in town.

An organization that we joined right away upon moving to town was St. Rose of Lima Roman Catholic Church. We became involved in the church right away, I helped out at Youth Group (being a former Youth Minister at another church) and our second and third sons were baptized there. Close to 60% of Newtown is Catholic. That is pretty amazing to me. Along with that it has a catholic school. I had the preconceived notion that when there was a catholic school at a church the public school children were second class citizens. This is not the case at St. Rose. We have never felt anything but welcomed and wanted in the church. I believe that there are 1,600 public school students in the Religious Education Program. What a group to organize! Being a teacher already I was asked to teach for the Religious Education Program. I volunteered for 14 years teaching Catechism.

Finally another big event in Newtown is St. Rose Carnival. Somebody came up to the pulpit one Sunday 14 years ago and asked for help in the food booth. I volunteered to help them out. Fourteen years later I'm still running the food booth. I love it! I love seeing people who come and volunteer to work in the food booth. They come year after year. We run a clean carnival and follow the health inspector's regulations, where we always get a great rating. It is a lot of work but it is worth it. We try and keep the prices reasonable so anyone can come to feed their families for a fair price. Many of the restaurants in town donate the food that we serve. Year after year they are giving us pulled pork, sausage and peppers, eggplant, meatballs, pizza and pasta to serve. These restaurants are asked for donations from every organization in town, yet they still give us a large tray of something every year. They are amazing!

The feeling I get when working with people in town is a warm feeling. We are in it for the right reasons. We are a loving, generous and caring community that I am so proud to be a part of.

Mary Jo Pecora-Runkle
Newtown Resident

December 16, 2012

My wife and I just spent most of the last two days at St. Rose Church. As the names of the victims became known to us, we all experienced a second wave of horror. I personally knew three of the victim's families, several families are close neighbors. On a more uplifting note, my wife (MB) and I have participated in the St. Rose Church Live Nativity reenactment for ten years. It was planned for December 15th, and we thought for sure it would be cancelled. After all, who could possibly celebrate anything a day after a tragedy like this. However, Monsignor Weiss (or Father Bob as he is known to us,) insisted that the Live Nativity be held as scheduled. So, last nite we gathered at St. Rose in Newtown; parents, clergy, citizens from Newtown and from around the world, to watch our children dressed as angels and shepherds, recreate the birth of Christ. I have never experienced a range of emotion like that before. In an hour's time, we cried, we laughed, we prayed and then we prayed some more. Some parents embraced their children as though they would never let go of them again. Everything took on a new meaning. While I was helping put up the Christmas lights, which spelled out "Peace on Earth," I became choked with emotion. We were bewildered by the news coverage. The parking lot at St. Rose for two days was home to dozens of news crews from all over the world. While setting up for the Nativity, I was approached by a reporter from the L.A. Times and then from a French news agency. They asked me what we were experiencing. I told them that our hearts were broken and our community was shattered, but the outpouring of support and prayers from around the globe has helped our citizens get through this, after all. When it is all said and done, all we have are other compassionate humans and God to look after us, and as Fr. Bob said at our Live Nativity, We now have 20 new angels and Six new saints that will perhaps look after us as well. Let us all pray for these families and pray that evil like this never happens again, anywhere in the world.

Gary L. Sippin

December 16, 2012

My wife and I just spent most of the last two days at St. Rose Church. As the names of the victims became known to us, we all experienced a second wave of horror. I personally knew three of the victims' families, several families are close neighbors. On a more uplifting note, my wife (MB) and I have participated in the St. Rose Church Live Nativity reenactment for ten years. It was planned for December 15th, and we thought for sure it would be cancelled. After all, who could possibly celebrate anything a day after a tragedy like this. However, Monsignor Weiss (or Father Bob as he is known to us,) insisted that the Live Nativity be held as scheduled. So, last night we gathered at St. Rose in Newtown; parents, clergy, citizens from Newtown and from around the world, to watch our children dressed as angels and shepherds, recreate the birth of Christ. I have never experienced a range of emotion like that before. In an hour's time, we cried, we laughed, we prayed and then we prayed some more. Some parents embraced their children as though they would never let go of them again. Everything took on a new meaning. While I was helping put up the Christmas lights, which spelled out "Peace on Earth", I became choked with emotion. We were bewildered by the news coverage. The parking lot at St. Rose for two days was home to dozens of news crews from all over the world. While setting up for the Nativity, I was approached by a reporter from the L.A. Times and then from a French news agency. They asked me what we were experiencing. I told them that our hearts were broken and our community was shattered, but the outpouring of support and prayers from around the globe has helped our citizens get through this, after all. When it is all said and done, all we have are other compassionate humans and God to look after us, and as Fr. Bob said at our Live Nativity, we now have 20 new angels and six new saints that will perhaps look after us as well. Let us all pray for these families and pray that evil like this never happens again, anywhere in the world.

Gary L. Sippin

Saint Rose Live Nativity, 2012

Ruth The Turtle

I smile from ear to ear when I hear the words "Ruth The Turtle!"

I met Ruth on February 14, 2013 and not by choice! As a police officer I was assigned to provide a presence at the Healing Arts Grand Opening. And while I did not really look forward to the assignment, I knew once I got there that I would enjoy the event.

The opening was a huge success and the place was filled to capacity. There were many beautiful pieces of art work displayed. And, as the event started to wind down and the crowd thinned out, I looked across the room and saw "Ruth" for the very first time! Ruth was a life size fiberglass loggerhead turtle that was painted in all primary colors! She was five feet tall and had a flipper span of four feet!

Without even realizing it, I vocalized what a neat piece of art that the turtle across the room was and I wondered where it came from. A gentleman standing near me pointed to a man

and woman near the turtle. I went over and introduced myself and that is when I heard their wonderful story of how Ruth the turtle came to be....
The man I met was Mayor Dietch of Surfside, Florida and the woman, Maggie Vidal-Santos an art teacher from Ruth K. Broad Bay Harbor K-8 Center also located in Surfside. When Maggie and her students heard of the sadness that spread through out town, they wanted to send a healing gesture to us.

Maggie and her students read the story that the children of Sandy Hook School had a REAL pet red slider turtle named Shelly. The students thought it would be a fun and whimsical gesture to send a "companion" for Shelly. Thus Ruth was born!

Ruth started out as a plain white figerglass turtle. The colors red, blue, and yellow were selected and each student designed and painted a section of the turtle. When Ruth was completed and "dressed" for travel she was sent to Newtown to meet her new family. Maggie and the mayor arrived shortly there after to make sure that Ruth got to us safely!

Aaah, but this is not the end of Ruth's story! You see, my sister lives in Florida about an hour away from Surfside. And, a couple of months after Ruth came to live in Newtown I went to visit my sister. I decided that I wanted to meet these special creators of Ruth who now had a bond with our town forever. Shhhhh! Only the principal knew that I would be visiting. To my suprise and delight, the day my sister and I arrived in Surfside we were welcomed by all of Ruth's relatives! Scattered throughout the streets and beaches of Surfside were 18 wonderfully painted fiberglass turtles! One more beautiful than the next; but none as beautiful as Ruth! The turtles were known as the "Tale of the Surfside Turtles" which is a public art project sponsored by local Florida artists. When I got to the school the principal had me sit among the students in the library as we all waited together for Maggie to arrive. (Maggie thought that she was making a presentation to her students of green wrist bands that I mailed to her earlier when she flew back home in February. The students were unsure of who I was or what was going on... Until their teacher entered the room with the principal, the Mayor and the Chief of police. Maggie immediately began to cry when she saw me "hidden" in the room!

There was a beautiful presentation that followed. I had the honor of thanking and hugging each boy and girl who took part in creating Ruth. Each were thanked and given a Newtown memorial bracelet. The School was also presented with a police challenge coin. This is a coin that has a very special meaning to military and law enforcement personnel. I told the students that they would be forever connected to Newtown. A video was shown that the students created that honored Newtown. Then each student shared one of their 26 acts of kindness that they had all worked on in the memory of Newtown.

And how was Ruth I asked the students? Well, I told the students that their plans for Ruth might have been to make a small school smile again.... But Ruth had BIGGER plans. Ruth I told them was displayed in the center of our town at the Healing Art Center making our town of 28,000 smile! Ruth was home.....

Yup.... Every time I hear about Ruth the Turtle I smile!

Officer Maryhelen McCarthy
Newtown Police Department

Ruth the Turtle

I smile from ear to ear when I hear the words "Ruth the Turtle."

I met Ruth on February 14, 2013 and not by choice! As a police officer I was assigned to provide a presence at the Healing Arts Grand Opening. And while I did not really look forward to the assignment, I knew once I got there that I would enjoy the event.

The opening was a huge success and the place was filled to capacity. There were many beautiful pieces of art work displayed. And, as the event started to wind down and the crowd thinned out, I looked across the room and saw "Ruth" for the very first time! Ruth was a life size fiberglass logger-head turtle that was painted in all primary colors! She was five feet tall and had a flipper span of four feet!

Without even realizing it, I vocalized what a neat piece of art that the turtle across the room was and I wondered where it came from. A gentleman standing near me pointed to a man and women near the turtle. I went over and introduced myself and that is when I heard their wonderful story of how Ruth the turtle came to be. . . .

The man I met was Mayor Dietch of Surfside, Florida and the woman, Maggie Vidal-Santos an art teacher from Ruth K. Broad Bay Harbor K-8 Center also located in Surfside. When Maggie and her students heard of the sadness that spread through our town, they wanted to send a healing gesture to us.

Maggie and her students read the story that the children of Sandy Hook School had a REAL pet red slider turtle named Shelly. The students thought it would be a fun and whimsical gesture to send a "companion" for Shelly. Thus Ruth was born!

Ruth started out as a plain white fiberglass turtle. The colors of red, blue, and yellow were selected and each student designed and painted a section of the turtle. When Ruth was completed and "dressed" for travel she was sent to Newtown to meet her new family. Maggie and the Mayor arrived shortly thereafter to make sure that Ruth got to us safely!

Aaah, but this is not the end of Ruth's story! You see, my sister lives in Florida about an hour away from Surfside. And, a couple of months after Ruth came to live in Newtown I went to visit my sister. I decided that I wanted to meet these special creators of Ruth who now had a bond with our town forever.

Shhhhh! Only the principal knew that I would be visiting. To my surprise and delight, the day my sister and I arrived in Surfside we were welcomed by all of Ruth's relatives! Scattered throughout the streets and beaches of Surfside were 18 wonderfully painted fiberglass turtles! One more beautiful than the next; but none as beautiful as Ruth! The turtles were known as the "Tale of the Surfside Turtles" which is a public art project sponsored by local Florida artists. When I got to the school the principal had me sit among the students in the library as we all waited together for Maggie to arrive. Maggie thought that she was making a presentation to her students of green wrist bands that I mailed to her earlier when she flew back home in February. The students were unsure of who I was or what was going on . . . until their teacher entered the room with the principal, the Mayor and the Chief of Police. Maggie immediately began to cry when she saw me "hidden" in the room!

There was a beautiful presentation that followed. I had the honor of thanking and hugging each boy and girl who took part in creating Ruth. Each were thanked and given a Newtown memorial brace-let. The school was also presented with a police challenge coin. This is a coin that has very special meaning to military and law enforcement personnel. I told the students that they would be forever connected to Newtown. A video was shown that the students created that honored Newtown. Then each student shared one of their 26 acts of kindness that they had all worked on in the memory of Newtown.

And how was Ruth *I* asked the students? Well, I told the students that their plans for Ruth might have been to make a small school smile again . . . *But* Ruth had *BIGGER* plans. Ruth I told them was displayed in the center of our town at the Healing Art Center making our town of 28,000 smile! Ruth was home. . . .

Yup. . . Every time I hear about Ruth the Turtle I smile!

Officer Maryhelen McCarthy
Newtown Police Department

Ruth the Turtle in her new home at the Healing Art Center

Remembering holidays in Sandy Hook and Newtown.

(from♥) THE KELLOGGS

Helen Kellogg   Bennett's Bridge Road   Sandy Hook   Connecticut   06482

When I meander back through the memories of the years that we lived in Newtown, images of festive holiday celebrations materialize at every turn in the pathway. They date back to 1967, when my wife, Helen, and I responded to a New York Times notice of a house for sale in Sandy Hook. The two of us were immediately enchanted by the serenity, warmth, and simplicity of the old farmhouse sitting beside a woodland pond and waterfall. The pair of red doors seemed to invite us to enter and nestle beside the large fireplace across the room. We remained in the benevolent glow of that fireplace for over three decades of Christmases, Thanksgivings, Halloweens, and family birthdays and weddings.

For us, the holiday joy that the house embodied overflowed into the nearby villages of Newtown and Sandy Hook. Walking at Christmas time on the magically illuminated streets elevated our hopes for peace on earth and sent our spirits soaring. During my years as a resident I was asked three times by our friend Scudder Smith to create illustrations for the cover of the Christmas issue of The Newtown Bee. These drawings gave me a chance to publicly express my enthusiasm for the holiday spirit of the town, and they were among my favorite projects during my long career as a writer and illustrator that evolved in the attic studio of the old farmhouse. I am grateful that I was able to work, and live, and raise my family in that inspiring house, and thankful for the fact that it happened to be located in such a beautiful and generous town.

With warmest regards and ongoing appreciation
to all of our neighbors and friends,

Steven and Helen Kellogg

Remembering holidays in Sandy Hook and Newtown. From the Kelloggs

When I meander back through the memories of the years that we lived in Newtown, images of festive holiday celebrations materialize at every turn in the pathway. They date back to 1967, when my wife, Helen, and I responded to a *New York Times* notice of a house for sale in Sandy Hook. The two of us were immediately enchanted by the serenity, warmth, and simplicity of the old farmhouse sitting beside a woodland pond and waterfall. The pair of red doors seemed to invite us to enter and nestle beside the large fireplace across the room. We remained in the benevolent glow of that fireplace for over three decades of Christmases, Thanksgivings, Hallo'weens, and family birthdays and weddings.

For us, the holiday joy that the house embodied overflowed into the nearby villages of Newtown and Sandy Hook. Walking at Christmastime on the magically illuminated streets elevated our hopes for peace on earth and sent our spirits soaring. During my years as a resident I was asked three times by our friend Scudder Smith to create illustrations for the cover of the Christmas issue of *The Newtown Bee*. These drawings gave me a chance to publicly express my enthusiasm for the holiday spirit of the town, and they were among my favorite projects during my long career as a writer and illustrator that evolved in the attic studio of the old farmhouse. I am grateful that I was able to work, and live, and raise my family in that inspiring house, and thankful for the fact that it happened to be located in such a beautiful and generous town.

With warmest regards and ongoing appreciation to all of our neighbors and friends,
Steven and Helen Kellogg

This is just a small sampling of what it was like in December 2012, and now how we look in September 2013.

December entering Treadwell Park

September entering Treadwell Park

December in front of Sandy Hook Hair Co.

September in front of Sandy Hook Hair Co.

December within Treadwell Park

September within Treadwell Park

Mourning Dove

The Mourning Dove is singing,
Her cry measured low and deep
As though she understands.
Only a fool would mistake this despair,
We know her song is ours.

It is hard to write because words unmoor us;
Because reality stills the pen
And silences the muse;
Because the unanswerable lies heavy
On the gnawing quiet night.

Emerson once said, "When it is darkest men see stars."
Let us bank on this hope.
And although the scale of our grief
Belies any dream of solace,
Let us hang on.

Everything we know is threaded by contrast:
The barkfly and the blue whale,
The nebula and the quark,
Stone and sea and sky.

We too are coiled in contradiction,
Our genes woven like loops of a braid
Laced with tragic and sublime.
We cannot fathom why.

But we can listen for the cry of the dove
Intoning our sorrow on the shifting wind
And we can hang on.

Lisa Schwartz

Mourning Dove

The Mourning Dove is singing,
Her cry measured low and deep
As though she understands.
Only a fool would mistake this despair,
We know her song is ours.

It is hard to write because words unmoor us;
Because reality stills the pen
And silences the muse;
Because the unanswerable lies heavy
On the gnawing quiet night.

Emerson once said, *"When it is darkest men see stars."*
Let us bank on this hope.
And although the scale of our grief
Belies any dream of solace,
Let us hang on.

Everything we know is threaded by contrast:
The barkfly and the blue whale,
The nebula and the quark,
Stone and sea and sky.

We too are coiled in contradiction,
Our genes woven like loops of a braid
Laced with tragic and sublime.
We cannot fathom why.

But we can listen for the cry of the dove
Intoning our sorrow on the shifting wind
And we can hang on.

Lisa Schwartz

MEAD TREADWELL

Anchorage, Alaska
September 1, 2013

In my heart, I'm a country kid who benefitted from living just far enough from the City. I love good hikes, hilltop vistas, ski trips, fishing, and a tromp in the woods. (These days, as an Alaskan, some of those tromps are to hunt moose, and I'm delighted only to have to be wary of bears, not Newtown's snakes or deer ticks!) My city skills aren't great, but I pay attention most to politics, art, and invention. I owe those interests to my surroundings as a kid in Newtown, attending elementary school in the 1960's and high school in the 1970's.

We lived close enough to New York to use its airports, see its museums, or make a day trip to the 1964 World's Fair, but we were far enough to be a world unto our own, away from the Mad Men of Madison Avenue, the halibut of Wall Street, the lights of Broadway. You had to live further west in Connecticut, the Gold Coast of Fairfield County, to be part of that world. Dad had grown up in the City, where his dad was a lawyer, and he lived for summers at his grandmother's home in Redding, where he perfected his woodworking skills, fished in the reservoir, and learned to cut brush, manicure a lawn, grow a vegetable garden, and harvest a wood lot for firewood. Those skills with our hands were the inheritances he left me and my two more talented brothers.

Newtown of my youth still had dairy farms, and I saw more woodchucks, cows and black snakes and copperheads, pheasant and white-tail deer on my paper route up Gelding Hill and Bennetts Bridge than I saw cars, commuters, or for that matter, customers.

Newtown's "famous" or "accomplished" residents were often the kind of New Yorkers who had made the escape, only had to make the trip to "the City" once a week or so, and had the time to enjoy the country, take some hikes, and mentor a kid or two along the way.

Next door to us on Parmalee Hill Road, where I lived until I was eight, was Lee Lorenz, a cartoonist and later the art editor of the New Yorker, who selected cartoons and

picked the magazine's covers every week. His
oldest son Christopher was my first best friend,
and Christopher was a railroad nut. I learned
to read from train timetables that Lee would
bring home from his weekly trip through Grand
Central Station; on our tricycles Chris
might be the New Haven line while I was
the conductor on the New York Central. If
you saw a five year old yelling "All aboard
for Utica" that's what that was all about.
We would ride over to Lee's Studio, a tiny
little guest house back behind our place, to
look at the cartoons he was drawing that day.
On Wednesdays, we'd race to be first to our
mailboxes to pull the New Yorker out of the
brown cover it was mailed in then to find Lee's
Cartoon in it. There was usually one by Dana
Fradon, another Newtowner, and I think by the
time I was conscious of it, cartoonist and
author James Thurber had come and gone from
our burg.

On the other side of our woods on Parmalee Hill
lived the famous photographer Andre Kertesz.
I did not know he was famous, just that he
had a darkroom that he took me into to see

pictures magically appear in a bath of foul smelling chemicals. He made some good ones of my Dad, my brother and me that we lost in the 1972 Zoar Road fire (more importantly, we lost Dad) and one of these days I will get the time to go to New York City and go through the Kertesz collection of negatives to find them. Later, the Newtown Bee's Scudder Smith hired me to work in the newspaper's darkroom, and I had one of my own at home in high school my Dad and I put together.

I caught my first fish in a pond owned by Elia Kazan in the Berkshire part of Sandy Hook, just across Route 34 from Zoar Road. It was a bullhead, or a sunny, I can't remember, because we caught lots of both in our quest for a rarer brown trout. Kazan, a friendly guy who let us on the property, we knew was a movie producer. I only learned later he was making his own escape for freedom, from an unforgiving Hollywood who thought Communism was kind of cool, when Kazan — an immigrant — knew more of the horrors of the real thing.

My paper route took me up Gelding Hill six days a week, often by foot. Regularly, I'd meet up with author and illustrator Steven Kellogg, who had put down his brushes to get a little exercise. His books for kids delighted my own when I had them. Some were about a Great Dane named Pinkerton; the Great Dane he was walking was named Oafie, whose antics inspired some of the stories in Steve's books.

At the top of Gelding Hill was a weekend house owned by a New York psychiatrist from England, Dr. Fiona Graham, who dated radio host Casper Citron. Casper had a nationally syndicated show heard on WQXR, radio station of the New York Times, but originating from the Algonquin Hotel in New York, famous for its literary roundtable. Citron's son Steve and I loved to build trails for motorbikes through the woods, both in Sandy Hook and at a property they owned in Roxbury. I had no iPod to soften my eardrums,... the sounds of chainsaws and motorbikes did the trick. In 1972, Casper dragged Steve and me to the

Democratic National Convention in Florida so we could carry his recording equipment. We interviewed Shirley MacLaine in her hotel room and Yippie Revolutionaries Jerry Rubin and Abbie Hoffman on the street; not to speak of the regular gamut of Senators and Congressmen on the Convention floor. Every week Casper arrived in Sandy Hook or Roxbury with a carload of books sent by authors who hoped to appear on his show; we got to paw through the pile and read before publication many of the sixties best sellers coming down the pike.

Investment bank founder Dan Lufkin bought a farm on Poverty Hollow Road, and did manage to make the commute to Wall Street, often in his own helicopter. Mom wanted to feed us kids raw milk, so Lufkin allowed her to regularly collect the creamy not-yet-Pasturized nectar of his Holsteins in clean jugs from his milk room. After Dad died, Dan had become Connecticut's first Commissioner of Environmental Protection. I spent a day with him at work, and wrote about it for The Bee.

That day in Hartford and on the Connecticut River near Long Island Sound looking at wetlands (I may have my geography off) was remembered often when I became Deputy Commissioner of Alaska's Department of Environmental Conservation 18 years later. I am grateful for the encouragement Lufkin made to this 17-year old that day about my education, and I had the chance to follow his footsteps at Hotchkiss for my senior year of high school, Yale and Harvard Business School on scholarship, before escaping to Alaska and avoiding Wall Street altogether!

Occasionally at our kitchen table would be a friend of Mom and Dad's who lived in Newtown. Robert Fulton was a raconteur, a descendant of the inventor of the steamboat and an inventor and artist in his own right. He'd made a movie called "One Man Caravan" about a motorcycle trip around the world, and had invented and built a flying car. He had his own landing strip and an office that looked like a control tower — in fact it had been one. His most famous invention was the Fulton Skyhook, which we saw first in the James Bond movie "Thunderball," later in one of the recent Batman films. It could be used to rescue downed fliers from the jungles of Vietnam, or U.S. spies who had snuck onto Russian ice camps left floating in the Arctic Ocean. When my Sandy Hook school friend Dickie Leonard's Dad was sent to fly in the war, we all hoped he wouldn't have to use it, but we thought it would be cool to try it ourselves.

In the seventh and eighth grade, before Newtown High School was finished, the town wasn't sure it wanted to foot the bill for a swimming pool in the new school. They had a referendum, and Otto Heise — a man whose Newtown factory had something to do with making mirrors for space telescopes like our spy satellites and the Hubble — offered an astronomical sum of money to match town funds and make sure we had a pool. I only remember meeting Mr. Heise once, but as a swimmer on Coach Tom Roberts' team at Newtown High I was sure glad we got that pool.

Enzo Domini was the Italian-born Dad of my oldest friend in the world, Tim, whose Mom and my Mom worked together as Girl Scout leaders. Tim and I would visit Enzo's office above Borodenko's market, next to the A+P at Newtown's center. Domini was a food entrepreneur, who imported colored pasta from Italy and later started a factory to make breaded eggplant. He should go down in history as the evangelist who brought soccer as a mainstream youth sport to America, where it now rivals Little League and Pop Warner football. Enzo was a gregarious Dad, and the Domini's song-filled Christmas Eve parties are a great memory.

Dad and my brother Albert liked to tell the story of visiting Mr. Brunot, who hadn't invented Scrabble, but had commercialized it. Brunot had in his Hattertown (?) garage the woodworking equipment used to carve letters into wooden Scrabble tiles. I was sorry to miss the visit, and as I can play a mean version of the game today, I like to think some of that rubbed off from knowing Mr. Brunot.

Another inventor who lived in Newtown was named Joe Engleberger, whose daughter Gay and son Jeff went to school with us. Joe was a pioneer of robotics. His company Unimation helped Detroit make cars more efficiently, and the movie he showed us in the sixth grade of those one-armed machines on the assembly line looked nothing like the robot blaring "Danger, Will Robinson!" on the weekly episodes of TV's "Lost in Space." But like Fulton, he showed me you could actually invent something, bring it to market, and change the world.

Roland Brandwein, another displaced New Yorker, mentored a group of us in the seventh and eighth grade. Our legendary math teacher, Mariette Paquin, was a woman of high standards who called us out as "flat tires" if we couldn't immediately cite a formula we were studying, or a conversion of a fraction to a decimal. But she too was amazed with what we could do with the telex machine Brandwein installed in the corner of our middle school classroom. It connected to a giant IBM computer far away in Poughkeepsie, New York. We could use that computer, after dialing the right number on the telex, and do all sorts of things with languages we learned like BASIC and FORTRAN. Brandwein foresaw a time we all might access a computer from our desks, and he'd invented a way to convert an IBM Selectric typewriter to hook up a phone line to do that. That was the late sixties. Later, in the late seventies when I had a computer terminal that hooked into the phone line, I realized Brandwein was thinking in the right direction even if he missed the mark. But he took away the mystery of computers for us, and helped our generation of Newtoners see the future.

Today, I am a Dad in Alaska, with three kids of my own to get excited about the size of the world and its possibilities. I moved out here in part because the fields in Newtown where I'd launched rockets and flown model airplanes and had fights with dried up cow pies were turning from wide open spaces to homes with manicured lawns.

I love the possibilities that come to mind with wide open spaces. The memories and experiences and acquaintances I have brought with me from Newtown have helped with our own endeavors, including serving as Alaska's Lt. Governor, or launching a few tech firms of our own based on smart people's inventions that have had global impact, like the spherical camera we used to start Streetview for Google or save lives of soldiers in Iraq or Afghanistan. I still look for Lee Lorenz's cartoons in The New Yorker, and am eternally grateful for the time he, Kellogg, Citron, Fulton, Domini, Heise, Engleberger, Brandwein, Paquin, and others, like Mom & Dad did for me in the crucible of Newtown.

Our world is full of opportunity, and to find frontiers sometimes all you need to do is take a drive, wet a line, or take a hike with a neighbor!

Mead Treadwell

In my heart, I'm a country kid who benefitted from living just far enough from the City. I love good hikes, hilltop vistas, ski trips, fishing, and a tromp in the woods. (These days, as an Alaskan, some of those tromps are to hunt moose, and I'm delighted only to have to be wary of bears, not Newtown's snakes or deer ticks!) My city skills aren't great, but I pay attention most to *politics*, *art* and *invention*, I owe those interests to my surroundings as a kid in Newtown, attending elementary school in the 1960's and high school in the 1970's.

We lived close enough to New York to use its airports, see its museums, or make a day trip to the 1964 Worlds Fair, but we were far enough to be a world unto our own, away from the Mad Men of Madison Avenue, the hubbub of Wall Street, the lights of Broadway. You had to live further west in Connecticut, the Gold Coast of Fairfield County, to be part of that world. Dad had grown up in the City, where his dad was a lawyer, and he lived for summers at his grandmother's home in Redding, where he perfected his woodworking skills, fished in the reservoir, and learned to cut brush, manicure a lawn, grow a vegetable garden, and harvest a woodlot for firewood. Those skills with our hands were the inheritances he left me and my two more talented brothers.

Newtown of my youth still had dairy farms, and I saw more woodchucks, cows and black snakes and copperheads, pheasant and white-tail deer on my paper route up Gelding Hill and Bennetts Bridge than I saw cars, commuters, or for that matter, customers.

Newtown's "famous" or "accomplished" residents were often the kind of New Yorkers who had made the escape, only had to make the trip to "the City" once a week or so, and had the time to enjoy the country, take some hikes, and mentor a kid or two along the way.

Next door to us on Parmalee Hill Road, where I lived until I was eight, was Lee Lorenz, a cartoonist and later the art editor of the New Yorker, who selected cartoons and picked the magazine's covers every week. His oldest son Christopher was my first best friend, and Christopher was a railroad nut. I learned to read from train timetables that Lee would bring home from his weekly trip through Grand Central Station; on our tricycles Chris might be the New Haven line while I was the conductor on the New York Central. If you saw a five year old yelling "All aboard for Utica" that's what that was all about. We would ride over to Lee's studio, a tiny little guest house back behind our place, to look at the cartoons he was drawing that day. On Wednesdays, we'd race to be first to our mailboxes to pull the New Yorker out of the brown cover it was mailed in then to find Lee's cartoon in it. There was usually one by Dana Fradon, another Newtowner, and I think by the time I was conscious of it, cartoonist and author James Thurber had come and gone from our burg.

On the other side of our woods on Parmalee Hill lived the famous photographer Andree Kertesz. I did not know he was famous, just that he had a darkroom that he took me into to see pictures magically appear in a bath of foul smelling chemicals. He made some good ones of my Dad, my brother and me that we lost in the 1972 Zoar Road fire (more importantly, we lost Dad), and one of these days I will get the time to go to New York City and go through the Kertesz collection of negatives to find them. Later, the Newtown Bee's Scudder Smith hired me to work in the newspaper's darkroom, and I had one of my own at home while in high school that my Dad and I put together.

I caught my first fish in a pond owned by Elia Kazan in the Berkshire part of Sandy Hook, just across Route 34 from Zoar Road. It was a bullhead, or a sunny, I can't remember, because we caught lots of both in our quest for a rarer brown trout. Kazan, a friendly guy who let us on the property, we knew was a movie producer. I only learned later he was making his own escape for freedom, from an unforgiving Holllywood who thought Communism was kind of cool, when Kazan—an immigrant—knew more of the horrors of the real thing.

My paper route took me up Gelding Hill six days a week, often by foot. Regularly, I'd meet up with author and illustrator Steve Kellogg, who had put down his brushes to get a little exercise. His books for kids delighted my own when I had them. Some were about a Great Dane named Pinkerton; the Great Dane he was walking was named Oafie, whose antics inspired some of the stories in Steve's books.

At the top of the Gelding Hill was a weekend house owned by a New York psychiatrist from England, Dr. Fiona Graham, who dated radio host Casper Citron. Casper had a nationally syndicated show heard on WQXR, radio station of the New York Times, but originating from the Algonquin Hotel in New York, famous for its literary roundtable. Citron's son Steve and I loved to build trails for motorbikes through the woods, both in Sandy Hook and at a property they owned in Roxbury. I had no iPod to soften my eardrums . . . the sounds of chain saws and motorbikes did the trick. In 1972, Casper dragged Steve and me to the Democratic National Convention in Florida so we could carry his recording equipment. We interviewed Shirley MacLaine in her hotel room and Yippie revolutionaries Jerry Rubin and Abbie Hoffman on the street; not to speak of the regular gamut of Senators and Congressmen on the Convention floor. Every week Casper arrived in Sandy Hook or Roxbury with a carload of books sent by authors who hoped to appear on his show; we got to paw through the pile and read before publication many of the sixties best sellers coming down the pike.

Investment bank founder Dan Lufkin bought a farm on Poverty Hollow Road, and did manage to make the commute to Wall Street, often in his own helicopter. Mom wanted to feed us kids raw milk, so Lufkin allowed her to regularly collect the creamy not-yet-pasteurized nectar of his Holsteins in clean jugs from his milk room. After Dad died, Dan had become Connecticut's first Commissioner of Environmental Protection. I spent a day with him at work, and wrote about it for The Bee. That day in Hartford and on the Connecticut River near Long Island Sound looking at wetlands (I may have my geography off) was remembered often when I became Deputy Commissioner of Alaska's Department of Environmental Conservation 18 years later. I am grateful for the encouragement Lufkin made to this 17-year old that day about my education, and I had the chance to follow his footsteps at Hotchkiss for my senior year of high school, Yale and Harvard Business School on scholarship, before escaping to Alaska for good and avoiding Wall Street altogether!

Occasionally at our kitchen table would be a friend of Mom and Dad's who lived in Newtown. Robert Fulton was a raconteur, a descendant of the inventor of the steamboat, and an inventor and artist in his own right. He'd made a movie called "One Man Caravan" about a motorcycle trip around the world, and had invented and built a flying car. He had his own landing strip and an office that looked like a control tower—in fact it had been one. His most famous invention was the Fulton Skyhook, which we saw first in the James Bond movie "Thunderball," later in one of the recent Batman films. It could be used to rescue downed fliers from the jungles of Vietnam, or US spies who had snuck onto Russian ice camps left floating in the Arctic Ocean. When my Sandy Hook school friend Dickie

Leonard's Dad was sent to fly in the war, we all hoped he wouldn't have to use it, but we thought it would be cool to try it ourselves.

In the seventh and eighth grade, before Newtown High School was finished, the town wasn't sure it wanted to foot the bill for a swimming pool in the new school. They had a referendum, and Otto Heise—a man whose Newtown factory had something to do with making mirrors for space telescopes like our spy satellites and the Hubble—offered an astronomical sum of money to match town funds and make sure we had a pool. I only remember meeting Mr. Heise once, but as a swimmer on Coach Tom Roberts' team at Newtown High I was sure glad we got that pool.

Enzo Domini was the Italian-born Dad of my oldest friend in the world, Tim, whose Mom and my Mom worked together as Girl Scout leaders. Tim and I would visit Enzo's office above Borodenko's Market, next to the A&P at Newtown's center. Domini was a food entrepreneur, who imported colored pasta from Italy and later started a factory to make breaded eggplant. He should go down in history as the evangelist who brought soccer as a mainstream youth sport to America, where it now rivals Little League and Pop Werner football. Enzo was a gregarious Dad, and the Domini's song-filled Christmas Eve parties are a great memory.

Dad and my brother Albert liked to tell the story of visiting Mr. Brunot, who hadn't invented Scrabble, but had commercialized it. Brunet had in his Hattertown (?) garage the woodworking equipment used to carve letters into wooden Scrabble tiles. I was sorry to miss the visit, and as I can play a mean version of the game today, I like to think some of that rubbed off from knowing Mr. Brunot.

Another inventor who lived in Newtown was named Joe Engleberger, whose daughter Gay and son Jeff went to school with us. Joe was a pioneer of robotics. His company Unimation helped Detroit make cars more efficiently, and the movie he showed us in the sixth grade of these one-armed machines on the assembly line looked nothing like the robot blaring "Danger, Will Robinson!" on the weekly episodes of TV's "Lost in Space." But like Fulton, he showed me you could actually invent something, bring it to market, and change the world.

Roland Brandwein, another displaced New Yorker, mentored a group of us in the seventh and eighth grade. Our legendary math teacher, Mariette Paquin, was a woman of high standards who called us out as "flat tires" if we couldn't immediately recite a formula we were studying, or a conversion of a fraction to a decimal. But she too was amazed with what we could do with the telex machine Brandwein installed in the corner of our middle school classroom. It connected to a giant IBM computer far away in Poughkeepsie, New York. We could use that computer, after dialing the right number on the telex, and do all sorts of things with languages we learned like BASIC and FORTRAN. Brandwein foresaw a time we all might access a computer from our desks, and he'd invented a way to convert an IBM selectric typewriter to hook up to a phone line to do that. That was the late sixties. Later, in the late seventies when I had a computer terminal that hooked into the phone line, I realized Brandwein was thinking in the right direction even if he missed the mark. But he took away the mystery of computers for us, and helped our generation of Newtowners see the future.

Today I am a Dad in Alaska, with three kids of my own to get excited about the size of the world and its possibilities. I moved out here in part because the fields in Newtown where I'd launched rockets and flown model airplanes and had fights with dried up cow pies were turning from wide open spaces to homes with manicured lawns. I love the possibilities that come to mind with wide open spaces. The memories and experiences and acquaintances I have brought with me from Newtown have helped with our own endeavors, including serving as Alaska's Lt. Governor, or launching a few tech firms of our own based on smart people's inventions that have had global impact, like the spherical camera we used to start Streetview for Google or save lives of soldiers in Iraq and Afghanistan. I still look for Lee Lorenz's cartoons in the New Yorker, and am eternally grateful for the time he, Kellogg, Citron, Fulton, Domini, Heise, Engleberger, Brandwein, Paquin, and others, like Mom and Dad did for me in the crucible of Newtown. Our world is full of opportunity, and to find frontiers sometimes all you need to do is take a drive, wet a line, or take a hike with a neighbor!

Mead Treadwell

Entrance to Treadwell Park, Sandy Hook

Basketball court, playground, pool, pavilion, and baseball field at Treadwell Park

Soccer field and tennis courts at Treadwell Park

I grew up in Sandy Hook. My childhood IS Sandy Hook. 18 years of my life is Sandy Hook. My memories are Sandy Hook. The deepest pain I have ever felt in my 30 years was in Sandy Hook. I am Sandy Hook. I had a baseball field on my street. I could walk to my best friend's house. We rode our bikes in Sandy Hook. We played football, baseball, and basketball in Sandy Hook. We grew up in Sandy Hook. We became men in Sandy Hook. I am Sandy Hook. I went to pre-school at Trinity. I went to Hawley School and Sandy Hook School. I had my first kiss at Sandy Hook School during recess. I walked the hallways of Sandy Hook School. I am Sandy Hook. I laid in Ram's Pasture. I ate at My Place Pizza. I went to the movies at Edmund Town Hall for $1. I went to the St. Rose carnival. I worked at Rock Ridge Country Club. I graduated from Newtown Middle School and Newtown High School. I drank my first beer in Sandy Hook. I fell in love for the first time in Sandy Hook. I am Sandy Hook. I swam in Lake Zoar. I've played soccer at Treadwell Park. I swam to the dock at Dickinson Park. I've stood at the flagpole at midnight. I've eaten at the General Store. I have seen the insides of Fairfield Hills. I am Sandy Hook. I trick-or-treated through all neighborhoods in Newtown. I attended Labor Day parades on Main Street. I went to the tree lightings. I've been to weddings in Sandy Hook. I've been to funerals at Honan's. I've seen every gym and field in Newtown. I've been to every park in Newtown. I am Sandy Hook.

Sandy Hook raised me. The people, the places, the things are part of me. Wherever I go and whoever I meet gets a taste of Sandy Hook. I am a man because of Sandy Hook. Sandy Hook has forever changed. My childhood and memories have not. I am and will always be Sandy Hook. I smile and get goose bumps when I think of Sandy Hook.

Nathan Daniel Gaines is Sandy Hook. And Sandy Hook is Nathan Daniel Gaines!